THE IMPERIAL MING TOMBS

THE IMPERIAL MING TOMBS

TEXT AND PHOTOGRAPHS BY
ANN PALUDAN

FOREWORD BY L. CARRINGTON GOODRICH

NEW HAVEN AND LONDON: YALE UNIVERSITY PRESS

Published in the United States of America
and England by Yale University Press and
in Hong Kong by Hong Kong University Press

Designed by Sally Harris
and set in VIP Garamond type by
The Composing Room of Michigan, Inc.
Printed in the United States of America by
The Murray Printing Company, Westford, Mass.

Library of Congress Cataloging in Publication Data

Paludan, Ann, 1928–
   The Imperial Ming tombs.

   Bibliography: p.
   Includes index.
   1. Shih-san-ling, China.   I. Title.
DS793.S5246P34   915.1'15   80-23829
ISBN 0-300-02511-4
(Hong Kong University Press ISBN 962-209-029-x)

10 9 8 7 6 5 4 3 2 1

For Janus
with love

Contents

Colourplates 1–13 and 14–31 follow pages 78 and 142 respectively

CHARTS (by Lucy Peck)

MING EMPERORS AND THEIR TOMBS

Name	Lived	Name and Date of Reign	Tomb Name	Temple Name
Chu Yüan-chang	(21/10/1328–24/6/1398)	Hung-wu, 1368–98	Hsiao-ling (Nanking)	T'ai-tsu
Chu Yün-wen	(5/12/1377–13/7/1402?)	Chien-wen, 1398–1402	Unknown	(Hui-tsung)
Chu Ti	(2/5/1360–12/8/1424)	Yung-lo, 1402–24	Ch'ang-ling (1)	T'ai-tsung (Ch'eng-tsu)
Chu Kao-chih	(16/8/1378–29/5/1425)	Hung-hsi, 1424–25	Hsien-ling (2)	Jen-tsung
Chu Chan-chi	(16/3/1399–31/1/1435)	Hsüan-te, 1425–35	Ching-ling (3)	Hsüan-tsung
Chu Ch'i-chen	(29/11/1427–23/2/1464)	Cheng-t'ung, 1435–49	Yü-ling (4)	Ying-tsung
		T'ien-shun, 1457–64		
Chu Ch'i-yü	(11/9/1428–14/3/1457)	Ching-t'ai, 1449–57	(Western Hills)	(Tai-tsung)
Chu Chien-shen	(9/12/1447–9/9/1487)	Ch'eng-hua, 1464–87	Mao-ling (5)	Hsien-tsung
Chu Yu-t'ang	(30/7/1470–8/6/1505)	Hung-chih, 1487–1505	T'ai-ling (6)	Hsiao-tsung
Chu Hou-chao	(26/10/1491–20/4/1521)	Cheng-te, 1505–21	K'ang-ling (7)	Wu-tsung
Chu Hou-ts'ung	(16/9/1507–23/1/1567)	Chia-ching, 1521–67	Yung-ling (8)	Shih-tsung
Chu Tsai-hou	(4/2/1537–5/7/1572)	Lung-ch'ing, 1567–72	Chao-ling (9)	Mu-tsung
Chu I-chün	(4/9/1563–18/8/1620)	Wan-li, 1572–1620	Ting-ling (10)	Shen-tsung
Chu Ch'ang-lo	(29/9/1582–26/9/1620)	T'ai-ch'ang, 1620	Ching-ling (11)	Kuang-tsung
Chu Yu-chiao	(23/12/1605–30/9/1627)	T'ien-ch'i, 1620–27	Te-ling (12)	Hsi-tsung
Chu Yu-chien	(6/2/1611–24/4/1644)	Ch'ung-chen, 1627–44	Sze-ling (13)	Chuang-lieh (Ssu-tsung)

CHRONOLOGICAL TABLE

Shang	ca. 1550–1027 B.C.
Chou	1027–221 B.C.
Ch'in	221–206 B.C.
Han	206 B.C.–A.D. 221
Three Kingdoms	A.D. 221–265
Chin	265–316
Northern and Southern Empires	316–589
Sui	589–618
T'ang	618–907
Five Dynasties	907–960
Sung	960–1127
Chin	1127–1280
Yüan	1280–1368
Ming	1368–1644
Ch'ing	1644–1911
Republic	1912–1949
People's Republic	1949–

Foreword

The Chinese arrange for their final resting places long before the end is near. I recall once, when on an excursion in October 1931 to an archaeological site in China's northwest, sleeping on the *kang* of a village farmer alongside an empty and well-made coffin prepared for the man's mother, who slept in an adjoining room. This foresight demonstrated his filial piety, and it seemed to please the old lady very much. So, too, was it with the highest in the land. Chu Ti (1360–1424), the emperor of the Yung-lo period, while still engaged in building Peking, selected a superb site twenty-six miles to the north of the capital and in 1409 erected his own mausoleum there. And there he was buried early in 1425.

This may well have been the custom as far back as thirteen centuries before our era. All we know about that distant time is that the kings of Shang were laid to rest magnificently. Professor Paul Pelliot, in his address to the Harvard Tercentenary in 1936 entitled "The Royal Tombs of An-yang," described the find, made only shortly before his visit in 1935, and told of the riches displayed. More recently Chinese archaeologists have brought to light some of the life-sized pottery figures, wooden chariots, and many other objects at the tomb of the first emperor, the redoubtable Shih-huang-ti, who died in 210 B.C.* These tombs were unquestionably fashioned long before. The sixth chapter of the *Shih-chi* (Records of a Historian) by Ssu-ma Ch'ien (145–ca. 87 B.C.) reports:

> From the beginning of his reign [247] Shih-huang caused to be dug and built Mount Li [said to be 150 ft. high]. Then when he had reunited under his control every part of the empire [221], workers were assembled from all over to the number of more than seven hundred thousand; they dug down to the water table; they poured molten copper to fashion the sarcophagus, and filled the grave with [models of] palaces and structures for all elements of his administration, with

*See, for example, Audrey Topping, "The First Emperor's Army: China's Incredible Find," *The National Geographic,* April 1978, pp. 440–59.

marvellous vessels and jewels, and rare objects transported thither. Artisans received orders to design crossbows and arrows which would be automatically released if any intruder ventured to enter the mausoleum. They fashioned with quicksilver innumerable streams including the Chiang [Yangtze] and the Ho [Yellow River], and had them run into a vast sea by mechanical means. Above [on the ceiling] were the stars of heaven, and below a [hydrographic] map of the empire. In addition, the workmen made torches of seal's fat calculated to burn indefinitely. . . .

Doubtless many another emperor in centuries to come followed Shih-huang's example, though on a less ambitious scale; the pattern nevertheless was set for selecting propitious sites and building imposing tumuli.

The first emperor of the Ming chose a beautiful area flanked by the mountain known as Chung-shan, three miles northeast of Nanking (his capital), and there in 1382 buried his faithful consort, Empress Ma. Ten years later, the heir apparent Piao followed; also numerous concubines and later empresses. The successor of the first emperor, his grandson, Chu Yün-wen (1377–1402) disappeared without a trace, possibly in the fire that consumed the Imperial palace following the capture of Nanking by the forces under the command of his uncle, Chu Ti. The third emperor, widely known by his reign title, Yung-lo, who much preferred his princely seat north of Nanking, in 1409 made Peking his capital, and there it remained until the fall of the Ming dynasty in 1644.

It is the description of the two areas near Nanking and Peking, particularly the latter, to which this book is dedicated. The author, taking advantage of several years at the Danish Embassy with her husband, has spent countless hours visiting the Shih-san ling, or Thirteen Tombs, outside of Peking. This accounts for the loving detail lavished on each one of them and also on descriptions of a few of the resting places of other members of the Imperial clan in the vicinity. No study so intimate has been made before. True, the noted Chinese scholar Ku Yen-wu (1613–82) had visited the tombs and made careful notes. So also, over two centuries later, did the learned Dutch scholar J. J. M. De Groot (1854–1921), in his multivolume work, *The Religious System of China,* and the French scholars Bouillard and Vaudescal in the *Bulletin de l'Ecole Française d'Extrême-Orient* (1920). But these studies are both out-of-date and hard to come by, and they do not include certain data which Ann Paludan gives us here. In addition, there are fine illustrations, and a bird list assembled by her husband. All this provides the reader with information on two notable sights of Nanking and Peking of which the Chinese themselves are justly proud. One can learn much here about Chinese architecture, ornamentation, and formal gardens. Ann Paludan is a charming and expert guide.

L. Carrington Goodrich
Dean Lung Professor Emeritus of Chinese
Columbia University

Preface

The idea of writing about the Ming Tombs came slowly. You could really say that this book was born of Sunday picnics. We lived in Peking from 1972 to 1976 while my husband was Danish Ambassador to China. During those years foreign residents were not allowed to travel farther than twenty kilometres from the centre of the town without permission. The two exceptions to this were the Great Wall and the Ming Tombs. The Great Wall is a fascinating place, but it is always full of tourists. It is not a place where you can rest or relax. The Ming Tombs, on the other hand, offer the perfect escape from town life. There are in all thirteen tombs—indeed the Chinese call the valley "the thirteen tombs." The first tomb, Ch'ang-ling, which has been restored to its full former glory, and the tenth tomb, Ting-ling, which was excavated in 1956, attract all the visitors. The other eleven remain almost entirely deserted. Unless you are unlucky, you will usually have the tomb to yourself. Even if there should be other people there, they will probably also be in search of quiet and you can easily find a place out of sight and sound.

The tombs make a perfect picnicking place. In the summer there is shade under the age-old trees or in the porches of the tile-covered doorways; in winter you can always find shelter from the wind, and use the various marble fragments lying around as tables and chairs. Inside the precincts of the tombs, the grass grows freely. There are wild flowers, and, best of all, the tall trees attract birds. Once, from the walls of the twelfth tomb, Te-ling, we saw Choughs and Golden Eagle. In other tombs Red-footed Falcons breed, and in yet another we saw a Roller. The tombs enclose a world of quietness and peace. The militia man who comes by on his bicycle does not disturb you, nor does the occasional elderly man or woman gathering wood or leaves. The combination of gentle decay and an unspoilt setting answers to the European love of ruins.

One advantage of being restricted to a very few places is that you get to know those places in depth. If we had been free to go wherever we liked, we would never have come to know and love the tombs as we did. Little by little, we gave the tombs names—"the bus stop tomb," "New Year's Day tomb," "the tomb you walk to." (Our sinologue friends, of course, never did this but rattled off the proper names, Yü-ling, Chao-ling, K'ang-ling, and so on). Then we started to notice architectural peculiarities or specialities. One tomb had strange urnlike objects near the altar which we had not seen anywhere else. Another tomb had an extraordinarily well-developed drainage system. One New Year's Day, one of the children and a friend disappeared down a drain from inside the walls around the central funeral mound and made their way underground to an exit in the outer wall. The guide books we had were remarkably uninformative. Since most visitors to Peking only have time to visit the restored and the excavated tombs, writers tend to dismiss the others with a sentence.

At the same time, we could not help seeing how, year by year, some of the smaller tombs were crumbling away. There is a great difference in the way in which individual tombs are being preserved. Whilst some are kept in an excellent state of repair, one or two of the more distant ones are gradually being incorporated into the life of the local village. Large stretches of the precinct walls have fallen down; the stones are being used for other buildings. Trees are being cut down, the stone-paved floors of the former funeral buildings are used for drying crops. In some cases the damage comes not from natural decay but from active vandalism by foreign visitors, who throw stones at the tiled roofs in the hope of getting a good decorated piece to take home with them.

After great searching, we got hold of a copy of Georges Bouillard, *Les Tombeaux impériaux Ming et Ts'ing* (1931) and were able to go through the tombs, one by one, checking their present state against his detailed descriptions. We discovered some things which Bouillard had not noticed and a few inaccuracies. In one case at least, a recent restoration did not conform to what he had seen. As we checked, I began to make a detailed photographic record of the individual tombs.*

The present book grew out of all those lovely Sundays we spent in the valley.

*My collection of negatives and slides recording the Imperial Ming Tombs as they looked in 1975 will be permanently placed with the Percival David Foundation of Chinese Art, School of Oriental and African Studies, University of London, 53 Gordon Square, London WC1. Unless otherwise attributed, the illustrations for this book are from this larger collection. The five photographs that show objects from the Ting-ling Museum and details of the funeral chambers in Ting-ling (figs. 156–160) were taken with the kind permission of the Chinese authorities.

Acknowledgments

A great many people have helped me with the research for this book. In particular I would like to thank Sir John Addis, Professor L. Carrington Goodrich, and Miss Margaret Medley, all of whom were good enough to read the manuscript at different stages and give me valuable advice, criticism, and encouragement.

I wish also to give special thanks to Dr. Wang Yeqiu, Chairman of the State Bureau of Museums and Archaeological Data, his colleague at the Palace Museum in Peking, Sheng Congwen, and Dr. Feng Cangyuan of the Kiangsu Provincial Museum, Nanking, for their generous and friendly help with research problems during my 1979 visit to China.

I wish to thank the following people for their very active help in different areas: Timothy and Richenda George for their help in the field in May 1979; Else Glahn, for constructive comments on the chapters on architecture; Rose Kerr and Frances Wood, for correcting the romanisation; Lucy Peck, for the beautiful charts that greatly elucidate much of the text; Jessica Rawson for advice on archaism; Leifur Thorsteinsson, both for his advice about taking photographs and for the very generous loan of his darkroom.

From our time in Peking I would like especially to thank Jan and Agnes Vixseboxse and Michael and Julian Morgan. With their knowledge and long experience of China they were the best possible companions in the Ming Tombs.

I would like to thank the Danish Foreign Service; I am well aware that without it I would never have had the chance even to see the Ming Tombs. Throughout this project I have received generous help from Danish colleagues in Peking and other parts of the world.

In carrying out the final stages of my work, I received valuable help from our Icelandic friends Henrik Sv. Björnsson and Sigurdur Helgason.

I also owe very great thanks to our Chinese friends at the Danish Embassy in Peking from 1972–76 and again in 1979; to officials and friends in the Western European

Department of the Chinese Ministry of Foreign Affairs and in the Chinese Embassy in Reykjavík, and indeed to the whole Chinese people, whose kindness, intelligence, sense of beauty, and stamina have been a great source of inspiration.

Finally I wish to thank the children, who have put up with this book through all its long and difficult stages and have always encouraged me. Above all I am grateful to my husband, Janus; it was he who first suggested writing about the Ming Tombs, and without him this book would never have been finished. The bird list is compiled by him.

A.P.

Danish Embassy
Reykjavík, October 1979

The Ming tombs in Ch'ang-p'ing undoubtedly formed one of the largest and most gorgeous royal cemeteries ever laid out by the hand of man. They yield the palm to the Egyptian pyramids in point of bulk, but certainly not in that of style and grandeur.

The greatest conservatism in matters of religion, ceremonies and rites having dominated the Chinese race through all ages, we were justified in our belief that those sepulchres were built on the same plan which had been transmitted to one another by successive dynasties as an heirloom from the ancients, so that they hold up before our eyes a clear image of the Imperial tombs of every epoch, beginning with that of Ch'in and Han. This fact . . . stamps them as monuments the historical and archaeological value of which it is hardly possible to overrate.

From Jan Jakob Maria De Groot, *The Religious System of China*, 1894

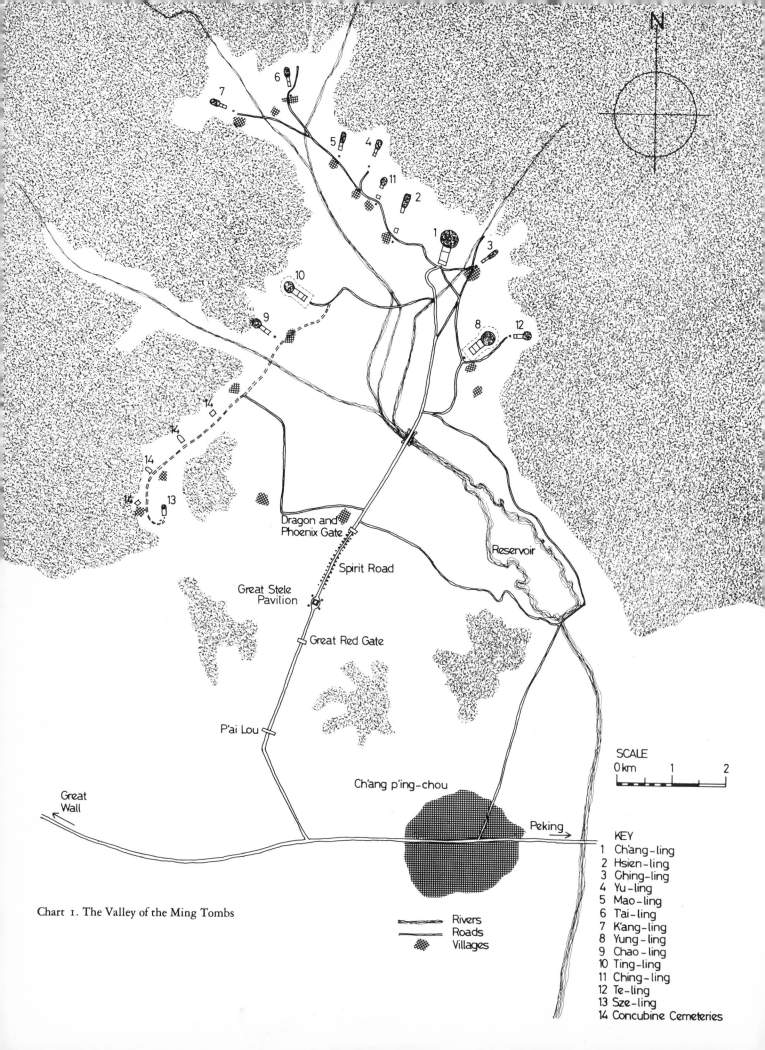

N

7

6

5

4

11

2

1

3

10

9

8

12

14

14

14

13

Dragon and
Phoenix Gate

Reservoir

Spirit Road

Great Stele
Pavilion

Great Red Gate

P'ai Lou

Ch'ang p'ing-chou

Great
Wall

Peking

SCALE
0 km   1   2

Chart 1. The Valley of the Ming Tombs

Rivers
Roads
Villages

KEY
1 Ch'ang-ling
2 Hsien-ling
3 Ching-ling
4 Yu-ling
5 Mao-ling
6 Tai-ling
7 K'ang-ling
8 Yung-ling
9 Chao-ling
10 Ting-ling
11 Ching-ling
12 Te-ling
13 Sze-ling
14 Concubine Cemeteries

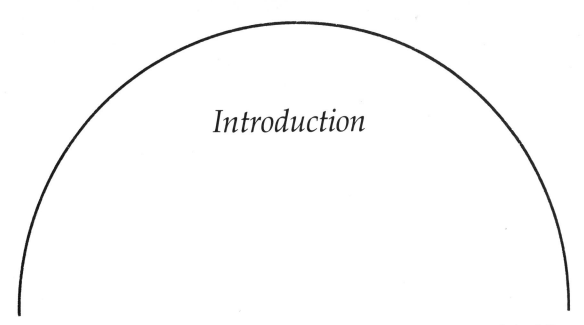

Introduction

The first Westerner to give a serious and comprehensive description of the Ming Tombs was the scholar Jan Jakob Maria De Groot, who devoted a whole section of his monumental *Religious System of China* (published in 1894), to this subject. The situation then seems to have been rather like that of today—the tombs were open to foreign visitors but most travelers concentrated on the first tomb, Ch'ang-ling, and made little attempt to consider the cemetery as a whole. A serious commentator such as the French consul in Canton, Camille Imbault-Huart, wrote scornfully in 1893: "Il n'est pas de touriste ou de globe trotteur qui, accomplissant religieusement l'excursion traditionelle à la Grande Muraille, n'ait été visiter les Tombeaux des Empereurs de la dynastie des Ming. . . . et ne soit hâté, de retour dans sa patrie, d'en donner une description plus ou moins fantasiste."[1] But he himself commited the same error and dismissed the twelve smaller tombs as inferior miniatures, placed like satellites around Ch'ang-ling.

De Groot gave us a firsthand account of how the mausoleum looked in 1894. He described the principal buildings and eight of the tombs in detail, giving a plan of Ch'ang-ling and several photographs. He checked what he saw against Chinese sources, relying mainly on the official Chinese records—Twenty-four Histories or Authentic Histories—including History of the Ming Dynasty and an account by the historian Ku Yen-wu, who visited the mausoleum in the 1650s, soon after the fall of the Ming dynasty.[2] Finally, and perhaps most important, he examined the role played by each building, tracing its historical background and symbolic significance in classical Chinese philosophy.

After De Groot, nothing serious was published on the subject until 1920, when *Les Sépultures impériales des Ming* by Georges Bouillard and Commandant Vaudescal came out in the *Bulletin de l'Ecole Française d'Extrême-Orient*. Bouillard and Vaudescal were a happy combination. The former was by training a railway engineer, for many years Chief Engineer and Technical Advisor to the Chinese government. When he retired, he chose to continue living in Peking and devoted his time to his real interests—mapmaking, topography, and archaeology. The latter, attached to the French garrison in Peking, was a serious sinologist and student of Chinese history. Between them they produced the first detailed account of all thirteen tombs with a chart of each, drawn to scale. For the general philosophical and historical background of the tombs, they relied heavily on De Groot, but their use of original Chinese sources about the tombs was more extensive. Where possible they preceded their own observations with a Chinese description of the tombs. Their main sources were Ku Yen-wu and the account of an earlier Chinese traveler, Sun Kuo-mi, who visited the tombs en route to the capital in 1622.[3]

Commandant Vaudescal was killed in the first year of the Great War in 1914, but Bouillard continued his researches into the tombs and in 1922 published a study, *Les Tombeaux impériaux des dynasties Ming et Ts'ing (avec cartes et plans),* in Peking. This was revised and reissued in 1931. In the introduction to the 1931 edition, he specifies that his main sources are original research, including that done with Vaudescal, De Groot's *Religious System of China,* and a description of the Western Tombs of the Ch'ing dynasty, *Si-ling, Etude sur les tombeaux de la dynastie des Ts'ing* (Paris, 1907), by E. Fonssagrives, a French officer stationed at these tombs from 1900–01, after the Boxer rising. Bouillard's later work gives much interesting material about Chinese Imperial graves in general, including information about the administration of the tombs and the sacrificial rites; but the topographical descriptions have been shortened, and they paint neither so full nor so vivid a picture of the cemetery as the 1920 publication.

This book starts with a brief account of who the Mings were and how they came to choose the site of their necropolis. Then follows a description of the impressive buildings at the entrance to the Ming Valley and the famous ceremonial way with its stone figures. Before dealing with the individual tombs, I give a short explanation of the principles of Chinese architecture in general and tomb architecture in particular, which I hope will make it easier to understand the layout of the different mausoleums. The thirteen tombs are then examined in detail; each chapter contains a description of the tomb as it was in 1975, a note on the drainage system, a brief account of the life of the emperor buried there, and a chart recording the state of the buildings in 1975. At the end there is a note on the traditional administration of the Imperial cemetery and the nature of the ceremonial and sacrificial rites performed at the tombs. The symbolism and characteristics of the "four intelligent creatures"—the unicorn, the phoenix, the tortoise, and the dragon—are briefly looked at in Appendix A. Appendix B gives a bird list for the Ming Valley.

The descriptions of the individual tombs are based on personal observation, but I have used Bouillard and Vaudescal's work as a point of departure. By checking present structures against the careful descriptions from 1920 and 1931, it has been possible to assess the extent and quality of the restorations. The charts of the thirteen tombs in the Ming Valley and the tomb of the first Ming emperor in Nanking are based on Bouillard's charts but have been redrawn by Lucy Peck on the basis of my notes from the field to show the present state of the buildings, and have been updated where the original charts no longer correspond to reality. In a few cases, noted in the text, personal observations and information given by Dr. Wang Yeqiu and Sheng Congwen at the Palace Museum in Peking and Dr. Feng Cangyuan of the Kiangsu Provincial Museum in Nanking have led me to question certain of Bouillard's findings. The comments on the drainage system break new ground.

For historical and biographical details I have relied heavily on the *Dictionary of Ming Biography* edited by L. Carrington Goodrich and Chaoying Fang. This dictionary gives full biographies of the first thirteen Ming emperors; the last three are covered by Arthur W. Hummel's *Eminent Chinese of the Ch'ing Period*. All dates and the chronological tables of the Ming emperors are taken from the *Dictionary of Ming Biography*. The Chinese characters for the principal sources, the names of the different parts of the mausoleum, the inscriptions on the grave steles, and some of the mythical animals mentioned in the text are given in the Glossary. With the exception of the names of present-day Chinese scholars, I have used the Wade Giles system of romanisation, since this is still more familiar to most Western readers than the official Chinese Pinyin.

The state of the Ming mausoleum is very different from what it was fifty years ago. Through Bouillard's work, and to a lesser extent through De Groot's, runs a distinct note of sadness—the tombs were already so decayed as to seem beyond restoration. No one can read their descriptions without being struck by the strong attachment both men felt for the Ming Valley. Their impressions are borne out by photographs taken by other travelers in the first half of this century. These show a landscape of desolation—stone figures stand in a wasteland and tomb buildings and courtyards appear to be completely abandoned (Fig. 18). The long years of war must have hastened the process of deterioration; but with the establishment of the People's Republic in 1949 the Ming Valley received a new lease of life. In the early 1950s the first tomb in the valley, Ch'ang-ling, was completely restored. In 1958 Ting-ling (tomb 10), tomb of the Emperor Wan-li, was excavated and partially restored. At least two other tombs, Ching-ling (tomb 3) and Yung-ling (tomb 8), have been partially restored; the remaining tombs have been cleaned up, and most show signs of maintenance and preservation. In some places, for example, the supports of a doorway have been renewed, in others, a new ramp has been built or the drains have been cleared. The Ming Tombs are recognized as great national monuments and, with the Great Wall and the Forbidden City, rank as one of the most popular tourist attractions for Chinese from all over the country, as well as for overseas Chinese and foreign visitors.

At the same time the landscape has come to life. The valley, integrated into the overall system of Peoples' Communes, is a flourishing example of Chinese agriculture, and the villages, still on the sites of the original villages set up for the guardians of the tombs in Imperial times, have been expanded and modernised with much new housing in the traditional style. In winter there are mass movements to transform the stony hillocks into level, fertile terraces. In spring and summer the valley looks like a vast vegetable garden. Corn is interplanted with beans, cabbages grow between apple trees. In early spring the fields flanking the ceremonial way are a sea of fruit blossoms. In autumn, the twelfth tomb, Te-ling, seems to lie in a bed of orange persimmons. Up the sides of the hills small children collect wood or leaves in curious high-wheeled barrows or straw paniers. The usual mixed herds of cows, donkeys, and mules graze on the hills that have been newly planted with pines.

In spite of all this movement, the valley retains an extraordinary feeling of serenity. You never feel that agriculture is spoiling the valley or that the tombs are out of place. Somehow the whole falls into a close-fitting pattern which is pleasing to the senses. It is all part of the Chinese idea of contrast and continuity. Not only is there the charm of sudden contrast between the bustle in the fields and the great stillness inside the tomb precincts. There is also the contrast between the newness of life outside and the preservation of an earlier civilisation inside, buried in the untouched funeral mounds. Against this background, I suspect that both De Groot and Bouillard would be happily surprised to see the Ming Tombs today.

This brings me to one of the most unusual features of the mausoleum. It was normal in Ming times to provide the dead with the sort of luxuries he had been used to in life, by placing clothing, jewellery, and other precious objects in the funeral chamber. Only one tomb has been excavated, and that belongs to the Emperor Wan-li who lived at a time of economic decline. His reign was by no means the most splendid of the Ming dynasty, yet the wealth uncovered in his tomb is breathtaking. The interesting point is that, as far as is known, most of the other tombs in the valley are intact. Similar or greater treasures may lie beneath the other funeral mounds. Whereas in any Western country they would all have been opened up long ago, the Chinese have as yet made no attempt to excavate them. The reasons given for this, to my mind highly attractive phenomenon, fit in with the whole Chinese idea of continuity in history. A man's life is part of a chain of lives—all those who went before him and all those who come after. No one epoch is all-important. Today the Chinese are busy excavating sites which have been discovered, often accidentally, in the course of land transformation schemes all over China. These already opened sites demand time and work. On the other hand, since it is known exactly where the Ming Tombs are and the sorts of things likely to be found in them, there is no particular hurry. One might just as well leave them for later generations to uncover. It is perhaps this feeling of an untouched part of the past being kept as a heritage for the future that gives the valley of the Ming Tombs its unusually peaceful atmosphere.

1

The Ming Dynasty and the Origins of the Tombs

"Ming" in Chinese means "brilliant." Chu Yüan-chang, the founder of the dynasty, was born in 1328, the son of poor peasants. Like the founder of the Han dynasty in the third century before Christ, his rise from poverty to the Imperial throne was due to sheer intelligence and an ability to take advantage of troubled times. At an early age, during a famine, he was sold by his parents to a Buddhist monastery where he learnt to read and write. Later he seems to have left the monastery and become a beggar; at twenty-five he joined one of the rebel bands that were springing up in China at that time. The Mongol dynasty, long hated for its harsh and alien rule and weakened by corruption and inefficiency, was slowly breaking up. A series of rebellions broke out; the Mongols were unable to suppress them and pulled their forces back towards their home territory in the North.

Chu Yüan-chang soon distinguished himself from the other rebel leaders by his ability to organise, and the areas which he overran were assimilated into a single system of administration, thus providing an evergrowing base for further advances. By 1356 he had crossed the Yangtze River and taken Nanking, which he made his capital. In 1368 he captured Peking and declared himself the first emperor of a new dynasty—the Ming.[1]

And brilliant it was. Under Hung-wu, as the emperor was now known, China was once again united under a Chinese dynasty.* The empire extended farther to the north than at any time since the T'ang; in the south, Yunnan was incorporated and settled for the first time. With the exception of Sinkiang, the Ming Empire covered roughly the same area as the People's Republic of China does today. After nearly one

---

*The whole question of names is very complicated. The emperor was given one name at birth, another "tomb name" after death. In addition to this, a name was given to the different "year periods" of his reign. Luckily, Chu Yüan-chang decided to revert to the habit of the old Chou kings and keep the name of his first reign period for the whole of his reign. His successors followed suit, and with one exception there is only one reign title for each Ming emperor; this title, which, strictly speaking, refers to a number of years rather than a person, is the one by which the emperor is usually known.

hundred years of foreign domination under the Mongols, there was a conscious return to Chinese traditions and a revival and revitalising of Chinese arts. As a moral precept to his successors, Hung-wu had engraved on his tomb: "Rule like the T'ang and the Sung." For 267 years, this empire of nearly two hundred million people, easily the largest political unit in the world, enjoyed comparative peace and stability.

It was an era of enormous vitality. Not only were the frontiers of the empire enlarged and consolidated, but for the only time in Chinese history, serious attempts were made to explore the rest of the world. In the reign of the third emperor, Yung-lo, naval expeditions under the great admiral Cheng Ho sailed to the East Indies, India, Ceylon, the Persian Gulf, the Red Sea, and finally reached the east coast of Africa. These explorers brought back rare objects and exotic animals; the courts in Nanking and Peking showed a wealth and sophistication unknown in the Western world.

In administration, taxation, and general fiscal matters, the empire was well organised. It was a highly centralised organisation with an elaborate network covering all the provinces. Taxation was graduated according to wealth and officials chosen competitively on the basis of academic merit. Later, under weak emperors and increasingly corrupt eunuch control, this system degenerated, but in the beginning at least, it led to a marked increase in economic activity. Trade and manufacturing grew apace and the arts and literature flourished. The technique of making porcelain reached new heights. It was under the Ming that western Europe started importing porcelain which not unnaturally came to be known as "china." Above all, however, the energy and exuberance of the age showed itself in its building activity. Most of what we today consider to be classical Chinese architecture is Ming architecture.

As we have seen, Hung-wu was a southerner; he therefore established his capital in Nanking. When he died in 1398, his grandson and heir, Chu Yün-wen, was twenty-one years old. Youth on the throne always led to weakness, and the new emperor was immediately challenged by his uncle, Chu Ti.[2] Chu Ti had been appointed "King of Yen" by his father, and in that position had been responsible for guarding the northern frontier against the Mongols. He was an able commander with experience in battle and administration. After five years of civil war the North, under his leadership, defeated the South, and Chu Ti declared himself emperor.

Later, many legends grew up about Chu Yün-wen. According to one of these, he escaped from Nanking disguised as a monk, and wandered around China for some forty years before being captured. It is said that he was then sent to Peking, where he was recognised by an elderly eunuch, Wu Liang. Wu Liang was at first reluctant to admit that he had known the former emperor, but when Chu Yün-wen began to recount certain stories from his youth, the eunuch could not help crying. In this version, the reigning emperor showed a clement attitude towards the former ruler and allowed him to live the rest of his life in peaceful obscurity in Peking. There is, however, no proof that Chu Yün-wen survived the fall of Nanking, and modern historians tend to believe that he died in 1402. It is not known where he is buried.

Meanwhile the victorious Chu Ti, better known by his reign name, Yung-lo, (Perpetual Happiness), felt more at ease among his own supporters in the North and therefore moved the capital to Peking. It is recorded that he employed one million men to build the new capital in ten years; in an interesting forerunner of the Great Leap Forward, they finished the task in five. The Forbidden City and old Peking as we know it are largely the creation of Yung-lo.

The decision to move the capital posed Yung-lo a very important question. Where were the Imperial family to be buried? In the Chinese philosophy of life, ancestor worship was all-important. Good government depended on achieving harmony between Earth and Heaven. The role of the emperor was to achieve this harmony. Although the emperor was called the "Son of Heaven," he was not considered divine in the Western sense of the word. He was a go-between. If he acted wrongly, heaven would send punishments in the form of natural calamities. By consulting the oracles one could often find out what was offending the gods and how they could be propitiated, but the only way to communicate with them was through the spirits of the ancestors. Ancestors provided the vital link between the living on earth and the spirits above. It was therefore essential to keep the spirits of one's ancestors happy; otherwise they would not cooperate. The spirit, however, could not survive without the body—hence the importance of the tomb.

The first duty of every son was to care for his father's tomb and to satisfy his father's spirit. This meant that the dead man should, if possible, lie surrounded by that to which he had been accustomed in life. If, for example, the father had lived in a palace, then his tomb must resemble a palace. And through sacrifices and the performance of the sacred rites, the son must continue to keep his father and all his earlier ancestors well provided with the necessities and luxuries they would expect. This applied to all people—high and low alike. The only difference was that whereas the spirit of a poor man could only wreak vengeance on his family, the dissatisfied spirit of an emperor could cause the whole empire to suffer.

The first Ming emperor, Hung-wu, had established an Imperial cemetery at Nanking. Yung-lo's wife, the Empress Hsü,[3] who had died in Nanking in 1407, was buried there in a temporary tomb, but it was obviously improper that she should continue to lie so far away. Nor would it be practicable for Yung-lo's successors if he were to be buried there. Yung-lo therefore gave orders that a propitious place be found for the Imperial cemetery near Peking. The question of site was all-important; if it was wrongly placed the spirits would be displeased, and this would affect the whole future of the dynasty.

For the Chinese, the choice of a site was a quasi-scientific matter based on geomancy or *feng-shui*. Literally, *feng-shui* means "wind-water," and the idea was to find a natural situation that would not disturb the good influences whilst being protected from the evil. The earliest extant record of feng-shui, which sets down ideas still widely accepted up to the establishment of the People's Republic in 1949, is the "Canon of Dwellings" from the Han dynasty, second century B.C. But this book ascribes its own origin to the mythical Yellow Emperor reckoned to have lived in the twenty-seventh century B.C. Feng-shui was all-embracing; no house could be built or altered, no road could be laid out, without consulting the geomancers. It was a system open to great abuse since the common man could not interpret the rules for himself. Not surprisingly, Western commentators have tended to regard it as irrational, absurd, and often downright harmful. De Groot typifies this attitude in his lively but malicious descriptions of a geomancer or "mountain cockroach" at work:

> He assumes all the airs of the literati and the gentry, dresses as they do, in a long gown, wears a pair of large spectacles, though not short-sighted, and awes his patrons into admiration and respect by scarcely ever opening his mouth, except to utter a few wise words, or a classic phrase borrowed from the books. Others on the contrary establish and keep up their reputation by loquaciousness, overawing everybody by speaking a mystifying learned jargon, and by apocalyptic utterances of which the ordinary man understands next to nothing.[4]

The choice of a grave site was a lengthy affair:

> Whilst wise discussions are being held on the contours of the country, and the hands are continuously moved up and down in all the directions of the compass, the party keep themselves under the shade of umbrellas of paper and silk; for around most towns scarcely a tree or shrub affords shelter against the scorching sun, all vegetation having in the course of time been radically destroyed under the direction of the geomancers. Now and then the professor brings forth his compass from a linen bag hanging from his shoulder, and lying full length, or creeping on the ground, he takes his bearings by placing over his instrument a so-called "thread for subtle measurement," which is a red cord, from each end of which dangles a copper coin to keep it stretched.[5]

And yet, when all this is said, there remains in feng-shui a sound core of common sense. The Chinese are a practical people, and from what I have been able to discover, the general principles of feng-shui are eminently sensible. The first principle is that the place must be protected from the evil spirits which come from the dominant— usually the north—wind. The second is that water should not run through the site of the building but should, if possible, run in front of it (because if the course of the stream is altered the spirit will take offense). The third is that it is desirable to have a view of mountains with auspicious shapes. These mountains should be continuous, that is, it should not be possible to see clefts or passages through them. In other words, the ideal site is very much what people would look for today—a sheltered place, facing in a southerly direction, dry but with a stream nearby and a good view.* As a result of

---

*The earliest European writer on feng-shui, E. J. Eitel, pointed out in 1873 that the Chinese in Hong Kong were convinced the Europeans knew all about feng-shui. "Why, they say [the Chinese], there is Government House occupying the best spot on the northern side of the island, screened at the back by high trees and gently shelving terraces, skirted right and left by roads with graceful curves and the whole situation combining everything that

1. Distant view of Ch'ang-ling (tomb 1)

2. View across the reservoir to foothills enclosing the southern end of the Ming Valley

feng-shui, not only is the Imperial cemetery in an incredibly beautiful place, but each tomb in the valley, with the exception perhaps of the very last, seems to fit exactly into the landscape (fig. 1). The outlook is always different but always pleasing, and you are left with the feeling that one could not have found a better site. In the Ming Tombs, you see more clearly than anywhere else the Chinese ability to achieve harmony between man and nature. The reservoir built in the Great Leap Forward in 1958 has done nothing but make the valley more beautiful (fig. 2).

It seems to have taken the geomancers several years to agree on a site, and records give conflicting accounts of how the final decision was reached. Both De Groot and Bouillard quote a Chinese report that at one time the emperor himself consulted a tortoise shell.[6] What is certain is that the mountain on the north side of the valley used to be called "Mountain of Yellow Earth" but was, once the decision had been taken, renamed "Mountain of Heavenly Longevity." According to one story, Yung-lo happened to visit the site on his birthday, and so many peasants came to wish him a long life that it led to the renaming of the mountain.[7] There is also a legend that at an early date in the dynasty twelve jade-coloured pigeons, flying from the south, settled on top of the mountain. This was interpreted to mean that the capital would be moved from the south to Peking and that twelve Imperial tombs would be built in the shelter of the mountain. The flaw in the story is, of course, that there are thirteen tombs, but the last tomb was in fact built by another dynasty.

The valley eventually chosen in 1409 is about five kilometres long from north to south and three kilometres wide (chart 1). The mountains are highest to the north, graduating downward to east and west. In the south they are little more than soft hills. Once the geomancers were satisfied about the site for the cemetery as a whole, the placing of the later tombs was comparatively easy. In these cases it seems only to have been necessary to consult the smaller points of feng-shui while paying a certain respect to the relationship between the newly deceased emperor and his predecessor—that is to say that the tomb of a son tended to be placed near to the tomb of his father.

---

feng-shui would prescribe, how is it possible that foreigners pretend to know nothing of feng-shui?" (*Feng-shui*, p. 3–4; In Hong Kong, for climatic and geographical reasons, the north rather than the south is the better aspect.) See also G. Schlegel's review of the relevant section of De Groot's book in *T'oung Pao* (Leyden), no. 9 (1898), p. 70.

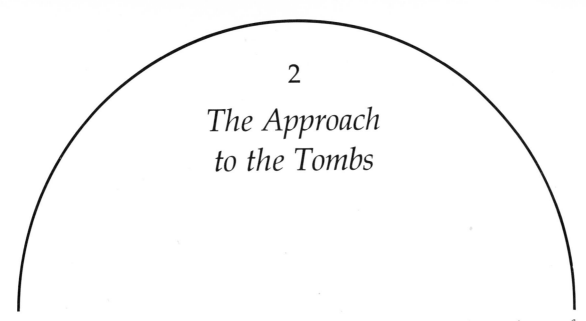

2

The Approach to the Tombs

The valley of the Ming Tombs lies some forty-five kilometres to the northwest of Peking. Once you have left the northern suburbs behind, the drive is a very pleasant one. The road runs more or less straight between avenues of trees; in the large, flat fields to either side, you can see the eternal cycle of Chinese agriculture. One Sunday the fields will be thick with people harvesting; the next Sunday half the road may well be covered with corn drying in the sun while small children watch to see that it does not blow away. Others will be patiently gleaning the fields for any straw or grain that may have been overlooked. Later, just before the frost, it will be cabbage time—cart after cart laden with bright green cabbages to be dried on the rooftops and balconies for use in the winter. The road is a busy one—long lines of horse-, donkey- or cow-drawn carts interspersed with khaki-coloured lorries.

You pass through two villages and cross two rivers and a canal. On an island in the middle of the first river there is a large white marble stele, which gives you the feeling you are on the right road. Up river on the far right bank are the remains of a mud fortress built in Ming times for troops to practise manoeuvres. The second village was an important staging post in Imperial times; even today it tends to be filled with horse-drawn carts and vehicles whose drivers are breaking the journey into Peking. Another marble stele stands by the second bridge, and then you come to the canal. This joins the Grand Canal that linked the grain-producing provinces in the south with Peking. Occasionally you can still see cormorant fishing from here. The fisherman uses a cormorant with a ring around its neck to catch the fish; the ring is so tight that the bird cannot swallow its catch but is forced to disgorge it into the boat. Farther along, on the left, is a small pavilion on a little hill; its bright yellow roof gleams through the pine trees. This was one of the resting places for the emperor on his way from Peking to the tombs.

After about an hour the road divides; the left fork leads to the Great Wall, the right, straight to the Valley of the Thirteen Tombs. At first the view is rather dreary. There are a few factories with tall chimneys along the foothills to the west. The road here is new and has not yet been planted with trees. Then quite suddenly, round a slightly hilly bend, you come to an enormous white marble archway. This is the P'ai-lou, a ceremonial Arc de Triomphe built in 1540 to commemorate the glory of the Ming dynasty (colourplate 2).

This P'ai-lou is said to be the most beautiful in all China. The white is dazzling against the blue Peking sky. The sheer size and beauty of the carved stone is overwhelming. The archway is made up of six square columns, each carved from a single marble slab, with single-slab lintels making five arches. The highest one, the central arch, is five and a half metres high. Above the lintels is an extraordinary superstructure of friezes and ornamental roofs, all carved in white marble. Right in the middle at the top is a blank surface; presumably this was left for an inscription which never materialized. The general effect of the upper part is of an unusually imposing palace style roof; all the intricate beams and crossbeams of the normal Ming roof are there, but in this fantasy, all are reproduced in marble.* Here and there are traces of colour, showing that this was once painted in bright colours as an ordinary roof would be.

The animals carved on the bases of the columns seem almost to be alive. On the four panels of the outer columns are two lions with a ball (fig. 3); on the second and fifth columns there are two "makara" sprouting vegetation (fig. 4); and on each of the innermost columns a dragon moves through the clouds (fig. 5). The lions are the traditional Chinese type; with their carefully frizzed-up hair and collars with little bell-like trinkets, they look more like large Pekinese dogs than lions. The role and origin of these lions will be discussed in more detail later. It suffices to note here that they were guardian animals of Buddhist inspiration, intended to keep evil spirits at bay. The ball they are playing with is probably the Buddhist "night-shining pearl"; this pearl symbolizes divine truth and the wisdom of Heaven and is found in the coat of arms of all emperors since the Han dynasty.[1] The background of these panels is carved with a trellis pattern of small flowers, giving the impression of an embroidered silk hanging.

The "makara" on the next two columns is of Indian origin, a mythical serpent god.[2] Originally derived from the crocodile, it is associated with hibernation and water and hence growth. These stone makara exude fertility—the tail branches out into large coiled leaves while an enormous flower on a long stalk spurts out through the mouth (fig. 6). Similar creatures can be seen on the beautiful stone arch at Chü-yung kuan at the Nan K'ou Pass on the way to the Great Wall. This archway, built in 1345, carries inscriptions in six languages, and its decorations are clearly Buddhist inspired.†

*Stone columns carved to imitate wooden and tile roofs are known from the Han dynasty onward. The habit of using one material to imitate a construction typical of another is very persistent in Chinese decorative art. A bronze flask from the Warring States period (480–222 B.C.), for example, is modeled in relief to look as if its sides are covered with a network of knotted rope.

†Under the Yüan dynasty, Buddhist influence, particularly in its Lamaistic or Tibetan and Mongolian form, was strong. Although the Ming, as restorers of the native Chinese civilization, supported Confucianism, they by no means rejected Buddhism. The founder of the dynasty had, after all, spent some years as a Buddhist monk, and the

3. RIGHT: Panel on column base of the P'ai-lou showing two lions playing with a ball

4. CENTRE LEFT: South side of a P'ai-lou column base showing reclining lion and panel with makara

5. CENTRE RIGHT: South side of a P'ai-lou column base showing ch'i-lin and panel with five-clawed dragon

6. Detail of makara head and flower on panel of P'ai-lou column base

The dragons on the two central pillars are full-fledged Imperial "lung," or five-clawed dragons. Of all the numerous Chinese mythical animals, the dragon is perhaps the most important. Its origins—both Chinese and Indian—and its symbolism as a creature of both the watery depths and the sky, are complicated and are examined in more detail in Appendix A. As the spirit of water and rain without which there can be no life on earth, the dragon was all-important and it was therefore natural for it to become the symbol of Imperial power. The dragon takes many forms and has numerous offspring. The five-clawed variety shown here was reserved by statute for Imperial use; lesser mortals might only use the four-clawed "mang." The carving of these panels shows the dragon in all its glory. Surrounded by clouds, as befits the bringer of rain, it moves effortlessly and timelessly, conveying a sense of freedom and eternal motion.

At the top of each column base, lying along the axis of the arch and facing inwards, there are two more animals. On the two outer columns on each side, these are lions of the same sort described earlier, only here they rest sedately. On each of the two central columns is a ch'i-lin. The ch'i-lin—like the dragon, the phoenix, and the tortoise—was one of the "four intelligent creatures" revered in Chinese classical tradition (see Appendix A). Scaly and cloven-hoofed, it takes many forms and in early times was often shown with only one horn. This led to its name being translated as "unicorn"—a cause of much confusion, as will be readily understood by anyone who looks at these stone figures. The ch'i-lin was a very popular mythological figure. It was gentle and good and rarely seen, appearing only when a ruler of the highest virtue sat on the throne or when a sage was about to be born. It was therefore natural that the ruling dynasty should choose it to ornament its memorial archway. All these carvings are in a perfect state of repair. The relief and delicate lines are so clear that it is hard to remember that they are four hundred years old.

The archway stands on a raised base of large stone paving. In photographs taken at the beginning of this century you can see a little stele just to the right, or east, of the P'ai-lou. According to Bouillard, this was put up in 1909 to record reparations done to the eastern side of the base, which was being eroded by water. At that time the whole P'ai-lou was surrounded by a low wall.*

It is hard to describe the full effect of the P'ai-lou. The grandeur of the arches, the delicate carving of the animals which almost appear to be moving, the intricacies of the marble mock roof, all seem to soar out of the flat plain and tower over you. The

---

Emperor Ch'eng-hua (1464–87) encouraged Buddhism, receiving Buddhist monks and Tibetan magicians at court. By cultivating the ruling lamas in Tibet and Mongolia, the Ming hoped to keep peace in these border regions. Contacts between Lhasa and Peking were maintained through visiting delegations, and in this way the Buddhist influence on Chinese art, which had received a new injection when the Yüan brought Tibetan craftsmen to Peking, was maintained. The very idea of a P'ai-lou is of Indian origin. Gateways or ceremonial doorways of this sort, such as the "toranas" or gateways of the Sanchu stupa, can be found in India as far back as the first century before Christ.

*In 1979 this wall was being replaced, and I understand that there is a plan to make a sort of garden round the P'ai-lou.

P'ai-lou stands very much alone. It is built on a slight rise, and the view through the arches, whichever way you look, is of the sky. Although it lies on a straight axis with the next two buildings—the Great Red Gate and the Stele Pavilion—it is in fact outside the necropolis. (There is a place, farther back on the road, from which in winter you can sometimes see the three buildings clearly in line, pointing toward the first tomb, Ch'ang-ling.) When the P'ai-lou was built by the Emperor Chia-ching in 1540, the Imperial cemetery had already been in use for more than a hundred years.

The Great Red Gate, one kilometre beyond the P'ai-lou, is the real entrance to the valley (fig. 7). When the necropolis was first laid out, the whole area was enclosed by a wall and a series of coloured posts.[3] In 1920 vestiges of this wall could still be seen on the sides of the hills and in some of the passes leading down into the valley. This huge triple gateway, almost certainly built in 1425, is painted the same deep red as the walls of the Forbidden City. The roof is covered with shining yellow tiles. (Yellow was reserved for Imperial use; all the roofs in the Ming Tombs, like almost all those in the Forbidden City, are yellow.) The central archway was reserved exclusively for the passage of a dead emperor; living emperors had to use the door on the left. Originally the encircling walls, which were also red with yellow roof tiles, joined the gate on both sides. To the left and right of the gateway were two stone tablets which said: "This is where officials and others should dismount from their horses." It was considered disrespectful to the spirit of the dead to ride or bring horses into the enclosed area; there was even an Imperial edict that all those passing in front of the gateway should dismount. The penalty for disobeying this edict in Ch'ing times was "one hundred blows with the long [bamboo] stick."

In 1931 the heavy wooden doors were still in place but the gate itself was in disrepair; the roof was crumbling and overgrown with vegetation, tiles falling to the ground. At that time the building, like the P'ai-lou, stood on a raised platform with steps. Today the platform is gone and the road leads through the two side arches. The building has been completely restored. The roof is in excellent condition but the wooden doors have been removed. Since the gateway stands on a small hill, you see a beautiful view of the mountains framed in the archway as you approach. From here you get the first real impression of the valley. The mountains circle in front, and on a clear day you can already see one or two of the yellow roofs of the tombs. (A straight line through the central arch northward would pass exactly over the highest peak on the north side.) To the east you can see the reservoir.

The Great Red Gate is the starting point for the official road up to the tombs. Originally there was a two-storied building just inside the gate where visitors could rest and brush away the dust; it was also here that the emperor donned his ceremonial robes for the sacrifices. From here the road leads directly to the Stele Pavilion and hence up the "spirit road" to the principal tomb in the valley, Ch'ang-ling (colourplate 1). As will be seen later, each tomb had its own smaller approach road; this one, leading to the first and largest tomb, is rather like the trunk of a tree with the memorial stele and row of attendant animals and figures intended to serve all those buried in the valley. Here and there you can still see traces of the old paving on both sides of the new road.

Half a kilometre farther on stands a large square red pavilion with arches opening to the four sides which houses the largest memorial stele in China (fig. 8). The idea of using a stele or tombstone to commemorate the dead dates from very early times. By the end of the Han dynasty, second century A.D., it was common practice. The stone tablet carried an inscription in memory of the dead; if the deceased belonged to one of the higher ranks, it was customary to decorate the top of the stele with a reclining "li," a hornless dragon (figs. 9 and 10). These mythical creatures were supposed "to shower down upon the buried man and his offspring all the blessings which dragons generally pour forth upon graves in their capacity of chief bearers of the beneficial influences of the universe."[4] By the sixth century there was a further development—nobles and officials of high rank were entitled to a stele placed on the back of a tortoise. The tortoise had since earliest times been regarded as a symbol of longevity, strength, and endurance, and its presence would therefore ensure long life to the descendants of the deceased. The earliest written reference to a tortoise stele is found in an edict by the first Sui emperor, who stipulated that: "To his officers in the Metropolis belonging to the three highest ranks and buried at seven or more miles from the city walls, a pei (stele) with a hornless dragon at the top, and a tortoise as a pedestal, might be erected, but it should not rise more than nine feet above the pedestal."[5] Lower ranks might only use a square pedestal.

The great memorial stele commemorating the Ming dynasty differs from its predecessors only in size. The stele tablet, some ten metres high, is cut from a single block of stone. The crowning border is carved with hornless dragons. Here and there you can see traces of red and green paint; it seems that originally the whole stele was painted. This tablet rests on a gigantic tortoise—4½ metres long, nearly 2½ metres wide, and 1.80 metres high—carved in one piece. With its scaly body, long supple neck, and small head, this mythical animal is clearly derived from a terrapin or turtle. It stands on a stone base decorated with waves. On one side of the stele there is an inscription: "Stele to the transcendent merit and saintly virtue of Ch'ang-ling of the great dynasty of Ming."*

Although the date at the bottom is equivalent to 5 May 1425, the stele itself was not erected until 10 October 1435, after the death of the Emperor Hung-hsi (Yung-lo's son and successor), who wrote the epitaph. On the reverse side of the stele there is a long poem, dated 1785 and attributed by De Groot to the great Ch'ing emperor, Ch'ien-lung. After a brief introduction, each line commemorates a different Ming tomb (figs. 11 and 12).

In 1538 the Emperor Chia-ching (the same who was responsible for the P'ai-lou) wanted to change the inscription on this stele. This would have involved erasing some of the characters and carving new ones; such an alteration could not be made without

*In choosing this name for his mausoleum, Yung-lo followed the example of Kao-tsu, the first Han emperor whose mausoleum name was Ch'ang-ling.

7. TOP: The Great Red Gate

8. RIGHT: Stele pavilion and two Columns Supporting the Sky, ca. 1910 (Yale Slide and Photograph Collection)

9. BOTTOM LEFT: Hornless dragons, or "li," on "east" face of tortoise stele, Te-ling (tomb 12)

10. BOTTOM RIGHT: Hornless dragons on "south" side of tortoise stele, Te-ling (tomb 12)

11. TOP LEFT: South face of the Memorial Stele

12. TOP RIGHT: North face of the Memorial Stele

13. LEFT: Base of tortoise stele, Yung-ling (tomb 8)

14. BELOW: Base of grave stele, Ting-ling (tomb 10)

authorisation from the Tribunal of Rites and the Han-lin Academy. Eventually permission was granted, but although a date was decreed for the work to begin, the change was never carried out. Later, in 1604, when the stele was damaged by lightning, the chief advisor of the new emperor, Wan-li suggested that since the stele needed repairing anyway, this would be a good moment to carry out the alterations. The emperor was furious. If Heaven saw fit to appear at the tombs of the ancestors in this way, it was obviously a sign of displeasure. To suggest dealing with this omen in such a practical way was worse than to deny the existence of Heaven![6] In this incident one can see both the slow-moving bureaucracy and the tremendous importance attached to everything that had to do with the tombs.

All Imperial tombs have two steles; the first, like this one, rests on a tortoise and stands at the entrance of the road to the grave. The other stands in a pavilion or small house on a fortified tower at the entrance to the grave itself; this carries an inscription to the deceased emperor and stands on a layered rectangular base (figs. 13 and 14). For simplicity I shall refer to these respectively as the "tortoise stele" and the "grave stele." In cemeteries such as the Ming Valley, where more than one person is buried, the first stele, at the start of the main sacred way, refers to the first and therefore the most important person buried there. With the exception of the first tomb, Ch'ang-ling, and the last tomb, Sze-ling, which were either restored or built by the Ch'ing dynasty, none of the tortoise steles in the Ming Valley carries an inscription. This is unusual; traditionally such a stele would have given the name of the deceased, beginning with the words: "road to the grave of. . . ."

Another curious feature of the tortoise steles in the Ming Valley is that, with the exception of the great memorial stele described above and the stele in the first courtyard of Ch'ang-ling (tomb 1), which was the subject of Ch'ing restoration, they are roofless. Ku Yen-wu, after his visits to the tombs in the 1650s, describes some of the tortoise steles as standing in a small pavilion with a double roof.* De Groot repeats this but is untypically vague: "In most cases, if not all, the tablet of fine white stone does not bear any characters and is supported by a tortoise and adorned with a crowning border on which dragons are engraved. In a few instances, the tablet stands under the open sky, the building sheltering it having disappeared in consequence of vandalism or want of care, or because no such building has ever existed."[7] According to Bouillard, the situation in 1920 was the same as it is today. He notes that, apart from the two steles referred to above, the tortoise steles were roofless, and that he could find no traces of any sheltering pavilions which may or may not have existed earlier. Today each of these roofless tortoise steles stands on a square stone terrace with a low surrounding wall; there is a short staircase up to an opening in the centre of the four side walls. The decorations on the slab base vary considerably and will be described later.

Around this first great Stele Pavilion, standing as if on guard, are four very beautiful

*Curiously enough, the "tortoise stele" of the Emperor Ching-t'ai, in the Western Hills, stands in such a pavilion.

15. LEFT: Column Supporting the Sky

16. ABOVE: Base of Column Supporting the Sky

17. FAR ABOVE: Ch'i-lin on Column Supporting the Sky

octagonal columns. These columns are exactly the same as those standing on either side of the Gate of Heavenly Peace, or Tien An Men, at the entrance to the Forbidden City in Peking. Here we come to a problem of names. Both sets of columns are Ming, but whereas those at Tien An Men are generally called "Hua Piao" or "flowery columns," those around the Stele Pavilion were known as "Ching Tien Chu," "columns supporting the sky" (fig. 15). According to Dr. Feng Cangyuan of the Kiangsu Provincial Museum in Nanking, wooden pillars of this shape were used in the Han dynasty to signal the staging posts for the postal system. This would perhaps explain their form, which is certainly calculated to catch the eye and perhaps, with their wings at the top, to indicate speed. Later, under the T'ang, these wooden posts were still in use but people started to use stone imitations of them to decorate palaces, temples, and tombs. As the purpose of these stone pillars was purely decorative, the exact name was not very important, a certain amount being left to the imagination. What looked like a "flowery pillar" in one place might well appear to be supporting the canopy of the sky in another.

These columns show the dragon in all its glory. The octagonal base, consisting of six layers, is alive with small dragons. Narrow ribbons of racing dragons encircle the whole socle; wide panels with horizontal dragons are interspersed with narrow panels with vertical dragons. The third and fifth layers are made up of decorated lotus petals, a clear example of Buddhist influence (fig. 16). Up the column itself, one enormous five-clawed dragon twines its way through clouds toward heaven. At the top, the column branches out into two large "wings," and above these sits an animal, clearly on guard (fig. 17). On the two southern pillars the animal faces south, on the northern pillars, north. Here again we are back to the problem of names. Is this a "lion" or a "ch'i-lin"? The head is leonine but the rest of the animal bears no resemblance to what we have come to think of as a Chinese "lion"; it is scaled and cloven-hoofed like a ch'i-lin, and since that name so clearly conjures up a mythical beast, I think it is easier to settle for that.* According to Dr. Feng, there is a legend that these animals welcomed those who came to perform the rites and reminded them, on their way out, to come again soon.[8]

*In both the Palace Museum in Peking and the Kiangsu Provincial Museum at Nanking, this animal was referred to as a "roaring toward the sky," but this, while highly descriptive, is a little cumbersome in English.

18. The Spirit Road at the turn of this century. (From
Mrs. A. Little, *Round About My Peking Garden,*
London, 1905, opp. p. 130)

19. Top of beacon showing dragon's head among clouds

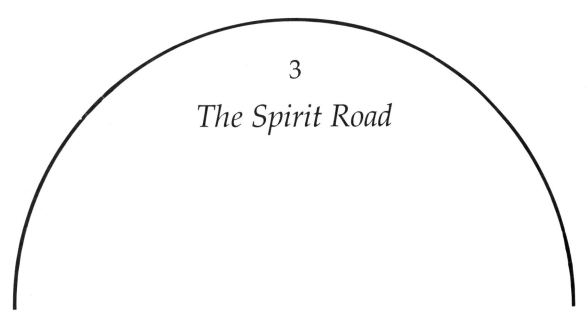

3

The Spirit Road

The P'ai-lou, the Great Red Gate, and the Stele Pavilion lie on a straight line pointing north. Continuing in this direction, the road beyond the Stele Pavilion becomes the famous "Spirit's Road for the Mausoleum in Common." This was the road that would lead the spirit home to its final resting place. After the splendour of the three approach buildings, the alley with its large stone figures provides almost a feeling of relief. There is always a slight holiday atmosphere here, and foreigners and Chinese alike climb up on the animals to have their photographs taken. At the same time there is a perpetual traffic of carts, peasants carrying firewood, or small children with little baskets and brushes to collect the precious manure that falls on the road. In a way the alley is a good example of the intermingling of the two aspects of the Ming Valley: here, side by side, are the monuments from four hundred years ago and the bustling new Chinese agriculture. Behind the figures stretch miles of neatly cultivated fruit trees; in spring the statues are framed in blossom. The contrast with pictures of this avenue earlier in the century is marked (fig. 18). The extraordinary thing is that the statues survived at all in such a state of desolation.

The entrance to the alley is marked by two stone beacons, hexagonal columns decorated with clouds (colourplate 3); a dragon peers through the clouds or smoke of the beacon head (fig. 19). Symbolically these beacons served a dual purpose: they showed the errant spirit the way home; and at the same time the warmth and brightness of their flames was believed to nourish the soul.*

*To understand the significance of these columns it is necessary to look briefly at the classical Chinese view of the universe. According to this view, which dates back to prehistoric times, nature consists of two fundamentally contrasting but coexisting parts, yang and yin. Yang, the male element, embraces light, warmth, and life and is identified with the heavens from which these blessings flow. Yin, the female element, belongs to the earth; it is associated with darkness, cold, and death. The soul, being vital, belongs to yang; the body, which, like the earth, is lifeless until the heavens act upon it, is clearly yin. By itself the soul would never be able to find its way through the regions of death in order to find the corpse and the sacrifices awaiting it—hence the beacons. Furthermore, the soul, which it was believed must be sadly weakened by its separation from the body, could receive sustenance from

This pattern—a tortoise stele, stone columns or beacons marking the entrance to a spirit road, and then stone figures to guard the tomb—was already well established in Han times, more than twelve hundred years before the Ming mausoleum was laid out. Frequently the early spirit ways began with a pair of stone columns carved like the watch towers of a city. Later, these towers and the stone beacons can be found together, as in the tomb built near Hsien-yang, some 90 km. northwest of Sian, by the T'ang empress Wu for her husband Kao-tsung. By Ming times, however, the watch-towers seem to have been dropped and only the beacons and figures remain. In the Ming tomb at Nanking the beacons stand halfway down the alley, between the animals and the men. This placing is unique and reinforces the theory that the beacons were intended to guide. After the animals, the Nanking spirit road makes a ninety-degree turn to the east; the beacons are clearly placed at the beginning of the second half of the alley to show the way.

Directly after the beacons come the animals. As we have seen, stone grave figures are known to have been used during the Han dynasty.* The practice spread rapidly and by the early sixth century A.D. had become so widespread that official decrees were issued restricting their use to those in the highest ranks. It is recorded in the Books of the Sui dynasty that in A.D. 507 "the rules of burial were officially expounded in this sense that no stone images of animals or men, nor inscribed slabs of stone might be made on ordinary graves, but only stone pillars, and a tablet bearing the name of the defunct."[1] The number and nature of statues was carefully regulated according to rank; a decree from the Sung dynasty prescribed that for officials: "One pair of stone sheep, one pair of tigers and one pair of stone beacons should be placed on their graves; but officers of the first, second and third degree might add two stone images of men."[2] Naturally no such limitations existed for Imperial mausolea, and the whole concept of a guarded or ceremonial spirit road was developed to the full under the T'ang and Sung. The spirit alley at the tomb of the T'ang Emperor Kao-tsung, mentioned above, is perhaps the largest and most splendid of its kind. Two kilometres long, it is flanked not only by horses and officials but by whole groups of figures said to represent emissaries from the provinces and tributary nations.

The spirit road in the Ming Valley, eleven hundred metres long, is flanked by twenty-four stone animals and twelve stone men, symmetrically placed in pairs and facing each other. Each animal is represented first sitting, and then standing. According to legend, this was to allow for the changing of the guard. At midnight, the pair that

---

the light and warmth (both yang elements) of the flame. This belief that the vitality of the soul can be nourished by a flame is found again in the underground grave chamber, where "everlasting" lamps of oil were lit just before the tomb was sealed (see De Groot, 3: 1088).

*The earliest group of stone grave figures yet discovered were found at a tomb in Shensi, generally recognized to be the tomb of Ho Ch'ü-ping, a celebrated Han general who died in 117 B.C. These show a surprising variety of subjects. The most famous is that of a horse trampling a barbarian; others, some only half-carved, portray a reclining water buffalo, a crouching tiger, a reclining and a rearing horse, and several fantastic creatures, including a large demon hugging and eating a small bear. These figures seem to have been placed around the tomb rather than along an alley.

had been standing on watch all day and is therefore nearest to the tomb, changed places with the pair that had been resting. However, the figures of the men are all standing because it was forbidden for a man to sit in the presence of the emperor. The carving is not very fine, but the figures have a good sturdiness about them. Here it should be remembered that in classical Chinese art a stone statue was not meant to be looked at in isolation. It was made for a purpose and for a particular setting. The animals were to stand in the spirit road; they represent the general rather than the particular idea of the animal. The very early custom of burying useful animals such as horses and sheep in the tomb to serve their master after death had been replaced by the idea of a stone image that would fulfill the same purpose. Seen in their proper setting, these enormous stone figures are attractive and impressive. Each one is carved from a single stone block, even the elephants, which are 3.40 metres high and 4.50 metres long.[3]

The animals, a mixture of the real and the fantastic, come in the following order: lions, hsieh-chai, camels, elephants, ch'i-lin, and horses. The camels, horses, and elephants (figs. 20–22) are obviously there for practical purposes. Camels were valuable beasts of burden. At that time, and indeed up to the 1950s, the camel was a common sight in the North China plain; in 1975 it was still possible to see the odd caravan outside the Great Wall. The horses were useful for transport in peace or war. They are of a heavy pony type, quite different from the high-legged, small-headed T'ang horse; with their short sturdy legs they recall Mongolian horses. The elephants might seem out of place today, but these animals served a ceremonial purpose throughout the Ming and most of the Ch'ing dynasties. In 1495 the Emperor Hung-chih built a special palace for them which was still visible at the turn of the century, and the French Deputy-Bishop of Peking, M. Favier, describes the superb elephant chariot he saw in 1900. At one time the elephants were numerous, but later they were limited to six. In 1884, however, an elephant went beserk. Charging down the street, it picked up an old deaf woman and threw her over the rooftops; it then lifted a donkey cart with its trunk and tossed it into a shop. After this escapade, Favier writes that the elephants were not used any more and died slowly from malnutrition.

The most easily recognisable of the fantastic animals in the alley are the lions (fig.23). The idea of the lion as a guardian of sacred buildings and defender of the law had come to China with Buddhism. The lion was not, however, an indigenous animal. Lions had been sent periodically from Persia as tribute ever since the Han dynasty, but these were kept in the Imperial zoos and few Chinese had ever seen them. The ordinary sculptor and artist had to rely on descriptions helped by imagination. Small wonder that the resulting animal bore little resemblance to reality. Although stone lions had been placed on tombs during the Han era—two lions, probably erected in A.D. 147 still stand on the shrine of the Wu family in Shantung—they did not become really popular until the fifth and sixth centuries. The stone lions from that period are magnificent winged beasts, standing on guard with head lifted and roaring. During the T'ang dynasty, the winged lion was at first accompanied and then ousted by the lion we

20. Camel, sitting, surrounded by sightseers
21. Horse, standing
22. Elephant, sitting, with small children
23. Lion, sitting
24. Lion's collar with hanging bauble

25. Hsieh-chai, standing
26. Hsieh-chai, full face
27. Ch'i-lin, sitting

see today—a lion clearly based on the Pekingese dog. The origin of these dogs is obscure; "short dogs" are mentioned in the records of the Chou dynasty, and by the first century A.D. "short-legged short-headed dogs" were recognised as a special breed whose proper place was under the low Chinese tables. Confucius referred to "short-mouthed" dogs. With time and the spread of Buddhism, these dogs became increasingly popular and were deliberately bred to reproduce all the characteristics of the semimythical Buddhist lion as the Chinese imagined him. The experiment must have been considered successful since from that time on the dog-lion became the accepted guardian animal. The stone lions in the Ming alley are in all important respects the direct descendants of the stone lion on the grave of the T'ang Emperor Kao-tsung, who died in A.D. 682. With the years the animal has become slightly more domesticated, less ferocious. Unlike the T'ang lion, the Ming lion does not roar; it is, moreover, the only animal in the mausoleum to wear a man-made object—an engraved collar with hanging baubles (fig. 24).[4]

The hsieh-chai is less well known. This creature has cloven feet, the thick legs and body of a heavy horse, and the face and mane of a Chinese lion, only here the hair is uncurled (figs. 25 and 26). Lying flat across the top of its head, almost obscured by hair, is a single horn. In classical mythology the hsieh-chai symbolized justice. It roared when it saw wrong-doing. Not unnaturally, it came to be associated with the Imperial censors and judges; hsieh-chai were embroidered on the caps of the latter during the third and fourth centuries and are found on the badges of the former throughout the Ming era. It is said to be white.

The last of the fantastic animals is the ch'i-lin, which we have already seen on the P'ai-lou (fig. 27). Its presence in the alley stressed the virtues of the deceased; it also augured that their descendants would be wise rulers (see Appendix A).

Beyond the animals, the road makes a definite swing toward the east. With our Western ideas of perspective, this seems very strange, almost as if the splendour of the alley were being deliberately spoilt. For the Chinese who laid it out, however, the turn was necessary and natural. It has already been seen how important it was to prevent evil spirits from disturbing the dead. Evil spirits traveled in straight lines, which were, said the geomancers, "like dangerous darts, which striking the grave to its core, may inflict a deadly wound."[5] By making the road change direction, the spirits could be foiled. To make doubly sure, this last stretch is guarded by stone men.

There are twelve stone figures: four warriors, four civil servants, and four Imperial councillors. Here again one is struck by the complete impersonality of the carving. These statues depict not the man but the office. The face is devoid of human expression; all the skill of the sculptor has gone into the clothing. This is extremely detailed because it was by a man's clothing that his position was known. Each decoration or ornament indicated rank and title and was carefully prescribed by Imperial decree. When, for example, the use of Mandarin squares or badges of rank was regulated by the sumptuary laws of 1391, it was specified that animal motifs, suggesting fierce courage, should be used for the military, and bird motifs, symbolizing literary elegance, for court officials.[6] All twelve figures have moustaches and beards, a convention indicating venerable age and wisdom. Traditionally the Chinese cultivated long beards. A description of the Emperor Yung-lo when he was fifty-eight years old says: "The Emperor was of middle height; his beard neither very large nor small; nevertheless about two or three hundred hairs of his middle beard were long enough to form three or four curls on the chair on which he was seated."[7]

The four warriors wear the court uniform of Ming generals (fig. 28).[8] The first pair hold a commander's baton in their right hand while the left hand rests on the hilt of a sword (fig. 29). They wear a long armour-robe consisting of several layers—part cloth embroidered with lotus flowers and other stylized patterns, and part armour (fig. 30).[9] A distinctive wing or ear-shaped piece sticks out from the back of the upper sleeve. In front the robe is either hitched up or cut to show a heavy but decorated pair of boots. The different parts of the garment are fastened with beautifully knotted thongs. The ferocious face of an animal holds the belt clasp in its mouth; similar faces can be seen on the epaulettes (fig. 31). The whole costume is a triumph of the Chinese art of reproducing the texture and pattern of different materials in stone. The helmet is shoulder-length, with cloud patterns, a large knob on top, and prominent winged ear-pieces (fig. 32). This helmet would have been metal, edged with gold or bronze, and painted golden.

The second pair of warriors are very similar to the first except that they stand with folded hands (fig. 33). The back and sides of the upper layer of clothing are no longer decorated with lotus but show galloping horses (a symbol of military vigilance) between waves and clouds (fig. 34). The fastenings on the front of the robe are more elaborate, but once again the carving has the extraordinary ability to make you feel the different materials. The clasp of the belt is held by a bull-like head, upside down with a ring through its nose. The helmet is the same as that worn by the first pair of generals, but with a slightly different badge in front (fig. 35).

The next figures, four civilian officers, wear the court uniform of a President of one of the Six Boards of State in Ming times (fig. 36). The civil administration of the country was divided among six boards or ministries: those of Personnel, Revenue, Rites, War, Justice, and Works; the six Presidents were therefore the core of the administrative structure. Their robes are long, extending down to the ground and with voluminous sleeves. There is a badge of office on the breast, and a wide band, tied in an elegant bow, hangs down from the back of the collar. The hat, which is fastened with a ribbon around the neck, appears to have been made from some ribbed material and has a highly decorated band. Originally there would have been a small knob sticking out from each side of the hat; you can see where these have broken off (fig. 37). From the belt a broad embroidered ribbon hangs down in front and five strings of beads show below the long sleeves on the right hand side. The robe itself is unadorned except for the back, which is beautifully carved with six cranes set in a panel of interlacing ribbons framed by clouds (fig. 38). According to the decrees of 1391 mentioned above, the white crane was prescribed as an emblem for civilian officials of the first two ranks.

28. LEFT: Warrior with baton

29. BELOW: Sword and sword fittings, warrior with baton

30. BELOW: Back of robe, warrior with baton

32. FAR BELOW: Upper back and helmet, warrior with baton

31. Centre front of robe with animal face and thonglike fastenings, warrior with baton

33. Warrior with folded hands

34. Back of robe with galloping horses, warrior with folded hands

35. Side view of helmet showing winged ear pieces and epaulette, warrior with folded hands

Each figure carries in his hands a tabula for taking down notes when in the presence of the sovereign. This tabula or "hu" is of ancient origin. De Groot quotes from the Han Book of Rites: "When a man of higher order shall go to his Ruler's mansion. . . . his secretary brings his 'hu' of ivory, that he may write down upon it what he intends to communicate to his master, and how he shall answer orders that he may receive from the latter."

"On visiting him (the ruler) to receive orders, one writes them on the 'hu.' This tablet is 2 ft. 6 ins. (in length). Its breadth is 3 ins. in the middle and it tapers away one-sixth at both ends."[10] While in the presence of the emperor the official might not look up; the "hu" was therefore always held below him in front so that he could write with bowed head.

The last four figures, standing nearest to the grave and therefore in the position of greatest importance, wear the robes of a Ming Grand Secretary, a member of the Grand Secretariat (fig. 39). This was a sort of cabinet whose members were the emperor's closest advisors; although they had no direct executive power, they were in fact senior to the members of the Six Boards and other state organs. Their costume is almost exactly the same as that worn by the Presidents of the Six Boards, but the hat is different (figs. 40 and 41). Here the hat is stiff and has a high flat top with a round button on it and two paneled sides. High on the left panel is a reminder of the expression "a feather in his cap," a small holder with a quill-shaped feather in it. The surface of the hat is highly decorated.

The classical nature of all these uniforms has led to some confusion on the part of Western writers in dating them.* This is not surprising. Court dress, and especially ceremonial dress, tends to be anachronistic. In England one has only to look at the robes worn at a coronation or, more mundanely, at the dress of the Beefeaters at the Tower of London or the choir boys in a village church to see how certain forms of dress may continue to be used for particular purposes long after common fashions have changed. When the Ming first came to power, they continued to wear the Mongol court uniforms, but as can be seen from the Yüan wall-paintings at Yung-lo kung in Shansi, painted in the early fourteenth century, the Mongols themselves had adopted many of the traditional Chinese features of court dress. In one of the murals the emperor can be seen flanked by two officials wearing the same sort of hats as those worn by the civilian officials in the Ming alley. Even more striking is the portrait of Duke Feng Chou, painted at about the same time, which shows him wearing a costume almost identical to that worn by a Ming Grand Secretary.[11] Once the Ming dynasty was firmly established, the general tendency of eliminating Mongol influence and returning to pure classical Chinese traditions was extended to clothing. The decrees of 1391 governing court dress ordered a deliberate return to the regulations of the T'ang and Sung dynasties.† T'ang and Sung costumes were, however, directly derived from

*Bouillard, for example, goes so far as to say: "Their costume is that of civil servants under the Han and no longer existed under the Ming" (Bouillard and Vaudescal, p. 29).

†Exceptions were made for the "Mandarin Squares," badges worn on the front and back of official robes that first appeared under the Yüan and were greatly developed by the Ming.

36. LEFT: President of one of the Six Boards

37. BOTTOM LEFT: Details of upper half of President of one of the Six Boards; note the hat, plaque of office, and "hu"

38. BOTTOM RIGHT: Back of robe with cranes, President of one of the Six Boards

42. LEFT: Dragon and Phoenix Gate, south side

43. ABOVE: "Wings," ch'i-lin, and "peach" on Dragon and Phoenix Gate

OPPOSITE

39. FAR LEFT: Grand Secretary

40. Side view of Grand Secretary's hat, with "feather"

41. Back view of Grand Secretary's hat

the Han. The long, cross-over robe with exaggeratedly wide sleeves, the cloth girdles and ribbons with jade or semiprecious stones hanging from the belt, and the carrying of the "hu" all date from the Han dynasty. In view of all this, it is not surprising to find a close resemblance between the dress of these Ming figures and that shown on T'ang and Sung grave figures or in murals or figurines from earlier dynasties.

The avenue ends at a short, free-standing wall pierced by three equal-sized doorways with large white stone frames. The official name for this gate is the "Ling-hsing men," the "linteled star gate," but it is commonly known as the Dragon and Phoenix Gate. On an early Chinese map it is marked as "the gate where fire is stopped by water."[12] The purpose of this gate is clear; standing free across the Spirit Road, it is yet another obstacle to straight-flying malevolent influences. Today the gate stands in an enclosure of thujas and the road divides to either side of it (fig. 42).

The wall of this gate is made of rough brick covered with red plaster and roofed with yellow tiles. The doorways are unroofed, consisting of two tall side pillars with a stone lintel some two-thirds of the way up (hence, no doubt, the official name). Each of the three lintels carries a carved frieze, and in the middle of this is a large stone petal-shaped object (fig. 43). De Groot suggests that this is a peach, the Taoist symbol of longevity.[13] (In the Taoist paradise, the tree of life was a peach tree whose fruit only ripened every three thousand years and conferred on mortals the gift of immortality.) Both the general form and decoration of the base, however, seem to me to show influences from Tibetan Buddhist art. I include for comparison a photograph of a gold-plated representation of the Buddhist wheel of life on the roof of the Jokhan

Monastery in Lhasa (fig. 44). Above the cross-beams the two columns branch out into stone winglike clouds; the columns are surmounted by a rounded block of stone carved with more clouds, and on each of these sits a ch'i-lin, facing inward, guarding the doorway. Originally these gates were closed with folding doors, presumably wooden. This type of door-arch is comparatively common in Chinese temple architecture; other examples can be seen in Peking at the Temple of Heaven and the Temples of the Sun and Earth.

From the Dragon and Phoenix Gate to the first tomb, Ch'ang-ling, there is still another four kilometres. In many places the modern road runs beside the ancient way and you can see the old stone paving. The road crosses a handsome new bridge built in Ming style at the head of the reservoir and then climbs through the terraced fields to Ch'ang-ling. If you look around the valley you can see most of the other tombs nestling in the foothills, their yellow roofs standing out brightly against the sombre green of the graveyard trees.

In a way there is something reminiscent of a stage setting about the whole approach to the tombs. First comes the P'ai-lou, a glorious monument without inscription that awakens the interest of the traveler. Then follows the Great Red Gate, forbidding and stately, showing that this is indeed an Imperial enclosure but still giving no indication as to what lies within. Not until reaching the Stele Pavilion do you learn that this is the mausoleum of the Ming. From there, with a flourish, you are led up the Spirit Road, circumnavigate the Dragon and Phoenix Gate, and climb slowly toward the imposing entrance to Ch'ang-ling.

44. Tibetan Buddhist Wheel, part of gilt roof decoration on Jokhan Monastery, Lhasa

4

General Principles of Chinese Architecture

Before considering the first tomb, Chang-ling, it may be useful to take a quick look at Chinese architecture in general and the developement of the Chinese Imperial tomb.[1] Part of the architectural interest of the Ming Tombs is that in all essential respects they are built on a pattern which had already been clearly established by the second century B.C. As De Groot points out:

> The greatest conservatism in matters of religion, ceremonies and rites having dominated the Chinese race through all ages, we were justified in our belief that these sepulchres (Ming Tombs) were built on the same plan which had been transmitted to one another by successive dynasties as an heirloom from the ancients, so that they hold up before our eyes a clear image of the Imperial tombs of every epoch, beginning with those of the Ch'in and Han.[2]

Andrew Boyd stresses the same theme and points out that the truly remarkable feature of Chinese civilisation, including Chinese architecture, is not so much its antiquity as its continuity. The Egyptian civilisations are earlier than anything yet known in China; the Bronze Age, which came to China in the second millennium B.C., flourished in Britain from 3000 B.C. "What there has been, however, is straight from the brilliant flowering of the Bronze Age in about 1500 B.C. right up to the present, a completely continuous, individual and self-conscious civilisation of an extremely high level: one might say, one nation with (basically) one language, one script, one literature, one system of ethical concepts, one tradition in the arts, including one architecture."[3]

The importance of this continuity is underlined by the fact that there are in fact few very old buildings in China. Since earliest times the common building material has been wood; the result is that very little remains of pre-Ming architecture.[4] Luckily however, there are abundant written records, and excavations in early tombs have produced clay models of contemporary houses, fortresses, and palaces. Clay models from the Han dynasty show a type of house which is, in important respects, the same as a small house in Peking today. These houses were rectangular with courtyards; the tiled roof was supported by a wooden frame the pillars of which rested on a raised base to keep out the damp. The walls consisted of packed earth held in an open wooden lattice or similar framework. One difference was that the multistory house seems to have been more common in the Han period than in Ming times.

The architectural ideas of the Han were developed and refined under the T'ang and Sung dynasties but the basic forms were not changed. With the Ming came a deliberate revival of the classical patterns; Ming architecture is exuberant, reflecting the strength of the new dynasty, but in all its detail it is consciously *Chinese,* that is to say, based on the earlier accepted forms. The Chinese view of history—"change within tradition"—applies to architecture. The Ming Tombs are a clear illustration of this; although the thirteen tombs were built over a span of two hundred and fifty years, it is practically impossible to pinpoint any change in style. Apart from size, what distinguishes the grander tombs from the more modest ones is the quantity and quality of decorative detail. As will be seen later, the only clear chronological development that can be followed is in a purely technical area: the drainage system.

The other interesting thing about Chinese architecture is that, with the exception of specifically religious buildings like the Temple of Heaven, pagodas (usually of Buddhist origin), and purely ornamental pavilions and follies such as can be seen in the gardens of the Summer Palace, virtually all Chinese buildings are built on the same model. The difference between a small house in a Peking lane or "hutung" and an Imperial palace is one of size, not of design. The basic unit is a courtyard with a single-story rectangular building set in the north wall. All windows and doors are on the south side of the building; the north side is blank. This north-south orientation is, as we have seen, based on the ancient principles of feng-shui. It is also eminently practical. The typical peasant's house in the North China plain is sheltered from the north wind and catches the low winter sun. In summer, the sun is too high to shine through the windows, and when it gets really hot, life moves into the courtyard.

The main building is never visible from the street entrance. If the house is small, there will be a short wall built directly in front of the entrance into the courtyard so that the visitor must go to the left or right before he can see the house. This wall is to keep out evil spirits which, it was believed, could only travel in straight lines. The screen wall dates from long before the Han dynasty. A ballad from the Chou era (1027–221 B.C.) describes a lover waiting for his sweetheart; the impatient young man has to wait three times, first between the gate and the screen wall, then in the courtyard, and finally in the front porch.

A small Peking house consists of one courtyard with one building divided into several rooms. Larger houses have two or three courtyards which may be flanked symmetrically on the east and west by secondary buildings; all buildings are however single-storied and the only way you can estimate the importance of a house from the street is by looking at the roofs. In a grand house you will see a series of roofs, one behind the other in ascending height and culminating in the hall in which the ancestral tablets would have been kept. This was always the highest part of any house; nothing must be allowed to look down on or disturb the dead.

A Chinese palace such as the Forbidden City is simply a vast enlargement of the peasant house. The central ingredients are the same; the buildings and courtyards have the same shape and orientation, but they are built on a colossal scale and repeated in different patterns. Here again there is an entrance in the south wall, a forecourt, then a hall or porch for receiving guests, another courtyard, and then the main building in which the ancestral tablets were housed and the rites performed. Until recently, the Hall of Supreme Harmony in the Forbidden City was one of the highest buildings in Peking but it was nevertheless only one story high. When the Ming Emperor Wan-li was shown pictures of European cities by the Jesuit priest Matteo Ricci, he is said to have commented adversely that these barbarians must be very poor if they were forced to live on top of each other up in the air; it must also be very dangerous for them. I am grateful to Nigel Cameron for permission to reproduce the diagrams which show the similarities in ground plan between a peasant house and the Forbidden City (fig. 45).[5]

45. Comparison of the basic plan of a Peking "hutung" house and the central section of the Forbidden City. "The entrance to this particular 'hutung' house is screened by the wall of the childrens' room, but there is an additional screen in the front courtyard (E). This is the counterpart to Wu Men (4) in the Forbidden City. Each plan shows water in a propitious place—(C) small pool and (3) the Golden Stream. The Guest Hall in the house is the equivalent in position and function to the Gate of Great Harmony (2). After this comes the most important part of the whole complex, the Parent's Room and the Hall of Supreme Harmony (1)."

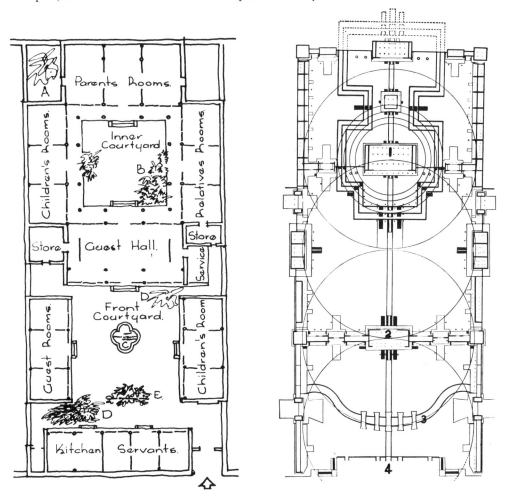

Not only the pattern but the method of building seems to have remained remarkably unchanged since Han times. While the foundation of the house was of stone or brick to keep out the damp, the framework was wooden.* This frame of wooden beams was then filled in with packed clay or bricks or stones covered with plaster, but it is important to remember that the walls were in fact only a filling. The size of a building was determined by the length, width, and number of beams. A large hall would consist of several bays—that is, several rows of columns each holding the necessary supports for the roof (e.g., figs. 46 and 47). The nature of the nonbearing walls made it necessary to protect them from the weather. Hence the development of the distinctive Chinese roof with its overhanging eaves. To carry the weight of the wide-flung and heavy roof while keeping as much width as possible between the rows of supporting columns, an elaborate system of bracketing was evolved. The roof rested on an intricate series of criss-crossing beams or brackets which could be extended in all directions. It was a simple and very flexible system; the building would not last forever since the wood might burn or decay, but it was always easy to rebuild an identical building: "Il n'y a que le provisoire qui dure."

This use of basic units had another advantage—there was no need for an architect or drawing. Since the unit was standard, it was enough to specify the size and quantity of the different components—how many bays, the size of the beams—rather as one does with certain prefabricated houses today. For this reason the role of the architect in China was very different from that of his European counterpart. The architect was above all a master builder or craftsman.†To say this is not to belittle the importance of his work. The Yüan, for example, went to great lengths to import skilled craftsmen from abroad, and when they decided to build their capital in Peking, an Arab and his son, Yeh-hei-tieh-er and Ma-ho-ma-sha, were put in charge of the works.[6]

Decoration was all-important. Generally speaking, it was concentrated on the roof, on the use of colour, and on the embellishment of the courtyard.

All the fantasy in Chinese architecture goes into the roof. The eye is irresistibly drawn upward. Whereas the lines of the hall are straight and simple, those of the roof are intricate and curved. A description of a palace in the Book of Songs (tenth to seventh centuries B.C.) includes the simile "like a bird with outspread wings," and this has been taken to refer to the wide spread of the roof. A Sung master builder, Yu Hao, on being shown a T'ang gate tower, remarked: "They were certainly capable enough in those days. The only thing is that they didn't understand how to curve up their eaves."[7] The two main styles of architecture in China, the "southern" style and the "northern" or "palace" style, are chiefly distinguished by the degree to which the roof

---

*There is a distinction here between the small hutung house and the larger palace-style houses. Many hutung houses are built of brick, with the walls directly supporting the roof structure. Larger houses, however, are built with the wooden framework described above.

†This practical approach to architecture persists today. When we visited the Red Star commune outside Sian in 1975, many of the old single-story houses were being replaced by two-story terrace houses. These were simple but attractive and well designed, with great attention to practical detail. We were told that there had been no need for an architect, that the plans were drawn up by local builders after discussing with the villagers what was needed.

46. ABOVE: Back and side walls of sacrificial hall showing clearly where supporting beams were positioned, T'ai-ling (tomb 6)

47. LEFT: Stone base and ventilation hole for wooden beam, K'ang-ling (tomb 7)

48. BELOW: Ch'i-wen holding roof ridge, Ching-ling (tomb 3)

49. Double roof on stele pavilion, Ting-ling (tomb 10)

50, 51. Details of roof construction, K'ang-ling (tomb 7)

is curved and the extent of ornamentation on the eaves and ridges. Ming roofs belong to the northern style. The swing of the roof corners is less pronounced than in Sung times; ornamentation is usually limited to the large ceramic head at each end of the roof ridge and a row of ceramic figures on the ridges that form the four corners of the roof.

The origin of the head, which Osvald Sirén calls a "fish-tailed owl" and which is made from a single tile, is a ch'i-wen, one of the many offspring of the dragon (fig. 48). The ch'i-wen was often carved on the beams of bridges because of its supposed fondness for water; its presence on a roof would help to preserve the building from fire. The present form of head with horns, bulging eyes, and a gaping mouth, dates from the Sung dynasty. Alexander Soper refers to contemporary evidence from the end of the eleventh century in which a Sung author notes that Buddhist and Taoist buildings from the T'ang era carried a "flying-fish shape with a tail pointing upwards"; the author mentions specifically that this form had now been superseded by a new shape with a large open mouth but was unable to give an exact date for the change.[8] It is interesting that C. A. S. Williams, in his study of Chinese art motifs, notes that the ch'i-wen was sometimes symbolized by the figure of a fish with uplifted tail.[9] Here is yet another example of a mythical figure which has retained its name and spiritual qualities while changing its physical appearance.

One way of accentuating the importance of a building was to give it a double roof. It will be seen that all the stele pavilions and the only remaining Sacrificial Hall have double roofs (fig. 49). Between the roofs a highly decorated frieze—sometimes painted on wood, sometimes made of coloured tiles—runs around the building. All roofs, single or double, rest on an extremely complicated pattern of interlocking wooden supports (figs. 50 and 51). These technical details, which are usually hidden in a Western building, are highlighted by decorative painting.

Chinese architecture is unusual in that colour plays an integral part in the design of the building. The rules governing the use of colour are as ancient and invariable as those governing orientation and form. In the Book of Rites, the Han chronicle of Chou customs, it is stated: "The pillars of the Son of Heaven are red." A clear distinction exists between the parts of the building which are monochrome and those which are polychrome. In Imperial buildings, roofs are yellow; precinct walls are red; columns are scarlet; and all staircases, terraces, and balustrades are white. Roof supports, beams, brackets, eaves, ceilings, and screens are polychrome; here the decorative pattern varies, but usually green, blue, and gold predominate. As one so often finds with Chinese customs, the origin of these principles is practical. Paint helps to preserve the wood, and Chinese archaeologists reckon that red mercuric oxide was being used as a timber preservative as early as the eleventh century B.C.[10]

The third decorative area is the courtyard. Here it is important to remember that the basic unit is not a building but a building with a space around it. In Europe it is perfectly common to find a building the beauty of which owes nothing to its surroundings. The Sainte Chapelle in the Palais de Justice in Paris is considered one of the

52. Marble terraces with balustrades, Ch'ang-ling (tomb 1)

53. Detail of marble balustrade, Ch'ang-ling (tomb 1)

masterpieces of Gothic architecture, but you can walk within five hundred metres of it and never suspect its existence. In classical Chinese architecture the relationship between the proportions of the building and the surrounding courtyard is paramount.

The basic form of the building may be monotonous; it is brought to life by its surroundings. Part of the beauty of Peking in the spring lies in the sudden sight of blossom over the grey courtyard walls. Trees are planted with infinite care, not only for giving exactly the right picture and colour when seen from different parts of the dwelling, but also for the shadows which the branches will cast on the courtyard walls in winter time. In Imperial architecture the buildings are set in an ornate framework of white stone or marble. There are elegant bridges with beautifully carved balustrades; the buildings themselves stand on gleaming white terraces (figs. 52 and 53). These rise in tiers, each with its own carved railings, broken only by formal staircases leading up to the main doorway. Here, as on the roofs, there is room for fantasy. Dragons and phoenixes twine around the marble posts; gargoyles smile out from the rain-water gutters. The courtyards are planted with decorative trees. In large palaces, these are also landscaped with ornamental rocks and small ponds: the mountains and lakes of the Chinese countryside are reflected in miniature.

The result of all this is to create an extraordinary harmony between the building and its surroundings. The original functional and very simple basic unit is expanded, embroidered, and overlaid with decorative details, but the essential symmetry and simplicity shine through. When successful, as in Ch'ang-ling or the Hall of Supreme Harmony in the Forbidden City, the art of China produces buildings easily able to compete with any other great architectural wonder of the world.

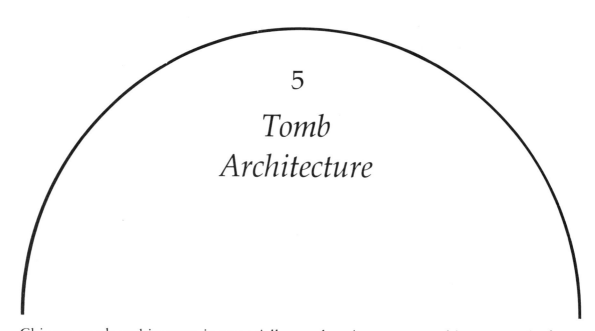

5

Tomb Architecture

Chinese tomb architecture is essentially secular. Ancestor worship was, as Andrew Boyd has pointed out, "in no sense a religious worship but a conservative social practice sanctioning and perpetuating the family and state structure."[1] The typical Confucian temple is laid out on the plan of the typical Chinese courtyard complex. The tomb is merely an extension of this plan, which takes into account the dual function of the grave. As we have already seen, the tomb in Chinese philosophy had both to please the spirit and to preserve the body. This division of functions is clearly reflected in the Ming Imperial tombs. Each tomb consists of two parts: first, a series of courtyards with palace-style buildings where the spirit will feel at home and the appropriate rites be performed; second, the funeral vault buried under an artificial hill and surrounded by a fortified wall. The first part is rectangular, the second, round. This corresponds to the Chinese conception of the universe: "heaven round, earth square." After death, man passed from the rectangular or square world of earth into the circular world of eternity. To quote De Groot once again, the general pattern was laid down under the Han: "Taking into consideration that a most rigid spirit of conservatism in regard to what has been established by the forefathers of the nation has always reigned supreme in Chinese state religion and in whatever is connected with it, we may be pretty sure that in all material points these mausolea (Imperial tombs of the Ming and preceding dynasties) have always closely resembled those of the Han dynasty."[2]

Recent excavations of tombs from the Han dynasty have justified De Groot's assumption. The distinctive features of the Ming tomb were already present during that era: the typical Han tomb had an underground funeral chamber covered by an artificial mound and enclosed by a fortified wall; surface buildings including a Sacrificial Hall; a walled park planted with trees; a stone grave stele; and an approach, usually from the south, involving a "spirit road" frequently flanked by stone figures, beacons, and/or watch-towers. Whereas in the Ming tombs the symbols for heaven and earth, the circle and the square, are placed next to each other, in Han tombs the circular grave mound was placed inside the square fortified wall.

The line from Han to Ming tomb architecture is, with the exception of a short break during the Yüan dynasty, who retained their Mongol funeral customs, continuous. It comes as no surprise to learn from the official records of the T'ang dynasty that: "When the Emperor Kao-tsung died (A.D. 683) an Imperial decree was issued, to the effect that, as to the style and dimensions of his burial place, the Ch'ang mausoleum of the Han dynasty should be taken as a pattern."[3] How closely these instructions were followed is not clear, but Kao-tsung's tomb, one of the most impressive Imperial graves in China, is a clear forefather of the Ming tombs. The layout is very much the same; the most striking difference is that in the T'ang tomb everything, from the stone figures in the spirit alley to the vast funeral mound, is on a much larger scale.

In the Ming tombs, the distinction between the two parts, the courtyards to the south and the northern grave enclosure, is very clear. The architectural layout of the first half is similar to what we have already examined; the order of the buildings, the method of construction, and the decoration are exactly the same as in a nobleman's house or small palace. The tombs fall into two groups: those with two courtyards and those with three. In the latter there is first a formal entrance with three doors, then a courtyard leading to a "Gate of Heavenly Favours." This is a hall built in the traditional style but open to north and south. It serves as a kind of front porch—a place for receiving those who were going to perform the rites. It was through this gateway that the satisfied spirit would send good influences out to its living descendants—hence the name. The Gate of Heavenly Favours leads to a second courtyard on the far side of which stands the principal building, the Hall of Heavenly Favours. This was where the rites were performed. In the centre of the hall was a small wooden tabernacle on which stood a wooden tablet bearing the name of the deceased. In front of this was a massive wooden table carrying the "five precious objects" necessary for the rites: two flower vases, two candlesticks, and an incense burner, all made of wood and painted red. Behind the Hall of Heavenly Favours a doorway, often with three arches and decorated with glazed tiles, leads into the third courtyard, the north side of which is formed by a large stone tower on which stands the stele pavilion and by the crenellated ramparts surrounding the grave mound.

In tombs with only two courtyards, the first entrance and the Gate of Heavenly Favours are amalgamated. The entrance is sometimes built in the form of a hall, and the Hall of Heavenly Favours (or Sacrificial Hall, as it is perhaps easier to call it), stands in the first courtyard.

The final courtyard has two interesting features: a protective "screen" door and a stone altar (fig. 54). Both of these play a symbolic rather than a functional role. The screen is a free-standing wooden door set in a framework of two marble columns surmounted by ch'i-lin. The door stands directly between the central entrance to the courtyard and the altar, and its sole purpose was to deflect evil spirits. The living could always walk around it and, indeed, paved pathways lead straight from the side arches

54. Protective screen door shown in relation to altar and stele pavilion, Yung-ling (tomb 8)

of the courtyard entrance to the terrace on which the stele tower is built. It is only the direct axis which is protected, the line leading from the altar through the centre of the stele tower to the heart of the tumulus where the deceased emperor lies.

The altar is a heavy rectangular table of stone or marble placed directly in front of the opening in the stele tower through which the body would have been carried for burial (figs. 55 and 56). The surface is plain; the sides are more or less decorated according to the grandeur of the tomb. The most common forms of decoration are lotus, knot, or "running cloud" motifs. This altar, clearly based on the massive wooden table in the Sacrificial Hall, is entirely symbolical since the actual rites were always performed inside the hall. It is reasonable to suppose that it dates from very early times when a tomb consisted of a mound without surface buildings and sacrifices were performed in the open air. Excavations from the early Bronze Age show that, at that time, the idea of satisfying the needs of the dead seems to have been taken in a very literal sense. Not only was the tomb filled with material goods such as food, household objects, precious clothes and stones, but concubines, slaves, and animals were buried alive to serve their owner after death.* Gradually the cruelty and wastefulness of this practice seems to have led to a shift in emphasis; it was the spirit of the deceased which had to be satisfied, and this could be done with symbols representing the idea of the object or through sacrifices in which the offerings—meats, silks, money—would be reduced to flame and smoke, a form more easily acceptable to the spirit. These

*The Mongols brought with them practice of immolating concubines with the deceased emperor, and this was continued by Ming emperors until the death of Cheng-t'ung in 1464.

sacrifices must have been performed in the open air, since the use of surface buildings is generally recognized to date from the Han dynasty.[4]

An early Han chronicler writes: "Anciently there was no sacrificing on the tomb but during the dynasty of Han a park with a temple was added as an appendage to each of the Imperial mausolea in imitation of the House of Ch'in."[5] (The earliest historically recognized emperor of China, Shih Huang-ti of the Ch'in, built a temple at the side of his tomb.) I am inclined to agree with De Groot, who asks "whether it is not somewhat improbable that such buildings should have come into vogue so suddenly, and whether it would not be more natural to consider them as the products of a gradual development of the altars which were erected on the graves of far earlier times?"[6] Once the functional altar with the genuine precious vessels was moved inside a temple, it seems likely that the general Chinese reluctance to modify established religious practices led to the retention of the old altar in a symbolic but more permanent form so that the spirits should not take offence.

Originally, stone copies of the same "five sacred vessels" (two flower vases, two candlesticks, and an incense burner) used in the rites stood on the altar (figs. 57–59). The pricket candlestick seems to have come from India; the flower vase and incense burner are archaistic—deliberate reproductions of two of the Shang or Chou bronze ritual vessels, the "hu" and the "ting." Archaism, a conscious and sentimental return to the past, probably began to be fashionable under the Sung. Under the Yüan it

55. Altar, Ching-ling (tomb 3)
56. Detail of altar pattern, Hsien-ling (tomb 2)

57. BELOW: Stone flower vase, K'ang-ling (tomb 7)
58. RIGHT: Stone candlestick, Ting-ling (tomb 10)

59. LEFT: Stone incense burner, Ch'ang-ling (tomb 1)
60. BELOW: Upper half of incense burner, Ching-ling (tomb 3)

flourished; maybe the Chinese, under alien rule, found consolation in returning to the purely Chinese forms of their early ancestors. The "set of five" were the vessels or ornaments that would have been used on ordinary household altars. Ancient ritual forms were considered appropriate for these vessels and were copied in porcelain and later in wood, lacquer, or even cloisonné. Archaic bronze vessels of the thirteenth and fourteenth centuries have two distinctive features: they are bold and squat and their decoration is thoroughly distorted.[7] The stone objects in the Ming Tombs are clearly based on these bronze imitations.

From photographs of "altar sets" on Ch'ing Imperial graves and from the description given by Fonssagrives during his period spent in the Western Tombs of the Ch'ing at the turn of the century, it is clear that at that time these objects were made in two parts. The lower part was made in the usual white limestone, the upper in a black stone, probably basalt. In De Groot's photograph of the altar at Ch'ang-ling, the candlesticks and incense burner have their upper halves, but as far as one can see these are made of the same stone as the bases.[8] This is borne out by the only example of an upper part remaining today: that of the central piece, the incense burner (fig. 60).

In the restored and the excavated tombs, the five bases have been replaced on the altar; in the other tombs they lie, whole or broken, scattered in the grass around the courtyard. The carving is heavy and formalised, and if one did not know beforehand what the objects were supposed to represent, it would be hard to guess. Nevertheless, there is something intriguing about them, especially the incense burner where a dragon's head peers through a stylised cloud of smoke with a diabolical grin.

Behind the altar begins the second half of the tomb, the grave enclosure. This is a fortified enclosure surrounded by crenellated ramparts; the entrance is guarded by a massive stone tower on which stands the stele pavilion housing the "grave stele." Since the spirit could not exist without the body, it was necessary to ensure the physical safety of the dead. The corpse must be defended against grave robbers or enemies of the state, hence the fortifications. The stele tower is modeled on the towers of a traditional fortified city wall, and a garrison of soldiers was attached to each Imperial grave.

The stele pavilions, which are all based on the great Stele Pavilion at the entrance to the necropolis, are the most striking feature of the tombs today. Standing high above the courtyards on their grey fortified bases, the red walls and yellow roofs dominate the grave enclosures. While many of the Sacrificial Halls and ceremonial gateways have crumbled away, all the stele pavilions except for the thirteenth remain. The pavilion is built in the same manner as the other precinct buildings, that is, with a wooden framework filled in with brick or stone and covered with plaster. There is an arched opening on all four sides, but in most cases only the arches to the north and south are open, the others are blocked a short way in. Hanging above the southern arch there is, or was, a wooden frame carrying a tablet with the name of the deceased emperor.

Inside the pavilion, on a rectangular pedestal, stands the grave stele bearing the name of the deceased emperor and giving him one flattering attribute such as "wise," "far-seeing," or "virtuous." This stele, like the tablet in the Sacrificial Hall, was thought to embody the spirit of the dead man; it was therefore of great importance that the number of characters in the inscription should be auspicious. Of the five ingredients in the classical Chinese view of existence—birth, old age, disease, death, and misery—only the first two were felicitous. To have a large number of sons and to live long were considered to be among the greatest blessings any human could hope for. If a grave stele was to confer these blessings on its owner and his descendants it was necessary that the number of characters, counted in multiples of five, should correspond to the numbers one and two in the series. In other words, inscriptions of one, two, six, seven, eleven, or twelve characters would bestow alternately many heirs and long life, whereas an inscription of three, eight, or thirteen characters would bring sickness. There were many ways of twisting this number play; sometimes the name of the dynasty would be included in the inscription; sometimes longer inscriptions would be divided into columns of both six and seven characters. All thirteen grave steles in the Ming Valley have seven characters, promising longevity, but the tomb of Emperor Ching-t'ai in the Western Hills has eleven if the name of the dynasty is included.[9]

Around the pavilion the crenellations of the stele tower form a small terrace from which you can look across the valley. All the pavilions have double roofs. These are in varying states of decay and enable one to see very clearly the different stages of roof construction.

The stele pavilion is perhaps the focal point of the whole tomb. Standing at the junction of the precinct and the grave enclosure, it belongs to both. When you look up through the courtyards, it is the stele pavilion which you see; when you look back from the ramparts, it is the pavilion which dominates the skyline.

The arrangement of the funeral enclosure shows certain variations that will be dealt with in the chapters on the individual tombs. In all tombs the underground vault is covered with a large hill which hides the entrance to the funeral chamber. This grave mound is reached either by a tunnel through the centre of the tower or by symmetrical ramps leading down from the back of the tower to a small area between the tower and the mound.

A description of the underground vault will be found in the chapter on Ting-ling, the only tomb to have been excavated. Here it is perhaps worth noting that while the ground pattern was similar to that of ordinary buildings, that is, a series of halls on a north-south axis with symmetrical wings to east and west, the method of construction was completely different. The tomb was built of stone; unlike the wooden-framed Sacrificial Halls, it was obviously designed to last for eternity. The roof was closely vaulted and there was an elaborate drainage system to keep the interior of the tomb dry.[10] Above the vaulted roof was a second layer of fitted stones, then rougher stonework and finally an outer protective wall. The result was that all water ran off the roof of the tomb and was collected in underground drains which carried it away from the mound. So successful was this system that when the vault of Ting-ling was opened over three hundred years after its construction, it was completely dry inside.

One important aspect of the grave enclosure was that it was essential for it to be planted with trees (fig. 61). Originally this seems to have been for defensive purposes—at the time of construction a wooded hill would have looked more natural and less likely to attract the attention of the enemy. It is noted in the "Historical Records" that when, in the second century B.C., the vast man-made tumulus over the grave chamber of the first emperor, Shih Huang-ti, was finished, "trees and shrubs were planted about the spot, to give it the appearance of a natural mountain."[11]

Once again, the practical was allied to the philosophical. From early times the wood of pines, and thuja, or cypress had been used for coffins because it was believed it contained certain properties that would help preserve the body. The same "Historical Records" state: "In the case of an Emperor, the funeral vault is made of cypress wood, cut from the foot of the trunk in pieces six feet long."[12] Long-lived and remaining green through the coldest winters, it was clear that pines and thujas were especially

61. "Cone" and trees on grave mound, Mao-ling (tomb 5)

vital and therefore capable of nourishing not only the body but the spirit. During the Han dynasty the ruling classes believed so strongly in the life-giving powers of the thuja that wine made from its leaves was given to the ruler on New Year's Day. At the same time it was common to pile extra pieces of the wood from its trunk around the coffin. From the Han dynasty onward, references to grave trees are frequent. A description of a fifth-century Imperial tomb of the Wei dynasty has a pleasant ring of familiarity: "The rows of cypresses on the four sides allure the birds and shade it from the sun."[13] Through successive dynasties the number and type of trees that might be planted on grave tumuli were subjected to Imperial regulation varying according to the rank of the deceased. The obligation of descendants to plant and tend these trees was taken as seriously as their duties to perform the rites and care for the tomb in general. Strict punishments were decreed for those who cut such trees down. A law of

Chart 2. Diagrammatic comparison between 2-courtyard and 3-courtyard tombs

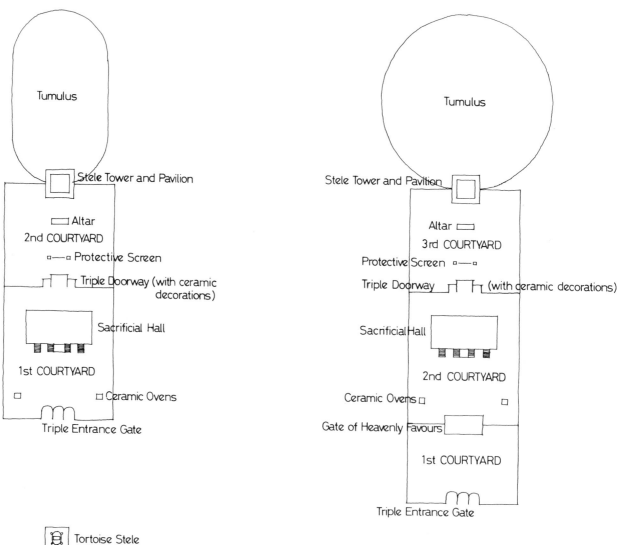

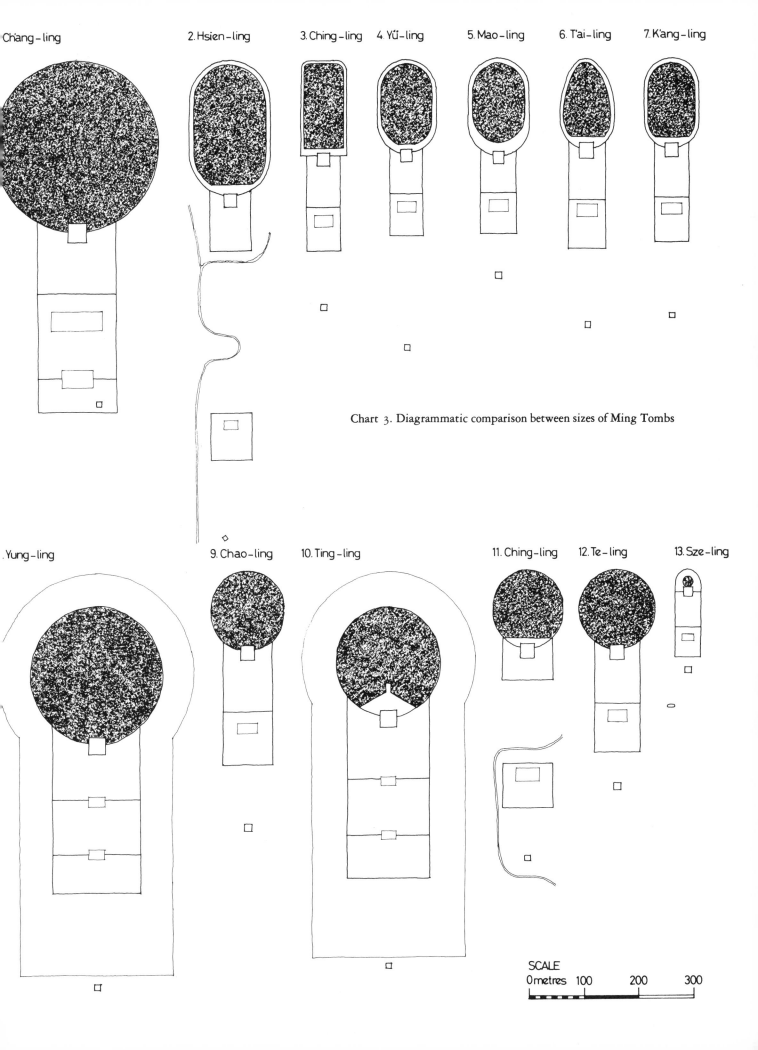

Ch'ang – ling 2. Hsien – ling 3. Ching – ling 4. Yü – ling 5. Mao – ling 6. T'ai – ling 7. K'ang – ling

Chart 3. Diagrammatic comparison between sizes of Ming Tombs

. Yung – ling 9. Chao – ling 10. Ting – ling 11. Ching – ling 12. Te – ling 13. Sze – ling

SCALE
0 metres 100 200 300

the Ch'ing dynasty dating from 1825 states: "Those who steal trees which grow in a mausoleum shall be punished with one hundred blows with the long stick and banishment for three years whether they have acted as chief culprits or accomplices."[14] Other violations of the mausoleum woods could lead to beheading, strangulation, and exile "to the most distant province with a malarious climate."[15]

As long as the Ming dynasty flourished, the mausoleum was thickly planted, but when the power of the central government waned, it was impossible to keep marauders out of the valley. By the middle of the seventeenth century the valley was already denuded; only the trees within the tomb precincts had been spared. Ku Yen-wu records: "Several hundred thousands of azure pines and green cypresses,* that studded the inner grounds beyond the Great Red Gate in numbers which even imagination cannot grasp, have now disappeared, being felled to the last."[16]

The two parts of the tomb, the courtyards and the mound, have very different characters. The first part, built on the same plan as a large residence, gives an impression of a decayed house in a beautiful but formal garden. It is very much the blending of man and nature. There are tall trees and wild flowers, but they grow between the ruins of buildings and the remnants of stone-paved paths. The second part, the tumulus, is more like an English park—a wooded hill enclosed by a crenellated wall. In the first, domesticated, half of the tomb, the eye is contained by the high red walls; where the gates and doorways remain, they are covered with brilliant green and yellow tiles. The charm lies very much in the feeling of being inside a sanctuary. In the second half, which is always on higher ground, the rampart wall is grey and unadorned; the eye is drawn outward to the mountains behind and the valley below. There is a peculiar pleasure in walking around a curved rampart: the countryside beneath changes continually but never abruptly. Thanks to feng-shui, the siting of each tomb is such that there is always a good view, usually including one or two of the other tombs spread out along the side of the foothills and sometimes of the whole valley. Nature and history merge in a profound harmony of life and death.

I hope this brief explanation will make it easier to follow the architectural descriptions of the individual tombs. Charts 2 and 3 show the traditional pattern of two- and three-courtyard Imperial tombs and the comparative size of the thirteen tombs. The majority of the tombs, in accordance with feng-shui, are built on a north-south axis. In some cases, however, where the lie of the land demands it, a northwest, southeast, or even an east-west axis has been adopted. For the purpose of clarity I have adopted a convention that all tombs lie on a north-south axis. Where this is not geographically correct, the words "north," "south," "west," and "east" are placed in quotation marks. The true orientation is marked on the chart of each tomb.

---

*The cypress mentioned in many translations of Chinese sources refers to the *Thuja orientalis* L. which, apart from the juniper is the only type of cypress to be found in North China. Very old thujas grow not only in nearly all the grave enclosures but also in all the parks and former religious centres in Peking, such as the Temple of Heaven. The most common pine is *pinus tabulae formis*, or the Chinese hard pine or red pine. In a few tombs there are also some *Pinus bungeana*, the Chinese lace-barked pine.

6

Ch'ang-ling

TOMB 1

BURIED HERE
Emperor Yung-lo, died 1424
Empress Hsu, died 1407

The approach to Ch'ang-ling leaves no doubt that this is the tomb of a great emperor. The large triple gate in the middle of the high, red southern wall is as imposing as any entrance to an emperor's palace (colourplate 4). The gateway and wall are surmounted by roofs of the Imperial yellow tiles. When you come through the gate, you find yourself in a completely different world, a world of formal gardens and formal architecture, of dazzling white marble terraces, flowering pomegranate trees, and brilliantly painted buildings with coloured tile decorations. This is Chinese architecture as one has always imagined it. Dragons and phoenixes twine round the balustrades, columns are scarlet and gold, dragons adorn the blue, gold, and green ceilings; the roofs are a network of interlacing painted wooden beams. Everything draws the eye upward to the sweep of the roof corners with their row of curious little yellow tile figures and the strange wide-mouthed, large-eyed heads that hold the highest roof beam in place.

This tomb was completely restored in the early 1950s. Apart from small changes such as the use of opaque glass in the windows instead of paper, the restoration of the exterior of the buildings seems to correspond exactly to early descriptions of the tomb. In 1920 Bouillard wrote of crumbling roofs and general decay, doubting whether it was not already too late to save the buildings (fig. 62). Today not only the buildings but the gardens are in pristine condition. The roofs are complete; the painted woodwork is as bright as it must have been in Yung-lo's time.

The great triple doors lead into a spacious courtyard on the far side of which stands the Gate of Heavenly Favours (colourplate 5). This gate is in fact a large hall, standing on a wide marble terrace and open to north and south. The hall has a double roof of glowing yellow tiles; three staircases of the purest white marble lead up to the doorway, and the flat coffered ceiling of small square panels, is a brilliant tracery of blue, green, and gold (fig. 63). The red columns supporting the building and the incredibly complicated coloured woodwork on which the roof rests complete a picture that

Chart 4. Ch'ang-ling (tomb 1)

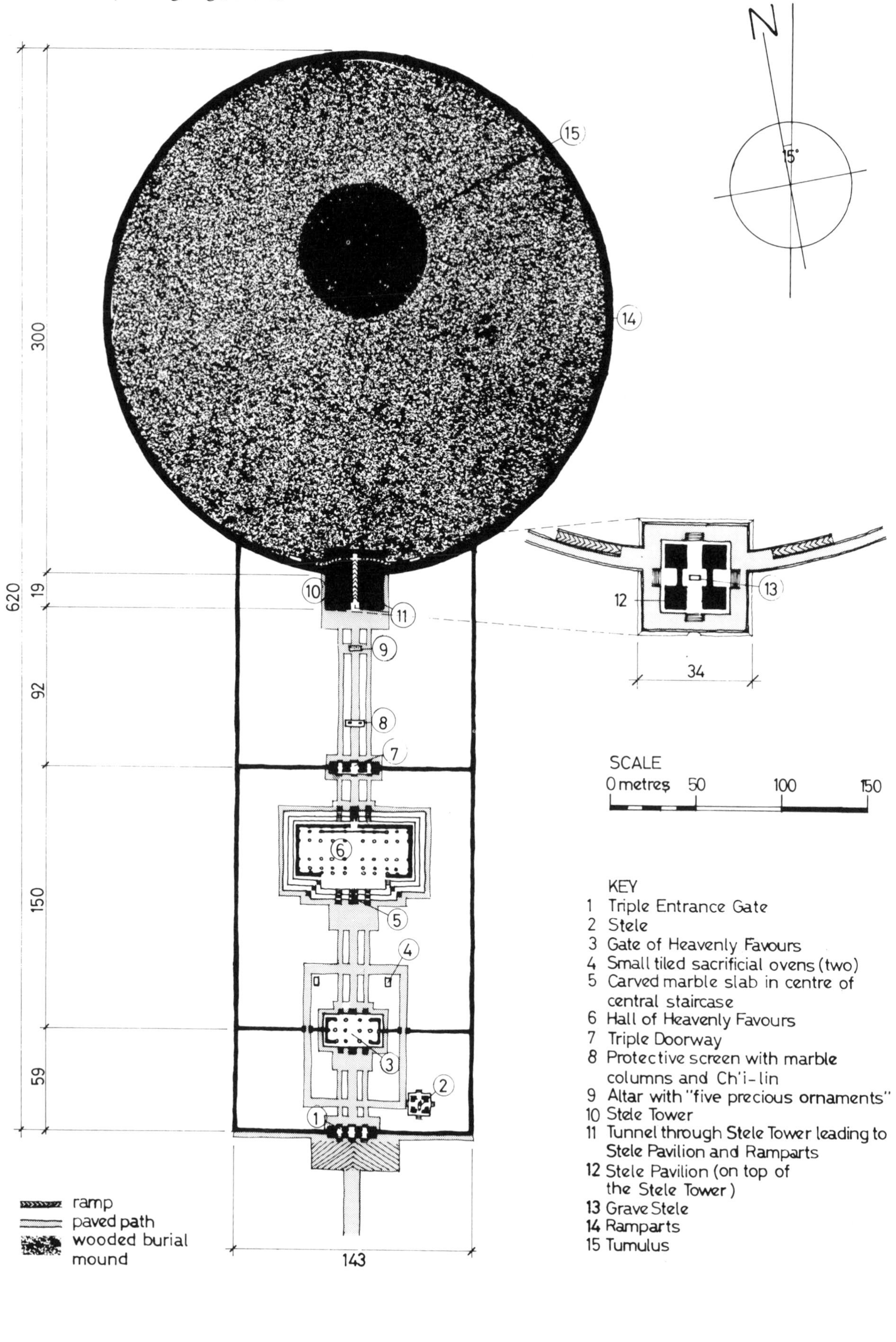

N

5°

15

14

10

11

9

8

7

6

5

4

3

2

1

12   13

34

300

620

19

92

150

59

143

SCALE
0 metres   50   100   150

KEY
1 Triple Entrance Gate
2 Stele
3 Gate of Heavenly Favours
4 Small tiled sacrificial ovens (two)
5 Carved marble slab in centre of
   central staircase
6 Hall of Heavenly Favours
7 Triple Doorway
8 Protective screen with marble
   columns and Ch'i-lin
9 Altar with "five precious ornaments"
10 Stele Tower
11 Tunnel through Stele Tower leading to
   Stele Pavilion and Ramparts
12 Stele Pavilion (on top of
   the Stele Tower)
13 Grave Stele
14 Ramparts
15 Tumulus

ramp
paved path
wooded burial
mound

62. Ch'ang-ling before restoration. (Yale Slide and Photograph Collection)

63. Details of roof on Gate of Heavenly Favours

稜恩門

64. Base of stele showing side view of tortoise

65. Top of tortoise stele, south face

reminds you of a particularly vivid kaleidoscope—a riot of colours which instead of clashing seem to have settled accidentally into perfect harmony.

This hall served as a sort of reception room or front porch. It was here that those participating in the rites were welcomed, paused to check that their robes were in order, perhaps received a cup of tea. In a way, the first courtyard and this building together acted as a sort of antechamber.

The courtyard itself is well planted with pines and a lot of fruit trees. In the southeast corner there is a very beautiful post-Ming stele pavilion (colourplate 6). Built on a square white stone terrace and open on all four sides, it has a double roof of yellow tiles. There are four little staircases leading up to the stele, which consists of a large marble slab resting on the back of a tortoise (fig. 64). The tortoise, which stands on a stone base carved with waves to represent the sea, is unlike the other earlier tortoises in the necropolis; in many ways it is more like a dragon, scaled with a dorsal ridge instead of a tortoise shell and with long flowing locks and distinctive horns lying flat on the head. The top of the stele, instead of showing the usual interlaced hornless dragons which we have seen in the great stele at the entrance to the valley, has been carved in the form of a large dragonlike creature with horns similar to the tortoise's except that here they are shown upright (fig. 65). The inscription on the stele is in both Chinese and Manchu characters. On one side is an edict dated 30 December 1659, prescribing certain repairs to the tomb and penalties for felling timber. The other side carries a description dated 1786 of further repairs undertaken in that year. On the right-hand edge of the stele is an Imperial edict from 1804; the left edge is blank.

There is some doubt about the origin of this stele, which has no counterpart in any of the other tombs. Ku Yen-wu mentions it: "In front of the kitchen stands a tablet house, facing south, inside which is a stone tablet, the crowning border of which is carved with a dragon and which has a pedestal in the shape of a tortoise but bears no inscription."[1] This shows that the pavilion and stele were standing in the 1650s. There is, however, something curious about this construction; none of the other tombs in the valley has a stele pavilion in that place, and since the great tortoise stele at the entrance to the mausoleum is dedicated to the Emperor Yung-lo who is buried in this tomb, it is difficult to see what purpose a second stele could have served. Bouillard deduces, to my mind correctly, that this was most likely a Ch'ing innovation.

The Ch'ing rulers were, from the beginning, anxious to demonstrate that they had taken the Throne of Heaven in the traditional way and not as foreigner usurpers. They were therefore punctilious in showing respect to the tombs of the previous dynasty. Some of the tombs had been damaged by the troops of the Chinese rebel leader Li Tzu-ch'eng, who captured Peking just before the fall of the Ming dynasty in 1644. One of the first acts of the new Manchu rulers was to see that these tombs were repaired and to issue edicts referring to the maintenance of the Imperial Ming Tombs and the importance of carrying out the proper rites. It is possible that during the course of these restorations they hoped to placate the local population by showing honour to the founder of the previous dynasty.[2]

Passing through the Gate of Heavenly Favours, you come into the main courtyard in which stands the Sacrificial Hall, the Hall of Heavenly Favours. Three paved pathways lead from the gate to the hall. The courtyard is planted with peonies, roses, fruit trees, and pines. To the left and right of the paths, facing each other, are two small buildings entirely faced with green and yellow tiles (colourplate 7). These were ovens for burning sacrificial offerings such as paper money and silks. Built like a miniature house, each oven is complete with a yellow tile roof decorated with the necessary roof animals; the tiles on the front of the oven around the opening are designed to look like lattice windows and doorways (fig. 66). In size and general effect they remind one of very pretty dolls' houses. These ovens are almost identical to an oven in the Ch'ing tomb, Mu-ling, photographed at the beginning of this century by E. Fonssagrives.[3] The only other surviving oven in the Ming Valley is in T'ai-ling (tomb 6), and there the roof has a much simpler form.

One of the original contributions the Ming made to Chinese ceremonial architecture was to develop the use of glazed tiles for decoration. Green glazed tiles had been used for roofs in the Han dynasty; the use of yellow tiles for Imperial buildings followed shortly afterward.* During the Ming era, there was a definite technical improvement in the art of glazing; for the first time tiles were baked in five colours to represent the five Buddhist precious jewels. Imperial potteries were set up in the Western Hills near Peking and in the mountains near Shenyang (Mukden). It became popular to use tiles to decorate walls, to create panels of flowers and leaves, or, as in the case of these sacrificial ovens, to imitate other building materials.

At the same time the practice of setting a row of little puppetlike figures on the corners of Imperial roofs was introduced. Each of these figures is cast in one piece with the tile on which it sits (fig. 68). Perched on the very edge of the roof is the figure of a man sitting on a hen. It is said that this represents the wicked Prince Min of the State of Ch'i, who in 283 B.C. was strung from the corner of a roof and left to die. His weight is too great for the chicken to fly to the ground. On the other hand, he cannot climb back up the roof because this is guarded by a ch'i-wen, which always holds the highest position in the row of figures. Between Prince Min and the ch'i-wen sits a row of small animals chosen in order from the following series: dragon, phoenix, lion, unicorn or ch'i-lin, and winged horse. The length of the series varies according to the importance of the building but should always be uneven and, as far as I know, never exceeds eleven.†

---

*Roof tiles were gutter-shaped and fixed on the roof in alternate concave and convex columns; the edges of each convex column overlapped the edges of the concave column on each side, thus providing a completely rain-proof covering. The tiles at the end of these columns, on the roof eaves, were whole or half discs decorated with different patterns which, on Imperial buildings, included a dragon (fig. 67). See W. P. Yetts, "Notes on Chinese Roof Tiles," p. 38.

†Uneven numbers belonged to the yang, or male, dominant element. I am grateful for this explanation of the roof animals to Arlington and Lewisohn, *In Search of Old Peking,* p. 29. Modern guides tend to be vague about the origin of the figures, often giving conflicting explanations. According to Dr. Feng, the importance of serial order was introduced by the Ming; before that, there was a greater variety of animals placed in a more haphazard way.

66. Details of lattice work on ceramic oven

67. Roof tile with dragon   68. Ceramic roof animals

The Hall of Heavenly Favours is very simple—a rectangular building running east-west, with doors and windows on the south side and only a concealed opening to the north (colourplate 8). The simplicity of the form is compensated for by the beauty of the proportions and the complexity of the decoration. This hall, standing on a spacious white marble terrace, was, until the introduction of Western styles of architecture, one of the two largest buildings in China; it is still one of the most beautiful.* The terrace has three layers, each with an intricately carved balustrade. The head posts of the balustrades are decorated with dragons and two different sorts of phoenixes (figs. 70–73). There appears to be no symmetry in the choice of motif, but this could be the result of restoration. Rainwater spouts are carved into horned gargoyles, small along the balustrades and large at the corners (fig. 74). Three staircases lead up the front of the terrace; there is an additional staircase near the southeast and southwest corners of the terrace. Running up the centre of the middle staircase is a beautifully carved marble slab (fig. 75). This is less stylized than the slabs in later tombs; between the waves and mountains run a couple of winged horses with antlers, while two enormous dragons play in the clouds above (fig. 76). When the emperor entered the hall, he was carried over this slab on his palanquin. The general effect of this terrace is that of an inspired tapestry, equalled only by the terraces in the Forbidden City and the Altar of Heaven.

*According to Liang Ssu-ch'eng, erstwhile professor of architecture at Tsinghua University, the surface area of the Hall of Supreme Harmony in the Forbidden City is very slightly larger than that of the Ch'ang-ling Hall of Heavenly Favours, but the roof of the latter contains the longest "ang" in existence, and its terrace is the oldest existing example of a triple terrace with marble balustrade. See figure 69.

69. Architectural drawing of the sacrificial hall by Liang Ssu-ch'eng. (Yale Slide and Photograph Collection)

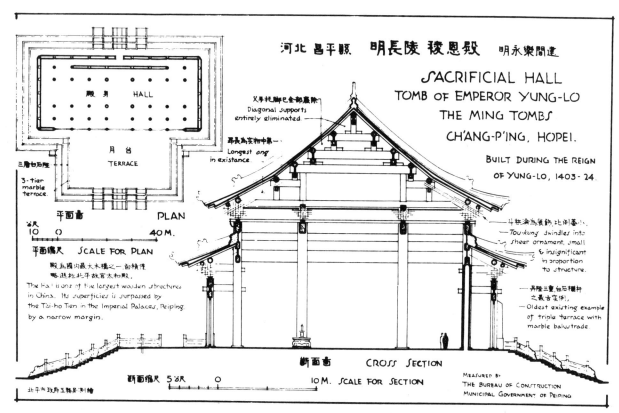

70. Triple terraces with marble balustrades, Hall of Heavenly Favours

71. Balustrade column with dragon, Hall of Heavenly Favours

72. Balustrade column with dragon's claw

73. Balustrade column with phoenix

The outside of the hall is a mass of colour. The enormous double roof of yellow tiles is supported by the usual highly intricate and brightly painted criss-crossing of small beams, each of which is carefully decorated. Beneath the roof-work is a painted frieze; below that, the latticed windows and doors which make up the front of the building are all painted red. Apart from the tiles on the roof, the whole construction of the front is made of painted wood.

The bright Peking light accentuates the contrast between the outside and the inside of the hall. Inside, there is a cool feeling of green. The roof is held up by rows of gigantic columns more than ten metres high and one metre in diameter (fig. 77). These beams of *Machilus nanmu*,[4] a sort of cedar, were brought from Szechuan, some four thousand kilometres away, by special order of the Emperor Yung-lo. Some light is cast on the way in which they were transported by Matteo Ricci, who traveled up the Grand Canal during the reign of the Emperor Wan-li, another of the great Ming builders. He records with amazement seeing huge beams, tree trunks and wooden columns, bound together sometimes for the length of two miles, and being dragged by many thousands of coolies. He was told that these were being brought from the province of Szechuan to rebuild part of the Imperial palace, damaged two years previously by fire. Their progress was so slow that Ricci reckoned the total time of transport would amount to almost three years.[5]

74. Gargoyle on terrace corner, Hall of Heavenly Favours

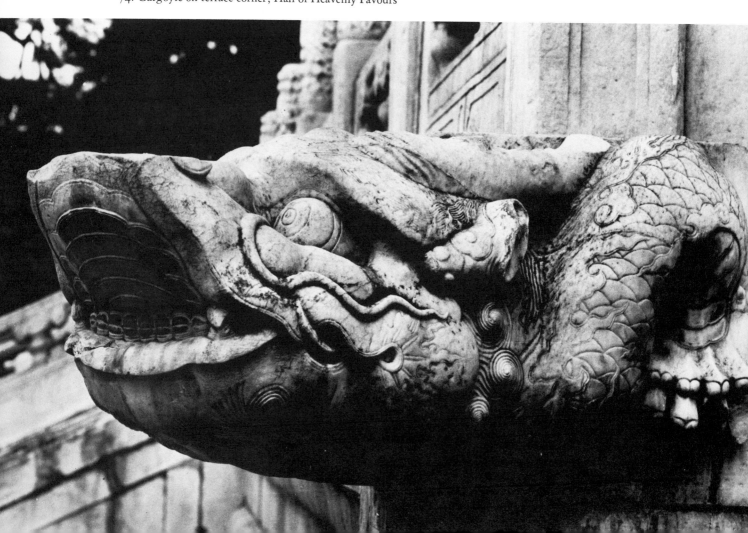

75. Triple staircase with carved marble slab
leading to Hall of Heavenly Favours, south side

76. Detail of figure 75, lower section

77. Interior of Hall of Heavenly Favours

The columns are a soft brown, and like all the other woodwork on the inside, unpainted. The only colour in the hall comes from the ceiling, which is made up of small squares similar to those in the roof of the entrance hall, painted green, blue, and gold (colourplate 9). Here it seems likely that the restoration has not been complete, since earlier descriptions suggest that the columns at least were painted red. It may be that there has been a deliberate decision to play down the religious significance of the hall's interior.

Today the hall is empty. In 1931 it still housed a wooden tabernacle with the five objects needed for the rites. Here the ceremonies were performed in honour of the dead emperor. Apart from his birthday and the day of his death, there were certain other fixed times in the year, particularly in spring and autumn, when the reigning emperor would come all the way from Peking to fulfill his duties. Sir Reginald Johnston, tutor to the last Ch'ing emperor, records that an officially recognized descendant of the Ming, the Marquis of Chu, visited the tomb to offer sacrifices twice a year until 1924. In September of that year he paid his last visit to the mausoleum and then followed the ex-emperor into exile.[6]

68 • Ch'ang-ling (Tomb 1)

The exit from the hall is concealed behind a high and very solid free-standing wall at the back, which acts as a protection against harmful influences from the north. Behind the building a triple marble staircase with a central slab similar to that on the south side leads down to a triple doorway in the courtyard wall. This doorway, which is decorated with green and yellow tiles, leads into a third and smaller courtyard; on the far side of this is an enormous stone tower—the stele tower. Between the triple doorway and the tower is the small, free-standing protective screen—a wooden door set between two marble columns topped with ch'i-lin. Beyond this is a large white stone altar on which stand stone replicas of the five ritual objects used in the sacrificial rites. As we have already seen, this altar was purely symbolic, since the rites were performed in the Hall of Heavenly Favours.

The altar is completely dwarfed by the stele tower and pavilion (fig. 78). Indeed, whereas the central courtyard gives a feeling of open space and lightness—it is the

78. Stele tower and pavilion with altar in foreground, seen from the south

width rather than the height which attracts attention—here everything is dominated by the combined height of these buildings. Built of great blocks of grey stone and joined by a high crenellated wall on each side, the tower looks exactly like a gate-tower in an old Chinese city. Firmly planted on the tower and looming over all else is the stele pavilion, a heavy, square, red-walled building with an imposing yellow tiled double roof, in which stands the grave stele of the Emperor Yung-lo.

Through the centre of the tower is a tunnel which rises steeply and then forks to the left and right leading onto a wide rampart surrounding the funeral mound. Here you are in a completely different world. Gone are all the bright colours and the rather elaborate decorations. In front is a large hill covering the funeral vault; at one end of this is a small conical tumulus just like the funeral mounds you see in the fields around Peking. The hill is planted with thujas and oaks. The grey rampart, three metres wide and one kilometre long, disappears out of sight behind the mound. There is an air of peace and quiet. This is a real grave—a place for the dead to sleep.

Behind you, standing squarely on the grey tower, is the pavilion. Here only the arches in the north and south walls are open; the other two are blocked about five metres in from the outer wall. The stele stands on a plain four-layered socle; it has been painted red and carries the inscription: "Tomb of the accomplished Emperor Ch'eng-tsu." The top of the stele is carved with two dragons surrounded by clouds and with two characters in chuan script:* "Ta Ming"—"the Great Ming."

*"Hsiao chuan," or "small seal script," was the standardized script introduced during the Ch'in dynasty (221–206 B.C.). It was based on regional variations of "ta chuan," or "large seal script," which developed in the Chou dynasty (1027–221 B.C.) and in which the original Confucian classics were written. In "hsiao chuan," the lines and structure of the characters were considerably streamlined, and this made it popular for seal engraving. See T. C. Lai, *Chinese Calligraphy,* University of Washington Press, 1973.

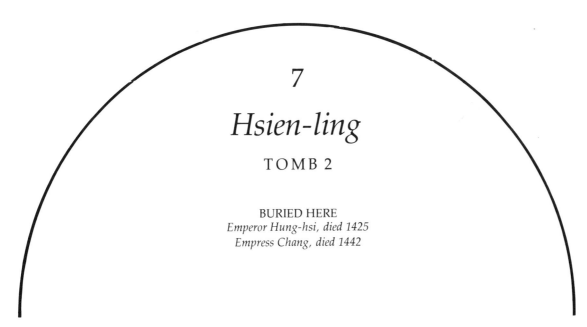

7

Hsien-ling

TOMB 2

BURIED HERE
Emperor Hung-hsi, died 1425
Empress Chang, died 1442

When the powerful Yung-lo died in 1424, he was succeeded by his son Hung-hsi. You do not need to read the histories to see that Hung-hsi was a modest emperor. His tomb, Hsien-ling, is as far removed from the grandeurs of Ch'ang-ling as a college chapel from a Gothic cathedral. In fact, the new emperor, who was already ailing when he came to the throne, lived for less than a year. On 29 May 1425, realising that he was seriously ill, he issued an edict expressing his last wishes: "I have reigned a very short time; I have not been able to bring any benefits to my people; I cannot bear the idea that they should be burdened with heavy works. My tomb should be constructed with great economy." Later that day he died.*

On acceding to the throne Hung-hsi's son immediately consulted his ministers on the question of his father's tomb. Obviously approving of his father's last wishes but afraid of being accused of lack of due respect, he quoted the examples of the early Ch'in and Han dynasties, who "followed the strictest rules of economy; pious sons thinking only of protecting the body and soul of their father, not wishing ostentatious funerals."[1] The ministers agreed that the dead emperor's wishes should be observed. The new emperor designed the tomb himself, and it was finished in the astonishingly short period of three months.

Hung-hsi was unlucky all round. Although at that time the whole of the rest of the valley was untouched, feng-shui seems to have indicated that he should be buried in an awkward spot, about 700 metres to the northwest of Ch'ang-ling where the lie of the land is such that the temple buildings were separated by a small hill. Indeed, not only were the two courtyards separated, but the tortoise stele does not lie on an axis with either of the two buildings. (This provoked Bouillard: "C'est assez choquant.") Unlike the tomb buildings, the stele lies on a true north-south axis. Maybe the shape of the hill, known as the Jade Table Mountain, and the direction of the little river that

*At the time of his death, in accordance with an old Mongol custom, ten of his concubines were forced to commit suicide and were buried with him. See *Dictionary of Ming Biography*, p. 340.

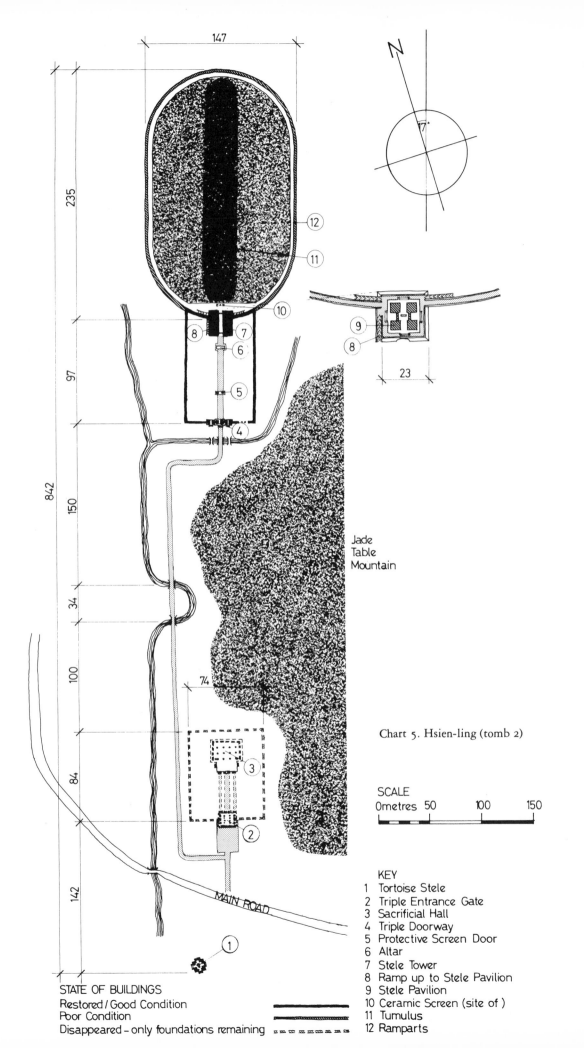

147

235

97

842

150

34

100

74

84

142

23

N

7°

⑫

⑪

⑩

⑧ ⑦

⑥

⑤

④

⑨
⑧

Jade
Table
Mountain

MAIN ROAD

①

Chart 5. Hsien-ling (tomb 2)

SCALE
0metres   50   100   150

STATE OF BUILDINGS
Restored / Good Condition
Poor Condition
Disappeared – only foundations remaining

KEY
1 Tortoise Stele
2 Triple Entrance Gate
3 Sacrificial Hall
4 Triple Doorway
5 Protective Screen Door
6 Altar
7 Stele Tower
8 Ramp up to Stele Pavilion
9 Stele Pavilion
10 Ceramic Screen (site of)
11 Tumulus
12 Ramparts

flows just to the south of the inner courtyard were considered auspicious; maybe it was decided to use the curious ridge which runs down the centre of the grave enclosure as part of the tumulus, possibly sparing some of the expenses of construction. In any case, perhaps as a result of the buildings being separated from each other, this tomb has suffered badly from decay.

Today the road runs between the stele and the remains of the first courtyard. The stele has been incorporated into the countryside (fig. 79); it stands in the middle of a large vegetable field and in autumn is often piled high with cabbages or bundles of corn. The flat uncarved surface of the stele carries a modern slogan to encourage more production in agriculture. (In 1979 the slogan had been removed.) To the right of the road is a copse of young pine trees. If you look among the trees, you can find the stone foundations of the former triple Entrance Gate and the Sacrificial Hall. The steps leading up to this hall and the central marble slab carved with mountains and clouds are still in place (fig. 80). The walls of the precinct and the buildings themselves have completely disappeared. Although they were standing in 1920, Bouillard writes: "The Hsien-ling is in a lamentable state. The roofs have crumbled, the tiles have fallen, the woodwork is rotten; complete ruin is very near."[2]

It comes as a pleasant surprise to find that the second courtyard and the tomb itself are in a relatively good state (colourplate 10). The approach is a pretty one, skirting the Jade Table Mountain and crossing a triple stone bridge just in front of the main doorway. Although this courtyard is built on the same plan as that in the other tombs, the fact that it opens straight off the road rather than off another courtyard gives it rather a naked impression. The altar, the little screen doorposts, and the stele tower (fig. 81) are all visible from the road and there is no privacy until you get up on the funeral mound behind the tower.

The central doorway, the roofs, and the precinct walls, with the exception of a large hole in the southeast corner, are in good condition and must have been restored since Bouillard saw them. The two side doors have lost most of their decoration. There are a few very large pine trees and a lot of young ones. The paved way is intact; of the protective screen only the lower halves of the marble doorposts remain (fig. 82). The altar is similar to that in Ch'ang-ling but smaller (figs. 55, 56); broken remnants of the altar objects can be found lying around on the grass.

The stele tower rises straight from the ground and can only be reached by a very steep ramp up the west side. The balustrade that was there in 1931 has gone, and the surface of the ramp is broken by the roots of two flourishing pine trees growing through its side. The stele pavilion is like the one in Ch'ang-ling only smaller. Of the four archways, only the north and south ones are open; those to the east and west are blind. The base of the stele is much more ornate than that in Ch'ang-ling, consisting of eight different layers; the lower layers are decorated with repeating cloud, lotus, and knot patterns, while the top row shows long-snouted, five-clawed dragons racing through clouds. The stele, which still bears traces of red and green paint, says: "Tomb of the illustrious Emperor Jen-tsung."

79. Tortoise stele in the fields

80. Marble slab and steps leading up to the overgrown site of the sacrificial hall

81. Stele tower, pavilion, and altar

82. White stone bases of protective screen door

The terrace surrounding the stele house is in fairly good condition. It is a pretty place to sit, with one view down into the courtyard and another onto the wooded tumulus. On both sides of the tower at the back, a very steep but short ramp leads down onto the mound itself. The surface and steps have fallen away, mainly because of the trees growing up between the paving stones. The roof of the stele pavilion is double and the tiles are nearly all in place, but the painting on the woodwork is very faded (fig. 83).

Going straight through the tower at ground level is an arched tunnel blocked by a brick wall a couple of metres from each end. De Groot thinks that these walls may have enclosed a special chamber for precious objects belonging to the deceased or used in the burying rites, but I have not come across any evidence to corroborate this. In some of the other tombs, similar brick walls have been breached and you can walk straight through to the mound. Opposite the tunnel exit on the northern side, i.e. inside the grave enclosure, there used to be a screen in green and yellow tiles with a small niche for burning paper offerings. No signs remain of this, nor of the wall which Bouillard describes as supporting the funeral mound.

The most extraordinary thing about the tumulus is its shape. Running north, straight up the middle of the hill, is a very steep ridge—a sort of hog's back—which appears to be natural. The top of this spine is covered with very old thujas; lower down on the slopes there are a lot of large-leaved Chinese oaks. The rampart around the mound is very narrow and low, climbing steeply at the northern end to a point as high

83. Roof on stele pavilion

as the roof of the stele pavilion. The whole area gives a wild and abandoned feeling; trees are growing through the ramp and the outer wall, which has fallen completely away in many places.

DRAINAGE. This is the earliest tomb in which you can see signs of the original drainage system. To ensure that the body of the deceased emperor was preserved safely, it was obviously important to have good drainage. In Ch'ang-ling, the drains have all been restored and it is not clear whether they have been rebuilt according to the original system. Here in Hsien-ling, the problem was a simple one; the steep fall of the land meant that water would naturally drain away. On the ramparts there are no signs of any water spouts, but at ground level there is a round drain-hole through the rampart wall every thirty metres. In the southwest corner of the courtyard there is a large drain-hole through the outer wall. Presumably there was a twin to this at the other end of the wall.

Hung-hsi, 1424–25

Hung-hsi, eldest son of the powerful Emperor Yung-lo, appears to have had almost nothing in common with his father. Whereas Yung-lo had been strong and famous for his physical endurance and military ability, Hung-hsi was fat and weak. It is recorded that when, in his youth, his father sent him along with the other young princes to review the troops at dawn, he surprised the court by returning almost at once. It was, he said, too cold. He would eat his breakfast first and review the troops afterward. This attitude did not endear Hung-hsi to his father, and he only managed to retain his position as heir to the throne by proving that he was a competent and responsible administrator. At least one of his reforms, that guaranteeing 40 percent of all civil service posts to northerners, lasted until the fall of the empire in 1911. Until then, the purely competitive nature of the civil service examination had led to an undue preponderance of the better-educated southerners.

Hung-hsi seems to have been a humane man with a serious wish to ease the burden on the peasantry. In times of hardship he cut ruthlessly through official red tape. When one of the Grand Secretaries tried to prevent him from remitting taxes in a distressed area, arguing that he should be patient and consult the Ministers of Works and Revenue first, the emperor retorted: "Be patient? Relieving peoples' poverty ought to be handled as though one were rescuing them from fire or saving them from drowning. One cannot hesitate . . . you be quiet, Sir!"

In order to save money, he stopped all foreign ventures—there were to be no more forays to the west to collect Mongolian horses, and no more naval expeditions. In the long run the latter decision had serious consequences. Hung-hsi reaffirmed the classical view that the Middle Kingdom was self-sufficient, that knowledge of foreign countries was unnecessary, and power on the seas irrelevant for a land whose security lay in its vast size and the Great Wall. Unfortunately, a side-effect of his decision was to weaken the army. A job had to be found for the leader of Yung-lo's naval expeditions, the great eunuch admiral Cheng Ho, who was therefore appointed Commander of the Garrison at Nanking. This was the first time a eunuch had been placed in a position of high military command during the Ming dynasty. It was an ominous precedent, widely followed by later emperors and eventually leading to the complete demoralisation of the Chinese army.

I Stele pavilion and Columns Supporting the Sky seen through the central arch of the Great Red Gate

2. South façade of the P'ai-lou

3. Beacon at the start of the Spirit Road

4. Triple entrance, Ch'ang-ling (tomb 1)

5. South façade of Gate of Heavenly Favours, Ch'ang-ling (tomb 1)

6. Stele pavilion in first courtyard, Ch'ang-ling (tomb 1)

8. Hall of Heavenly Favours, Ch'ang-ling (tomb 1)

7. Ceramic oven, Ch'ang-ling (tomb 1)   9. Ceiling detail in Hall of Heavenly Favours, Ch'ang-ling (tomb 1)

10. Second courtyard with stele tower and pavilion, Hsien-ling (tomb 2)

11. View over courtyards from stele pavilion, Ching-ling (tomb 3)

12. Protective screen door, Ching-ling (tomb 3)

8

Ching-ling

TOMB 3

BURIED HERE
Emperor Hsüan-te, died 1435
Empress Sun, died 1462

The new emperor, Hsüan-te, was Hung-hsi's son. He had two wives, one of whom was buried in the same tomb, Ching-ling; the other, the Empress Hu, degraded from the rank of empress because she failed to produce a son, was buried in the Western Hills, where there was a cemetery for princes, princesses, and concubines.

Hsüan-te seems to have been impressed by the modesty of his predecessor, and on an early visit to the Ming Tombs, ordered that his own tomb should in no way exceed Hsien-ling. In fact, the area covered by the courtyards and buildings is somewhat larger than that in Hsien-ling, but the funeral tumulus is smaller. The tomb is laid out on exactly the same plan, only in this case it is in one continuous unit. The axis of the tomb is northeast-southwest, but as already explained, I will refer to the directions as if it lay on a true north-south line.

Although architecturally this tomb and Hsien-ling are practically identical, they make a very different impression. Hsien-ling is much more abandoned; it is common to find cows and sheep grazing even in the second, rather well-preserved courtyard. Ching-ling, on the other hand, gives a feeling of neatness and order (colourplate 11). It is small but elegant—a sort of Petit Trianon. Although the village comes right up to its gates and the tortoise stele is surrounded by houses, the tomb and its precincts are much better preserved than Hsien-ling. The tortoise stele stands on a stone paving carved with waves and snail-like coils in the four corners; the small surrounding wall has gone (fig. 84). A cobbled path leads from the stele between two thorn garden hedges and up a ramp to the main entrance. This entrance has been completely restored since 1931 but not according to the original design. In 1931 there was still a triple door such as we have seen in Ch'ang-ling and Hsien-ling. Today the opening is flanked by two square brick or stone doorposts, slightly higher than but joining onto the precinct walls (fig. 85); like the walls, they are painted red and have yellow tiled roofs. On the ground between these posts, you can see the stone foundations of the

13. OPPOSITE: View of Yü-ling (tomb 4) from the ramparts of Mao-ling (tomb 5)

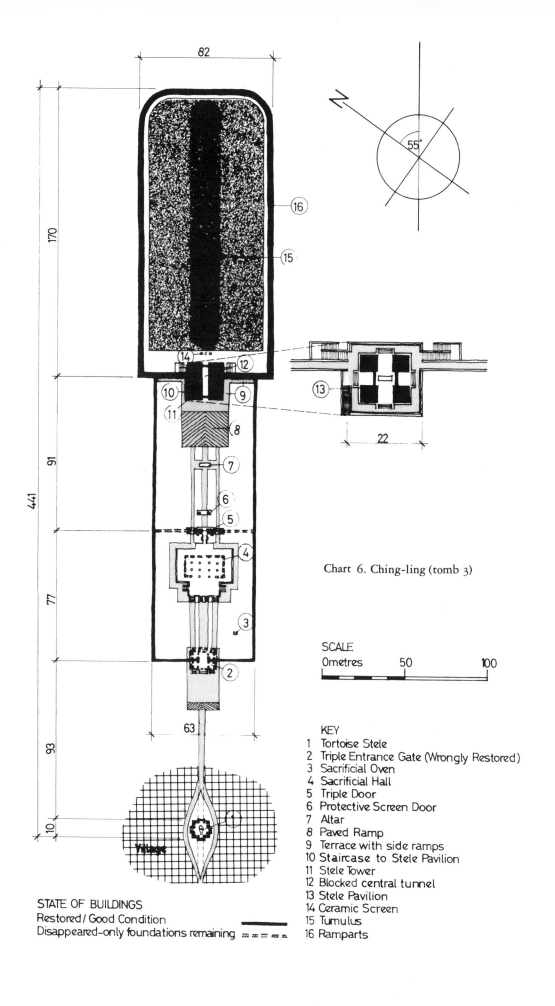

Chart 6. Ching-ling (tomb 3)

SCALE

0 metres   50   100

KEY
1 Tortoise Stele
2 Triple Entrance Gate (Wrongly Restored)
3 Sacrificial Oven
4 Sacrificial Hall
5 Triple Door
6 Protective Screen Door
7 Altar
8 Paved Ramp
9 Terrace with side ramps
10 Staircase to Stele Pavilion
11 Stele Tower
12 Blocked central tunnel
13 Stele Pavilion
14 Ceramic Screen
15 Tumulus
16 Ramparts

STATE OF BUILDINGS
Restored/Good Condition
Disappeared–only foundations remaining

84. Tortoise stele with village and stele pavilion in background

earlier triple doors conforming to Bouillard's description. The triple staircases on both sides of the doorway are in good condition.

The first courtyard is well planted with pine trees, and on the right of the paved way the stone foundation of the former oven or small building for burning paper offerings can be traced. Although the Sacrificial Hall has completely gone, the foundations have been cleaned up and the stone column bases, door sockets, and bases for the beams that would have held up the walls and roofs are clearly visible. For most of the year grass and wild flowers grow up between the stones, heightening the generally peaceful effect. A triple staircase, with a very fine marble slab carved with dragons in the centre of the central stair, leads up to the hall foundations (fig. 86). In 1931 the building was in good condition with the roof intact. The present terrace on which the Sacrificial Hall stood was built about a hundred years after the rest of the tomb. In 1536, the Emperor Chia-ching (the one who was responsible for the P'ai-lou) visited Ching-ling and was displeased by what he saw: "Ching-ling has been built very small; moreover, it is in a very bad state; this does not correspond to the virtues and merits of the Emperor Hsüan-tsung [Hsüan-te]."[1] He therefore ordered that the Sacrificial Hall be rebuilt and a terrace added. This may explain the unusual shape of the terrace. In all other tombs the "north" side of the terrace runs in a straight "east-west" line. In some cases there is a staircase, but the top of the staircase does not jut out from this line and there is always a considerable gap between the terrace and the triple doorway into the next courtyard. Here the central part of the terrace has been extended right up to the triple doorway, the level of the second courtyard being the same as the height of the terrace (fig. 87); two short staircases lead down from this platform to the right and left just before the door.

Today the doorway stands free and all traces of the original dividing wall have gone. The doorway itself is in unusually good condition; the wooden door-frame and lintel are still in place, the green and yellow tile decorations are very fine, and the tiled roof is complete with the ch'i-wen and smaller roof animals in place (fig. 50).

Ten metres on, you come to the protective screen door (colourplate 12). This is one of the very few tombs where the door framework is complete. The marble columns and two ch'i-lin are intact; the woodwork is brightly painted with a flower motif and a row of Buddhist "eyes" just under the crossbeams. (Similar "eyes" can be seen in the Temple of the Sleeping Buddha near the Western Hills.) The altar beyond is of the usual style; the upper half of a stone incense burner lies on the ground (fig. 60).

The stele tower and the "southern" end of the wall around the tumulus show two innovations. The first is that the tower does not rise straight from the ground as in Ch'ang-ling and Hsien-ling, but is built on a wide terrace reached by a broad ramp. The second, repeated in all subsequent tombs except for the last, is that, leading off this terrace and running along the tumulus wall between two to three metres from the ground on both sides of the stele tower, is a ramp wide enough to walk along (fig. 88). Nowhere have I been able to find any reference to this ramp, which is completely ignored by De Groot and Bouillard. In this and most of the other tombs, it ends at the

85. Rebuilt entrance door

86. TOP: Terrace, triple doorway, and stele pavilion

87. BELOW: Sacrificial hall terrace leading to triple doorway

88. RIGHT: "Sidewalk" leading from the terrace of the stele tower to the courtyard outer wall

outer wall of the precinct; it could, perhaps, have been designed for a guard patrolling the approach to the grave mound.

The stele tower is reached by an obviously new stone staircase on the "west" side. (In 1931 there was a ramp similar to that in Hsien-ling.) Through the centre of the tower is a blocked tunnel exactly like that in Hsien-ling. The "north" and "south" arches of the stele pavilion are open; the side arches are blind. The base of the stele is less decorated than its predecessor but has the usual lotus and knot motifs with running dragons round the top layer. The stele bears the inscription: "Tomb of the illustrious Emperor Hsüan-tsung." The tiles on the double roof are complete, and here for the first time the frieze between the roofs is ceramic and not painted wood. The ramps extending from the back of the tower down onto the funeral mound are in good condition. It looks as if the "south" end of the mound enclosure, between the stele tower and the mound itself, was once paved. The mound does not go right up to the ramparts but is held by a low supporting wall. In 1931 there was a ceramic screen opposite the entrance of the blocked tunnel, but of this nothing remains.

As in Hsien-ling, the tumulus is a very strange shape. Once again, the centre of the mound rises sharply to form a steep, spinelike ridge running "north-south" up the side of the hill. The whole length of this ridge is planted with thujas. The ramparts around the tumulus are wider than those of Hsien-ling and in much better condition. It seems likely that these ramparts benefited from the general restoration and improvements made to the tomb after the Emperor Chia-Ching's visit in 1536. In all other tombs the corners of the ramparts are rounded, but here, exceptionally, the "southern" corners are right angles. The "northern" end is in the usual circular form.

This tomb and its predecessor should be considered together. They are, after Sze-ling, the smallest of the tombs, are built on the same plan, and have the same curious spinelike formation running through the centre of the funeral mound. Whereas Hsien-ling is one of the more decayed tombs, Ching-ling has obviously been restored at different times. They are, in a way, two sides of the same coin. Although, at least as far as the entrance is concerned, the latest restoration is not accurate, the tomb is in a much better state than twenty-five years ago and has lost none of its charm. A decision must have been taken to keep only those buildings which could be put in good order; all that was decayed beyond repair has been cleared away. This absence of rubble gives the courtyards the soft air of a slightly overgrown garden. The protective screen is the best in the whole valley.

DRAINAGE.   As in Hsien-ling, the problem has been a simple one. The whole grave enclosure is built on such a steep slope that water will naturally drain away. For the first time, however, there are provisions for water to run off the encircling rampart. On each side of the "south" wall of the rampart, is a drain spout through which the rainwater falls down to the paved area behind the stele tower. Beneath each of these spouts, at ground level, is a large drain built under the rampart wall. It looks as if there has been a shallow paved gutter the whole way around the mound at the foot of the rampart wall.

Hsüan-te, 1426–36

There is something of the Renaissance idea of the perfect man in Hsüan-te. The eldest of his father's ten sons, he seems to have excelled in everything. From an early age his skill in riding and in solving military problems made him a favourite with his grandfather, the great Yung-lo, who took him on expeditions to Peking and the Mongolian frontier. As a ruler, he showed administrative ability and a sense of responsibility for his people. Above all, however, he is known as a patron and amateur of the arts. During his reign the classical "blue and white" decoration of porcelain was developed at the famous kilns at Ching-te-chen. For the first time, reign marks on porcelain were widely used.* His court encouraged poets and painters. He wrote verses himself and painted birds, flowers, and animals in the Sung style, sometimes signing his scrolls "playfully painted by the Imperial brush."[2] And like a Renaissance counterpart in western Europe, he was a collector. Messengers were sent throughout the empire to search for rare and beautiful objects. The Imperial palace blossomed with exotic flowers, silks, fish, porcelain, and unusual manufactures. The gardens and menageries were filled with falcons and leopards, and the harems with Korean virgins exacted as tribute.

From his father Hsüan-te inherited good political advisors, and these he cultivated in the Taoist tradition by combining philosophical discussions with good wine. During his reign, the institution of the Grand Secretariat was further developed. Hsüan-te tried to keep the taxes down, avoided military adventures, and, after a Chinese defeat in Annam in 1428, withdrew from that area, concentrating the army in the north against possible Mongolian incursions. At the same time, however, he allowed a brief revival in naval expeditions. The famous eunuch admiral Cheng Ho, who had been grounded as garrison commander at Nanking by Hsüan-te's father, was recalled to the navy. Cheng Ho's seventh and last expedition from 1431–33 took him through the Indian Ocean and down the east coast of Africa, while yet another Chinese fleet visited Sumatra.

Nevertheless, the emperor's chief interest was to improve internal administration. He was anxious to keep check on what was happening throughout China and started sending "Grand Coordinators" out to the provinces, "to tour and soothe." He was also responsible for beginning interprovincial cooperation on the Grand Canal grain transport system. In times of natural disaster, he followed his father's example of tax remissions and grain distributions.

Hsüan-te's weakness was that he trusted the eunuchs. Hung-wu, founder of the dynasty, had been well aware of the harmful role played by eunuchs in earlier dynas-

*There are rare examples of reign marks on porcelain from the Yung-lo period.

ties, in particular the Han. He had an iron tablet made, one metre high, saying: "Eunuchs must have nothing to do with administration." More effectively, he controlled by edict their numbers, the ranks and titles they might assume, and their style of clothing. Eunuchs were not allowed to meddle in politics, must not give advice or handle official papers, and—above all—they must remain illiterate. "Anyone using eunuchs as his eyes and ears will be blind and deaf. . . . The way to manage them is to make them fear the regulations. Don't give them the rewards of merit."[3]

This was all very well in the time of a strong ruler; but in the long run the whole closed-court system, with the emperor's dependence on male heirs and hence the need for a harem, gave the eunuchs a built-in advantage. They were needed to administer the vast complex of the Forbidden City. Apart from the emperor, they were the only contact the empresses and the young princes had with the outside world. When a young prince ascended the Throne of Heaven, it was only natural that he should turn to those who had instructed him during his youth—the eunuchs.

As we have already seen, Hsüan-te's father had taken the first step by appointing a eunuch commander of the military garrison at Nanking. Hsüan-te carried this further and appointed eunuch commanders in nearly all the leading provinces. This was bitterly resented by the army; however intelligent the eunuchs may have been, they had no military experience and the regular officers distrusted their new commanders' direct link to the palace. In 1426, a School for Palace Eunuchs was set up in the Forbidden City, and from that time on, eunuch power was virtually uncontrolled. At the time of Hsüan-te's death, his use of eunuchs as "Grand Coordinators" was already so unpopular that one of the first edicts of the regent, his mother, was to recall them to court.

Hsüan-te died unexpectedly after a short illness, leaving two sons and two daughters. His eldest son was only eight years old and the old empress dowager became regent. It is said that ten concubines were forced to accompany him after his death.[4]

9

Yü-ling

TOMB 4

BURIED HERE
Emperor Cheng-t'ung, died 1464
Empress Ch'ien, died 1468
Empress Chou, died 1504

This tomb is one of the most beautiful of the thirteen. Driving west past Hsien-ling, you turn right up a small cobbled road just by a bus stop. The road is very bad and there is no village on this side of the main road. As a result this tomb is seldom disturbed. It is beyond the reach of the village loudspeakers and only the determined sightseer or picnicker will go there. The tomb, cradled by the foothills which rise directly behind the funeral mound, makes a striking contrast to the land around it (fig. 89). The red walls and tall, dark green pines stand out against the brown fields and carefully pruned fruit trees in winter, the brilliant green of the young wheat and the fruit blossom in spring (colourplates 13 and 14).

The Emperor Cheng-t'ung, who is buried here, had a chequered career, being the only Ming emperor to reign twice. In 1449, the Chinese army was disastrously defeated by the Mongolians and the young emperor was taken prisoner. A palace coup in Peking placed his younger half-brother, Ching-t'ai, on the throne.* Although Cheng-t'ung was released by the Mongolians after a year and a half, it was not until 1457 that his supporters at court were sufficiently strong for him to regain the throne.† During the intervening years, Cheng-t'ung was virtually held prisoner in the Forbidden City.

In his testament, Cheng-t'ung broke with tradition by insisting that his first wife be buried in his tomb even though she had not borne him a son. Yü-ling is therefore the first tomb in the valley to house two empresses. It is known that when it was built, there were three separate underground entrances, one to each crypt. The only tomb

*The short interregnum of Ching-t'ai explains one peculiarity in the placing of the tombs. As can be seen on the map, tombs 2 and 3 are respectively to the west and east of Ch'ang-ling. Beyond tomb 2 lies tomb 11, then tombs 4, 5, and 6. The reason for this curious order is that tomb 11 was originally built for Ching-t'ai. When Cheng-t'ung regained the throne, he refused to allow his half-brother to be buried in the Imperial cemetery and the tomb stood, half-destroyed and unused, until 170 years later. Then, when an emperor died unexpectedly after ruling for only a month, it was decided to adapt the tomb for his grave. Ching-t'ai was buried in the Western Hills (see chapter 19).

†During his second reign, 1457–64, he took the name T'ien-shun, but to avoid confusion I will use the name Cheng-t'ung to cover both periods.

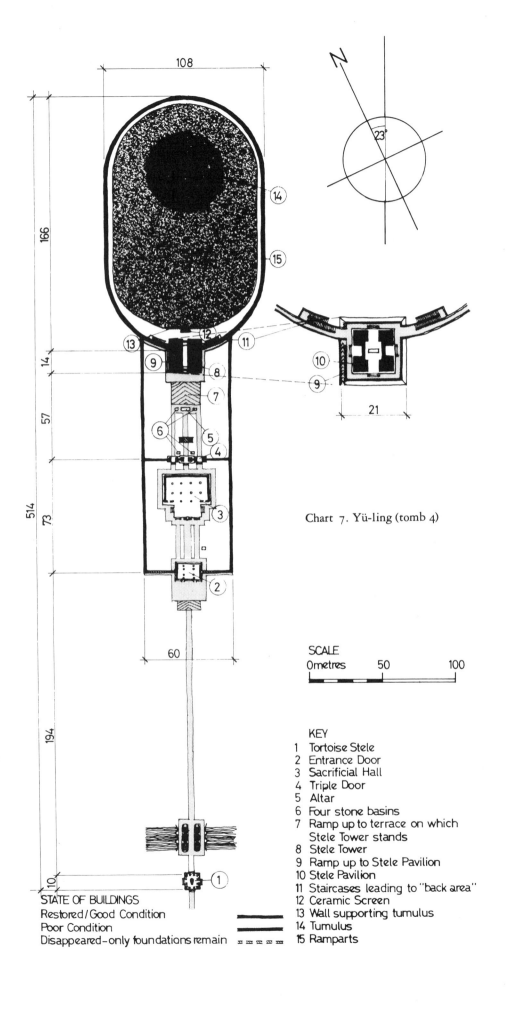

108

166

14

57

514

73

194

10

60

23°

N

21

Chart 7. Yü-ling (tomb 4)

SCALE

0 metres   50   100

KEY
1 Tortoise Stele
2 Entrance Door
3 Sacrificial Hall
4 Triple Door
5 Altar
6 Four stone basins
7 Ramp up to terrace on which
   Stele Tower stands
8 Stele Tower
9 Ramp up to Stele Pavilion
10 Stele Pavilion
11 Staircases leading to "back area"
12 Ceramic Screen
13 Wall supporting tumulus
14 Tumulus
15 Ramparts

STATE OF BUILDINGS
Restored/Good Condition
Poor Condition
Disappeared–only foundations remain

to be excavated, Ting-ling, has the same arrangement, and it seems probable that this was the pattern in most, if not all, the later Ming tombs. The question of whether an empress who outlived her husband should be buried with him in the Imperial grave was much disputed. Empresses who predeceased their husbands posed no problems; they were moved to his side at the time of the Imperial funeral and the grave was then closed. There was a strong school of geomancers who held that it was extremely inauspicious to reopen an Imperial grave; according to this view, it was equally harmful to build separate entrances to the grave chamber for later burials of the empress and possibly the consort mother of a future emperor. Historical precedent varied from dynasty to dynasty. The T'ang Empress Wu was buried beside her husband who had died twenty-three years previously, but in spite of the powerful position she had held up to the time of her death, this action was bitterly attacked by one of the Chief Ministers. He pointed out that an emperor's tomb was never reopened during the Han dynasty, which had prospered for four hundred years; later dynasties, such as the Wei and Chin, which allowed deceased emperors to be disturbed were relatively short-lived.[1]

Yü-ling lies somewhat higher than the earlier tombs, on a nearly north-south axis. The cobbled road, probably following the same route as the original "spirit way," leads through orchards to the tortoise stele which stands on a stone platform without walls

89. View of stele pavilion from southeast

(fig. 90). From there, the original paved way crosses three arched bridges and continues up a gentle ramp to the terrace on which the triple entrance once stood. Today the doorway has gone. On the west side, the remains of the outer doorpost have crumbled to less than a metre high. The east side is in a slightly better state, but the plaster has gone, revealing the rough brickwork. The red precinct walls are complete and most of the yellow tiles in place. In the door opening are the stone column bases and door sockets corresponding to the description of the original doorway.

From the entrance, steps lead down to the first courtyard. A large part of the courtyard, which has a few very old pine trees and a lot of young ones, is paved. The Sacrifical Hall, standing on a wide stone terrace, still has its walls. The roof has gone, but it is easy to see the shape of the building and the place where the supporting beams stood (figs. 91 and 92). In 1920 Bouillard noted: "the roof is nothing but a ruin; the little that is left will disappear very shortly."[2] The walls, made of rough brickwork filling between the beams, have been faced with stone up to a metre high; above that they have been plastered and painted a light yellowy-brown. The stone paving of the terrace is in excellent condition except for a small, perfectly conical thuja growing through the southwest corner. On the south side of the terrace there are three staircases, the central one with a fine marble slab engraved with mountains and clouds (fig. 93); to the east and west are two side staircases. There is no exit from either terrace or hall to the north.

Walking round the back of the Sacrificial Hall, you come to the triple doorway leading to the second courtyard. The doors are in very good condition and look as if they have recently been repaired; almost all the green and yellow decorative tiles are

90. Courtyards and tortoise stele in spring seen from stele pavilion

91. TOP: Stele tower and pavilion with back wall of sacrificial hall in foreground

92. LEFT: Wall of sacrificial hall showing where wooden beam was positioned; note the stone base and ventilation hole for the beam and the wall filling of brick and rubble

93. BELOW: Marble slab with mountains and clouds

in place, and the tile roof is nearly complete, with two ceramic heads still holding the roof ridge of the central door. The courtyard is grassy and wild flowers grow under the tall pines. Three paved paths lead from the door to the stone altar. To the west and east of these paths, just inside the triple door and then again just short of the altar, are four stone basins (see chart). All are cracked or broken—one has a small tree growing through its centre—but it is easy to see their form (figs. 94–96). The outside of each basin is decorated with some rather simple carving. A similar basin can be found in Mao-ling (tomb 5) to the east of the altar, and in Chao-ling (tomb 9) there are four similarly placed square stone bases but no trace of any basins. (Bouillard believed these basins to be unique to Yü-ling.) These are the only tombs in which such an arrangement is visible, and I have not been able to find any explanation of their use.

Beyond the altar, a steep ramp dotted with young pines leads up to the terrace on which the stele tower stands. Leading off the terrace to east and west along the outer wall of the funeral enclosure, run the same narrow walks we saw in Ching-ling. There is a blocked tunnel through the centre of the tower; in one place the orange plaster has broken and you can see through to a brick wall and a lot of rubble (fig. 97).

The tower is approached by a very steep ramp up the west side. This ramp still has part of its balustrade, but the paved surface has nearly all gone and you can climb up over rough stones. Pine trees are growing through the stonework on all sides— through the sides of the ramp, from the crenellated walls, and up through the little terrace around the stele pavilion. Another small tree is growing out of the roof; in winter this is often packed with Bramblings.

The pavilion housing the stele is the same as in the other tombs we have seen; the arches to the north and south are open, those to the east and west are blind. The inscription on the dragon-decorated stele reads: "Tomb of the far-seeing Emperor Ying-tsung." The stele base has six highly decorated layers (fig. 98).

From the terrace there is a lovely view over the valley to the reservoir. The double roof of the stele house is picturesque but very decayed. Nearly all the tiles have fallen off, making it easy to study the intricate criss-crossing of wood beams of which a typical Ming palace-style roof consists. Two green and yellow ceramic friezes that run around the building just below each roof are more or less complete.

Behind the tower, two right-angled staircases lead down into what appears to have been a paved back area. Standing free, opposite the blocked tunnel, are the remains of a ceramic screen. Behind that, two steps lead up onto the wall which supports the southern end of the tumulus.*

The tumulus and the surrounding ramparts create a very different impression from those in Hsien-ling and Ching-ling (colourplate 15). This tumulus is much more like a soft natural hill with a little artificial cone at the northern end. The slope is gentle, and for the most part the ramparts are much higher than the mound. The whole area is beautifully planted with very large oak trees and a few thujas; young pines grow from

*This wall does not surround the tumulus as Bouillard suggests; a specially carved stone marks the end on each side, just round the bend to east and west.

94, 95, 96. Stone basins

97. BELOW LEFT: Blocked tunnel through stele tower
98. BELOW RIGHT: Grave stele base

the side of the small cone. The outer wall of the ramparts is crenellated and fairly complete; the inner wall, which is low and smooth, has fallen away over long stretches. The walk around the hill is very lovely: to the north, the hills come right up to the edge of the ramparts; to the east, orchards stretch across to Hsien-ling and farther south you can see the golden roofs of Ch'ang-ling.

The second courtyard of this tomb is one of the most beautiful places in the whole valley. The tall trees seem to attract the birds, and in summer the triple doorway provides shade from the sun and shelter from the rain. The soft red colour of the walls, the gentle air of decay—white chunks of stone and marble lying on the green grass— the old, rather crooked trees, and the complete quiet give you a curious feeling of timelessness. Here, on our last day in Peking, a Sunday in early April, we sat with our Dutch friends and watched Daurian redstarts, red-flanked Bluetail, and Great Tits hop on the ground around us. Blue Magpies crossed to and fro, a sudden spot of red and a long streak of pale blue with a familiar screech. For a short while it was as if we had wandered into an enchanted garden; the outside world had ceased to exist.

DRAINAGE. This tomb was built on a gentle slope and so natural drainage was not enough. For the first time a system of stone ridges and spouts to carry the rainwater away from the ramparts was used. The ridges, twenty-two on each side, run at an angle across the rampart and lead to a hole in the inner rampart wall about 15 centimetres wide. On the other side of this wall is a small stone spout. In this way all rainwater is channeled into a shallow, paved gutter that runs around the mound alongside the inner rampart wall. At the southern end of the enclosure there is a large drain and spout carved from a single stone facing inward on the ramparts on each side of the tower. Directly below this, catching the water from the gutter, are two large, square drain holes that lead right under the rampart walls. There are two similar large drains at each end of the south wall of the first courtyard. No doubt there was once a channel connecting these with the small stream running under the three bridges. The sides of this stream have been lined with large stone blocks.

Cheng-t'ung, 1435–49, 1457–65

Great grandson of Yung-lo, Cheng-t'ung became emperor at the age of eight, the third emperor to ascend the throne in eleven years. Inevitably, the frequent change of rulers and his own youth weakened the central government. As we have seen, his father had encouraged the eunuchs. Now, with the old empress dowager as regent and a minor on the throne, they took complete control. The establishment of the Palace School of Eunuchs in 1426 had greatly strengthened their position, and by the second half of the fifteenth century it was said that the number of eunuchs had risen to thousands, some say tens of thousands.[3] The eunuchs ran their own secret service, which kept special files, available only to the emperor, on all government officials. This led to a disastrous rivalry between the eunuchs and the Grand Secretaries, the so-called "Inner Court" and the "Outer Court," or top officials of the Imperial bureaucracy. Even more serious, it exacerbated the hostility between North and South. The eunuchs were nearly all northerners; most of the high officials were southerners. As the eunuchs tightened their grip on the administration, they used their new strength to make money. Official positions were sold and office holders were expected to pay a yearly tribute. Provincial officials, who already found it virtually impossible to get through to the emperor, were driven to levying illegal taxes from the peasantry. In this way everyone suffered—the peasants who were badly governed and overtaxed, the officials who had bought their jobs and could not function efficiently, and the emperor, who was effectively screened from all reality.

When Cheng-t'ung came of age at fifteen, he entrusted all power to his earlier tutor, Wang Chen.* In 1449, Wang Chen, wanting to impress his family with his power, persuaded the emperor to send a punitive expedition against the Mongols who had been raiding the Chinese Empire in the north. En route, Wang Chen intended to entertain the emperor at his own home near Huai-lai, which is just the other side of the Nan-k'ou Pass in the Great Wall, some eighty kilometres to the northeast of Peking. The expedition was an unmitigated disaster. Although Wang Chen had no military experience, the emperor appointed him general, thus alienating all the professional officers. The Mongols defeated the Chinese; Wang Chen, instead of retreating, kept the army at Huai-lai so that he could entertain the emperor. As a result, the Chinese army was annihilated. Wang Chen and most of the other officers were killed and the emperor himself was taken prisoner. It is said that the Mongol chief found the young emperor sitting calmly on the floor of his tent, apparently unconcerned by the slaughter of his bodyguard around him.[4] This military defeat had a lasting effect on the Ming dynasty, which was henceforth on the defensive on the northern frontier.

Thus ended Cheng-t'ung's first reign. While he was in Mongolian hands, a new clique seized power in the palace and his younger half-brother, Ching-t'ai, who had been acting as regent during the campaign, was created emperor. Later, when the Mongols heard this, they set Cheng-t'ung free, realizing that he was no longer any use as a bargaining counter. Cheng-t'ung returned to Peking, where for six years he was held prisoner in the Forbidden City by his brother's supporters. In 1457, Ching-t'ai fell mortally ill, and with a new coup d'etat, Cheng-t'ung regained the throne.

Despite all these vicissitudes, Cheng-t'ung seems to have been a likeable man. It is recorded that he made friends among his Mongol captors. He was lastingly faithful to his first wife and, as we have seen, broke with precedent by insisting that she be buried in his tomb, even though she had not given him an heir. This first empress, the

*Wang Chen had been one of the first students at the Palace School for Eunuchs. His rise to power was rapid; he was appointed one of the chief officials of the all-important Directorate of Ceremonials and, with the emperor's open support, was soon recognized as the most powerful figure at court. It was he who ordered the first Ming Emperor Hung-wu's tablet forbidding eunuchs to take part in politics to be removed from its conspicuous place on one of the palace gates. Chinese historians, with the natural bias of the scholar-official against the eunuch official, have tended to blame Wang Chen for most of the disasters that occurred during Cheng-t'ung's first reign. See *Dictionary of Ming Biography*, pp. 1347–49.

Empress Ch'ien, had a strong character. Although her family were poor and obscure, she refused to allow the emperor to ennoble them.[5] While the emperor was captive in Mongolia "she sacrificed all the treasures of the Central Palace . . . to help him come back; during the night she invoked Heaven, wailing and weeping; when she tired she slept on the ground, so that she injured a thigh; and by her wailing and weeping she impaired the sight of one of her eyes." During his years of confinement in the Forbidden City, she was "his consolation in the wrong done to him." No wonder that in his last will the emperor insisted: "The Empress Ch'ien shall lie with me in the same grave for more than a thousand autumns and ten thousand years."

But it was not to be as easy as that. The new emperor, son of the first concubine, raised his mother to the rank of empress; the leading Grand Secretary ordered that since the two empresses were equal in rank, Cheng-t'ung's tomb should be built with three crypts so that one could lie on each side of the deceased emperor. When, however, the Empress Ch'ien died, the Empress Chou refused to allow her to be buried in Yü-ling, and the emperor, against the advice of his ministers, supported her. At this uproar broke out. The ministers refused to leave the Council Chamber and were joined by a group of followers who banged their foreheads and wailed from nine o'clock in the morning until five in the evening. Finally the emperor gave way, and in the following month the Empress Ch'ien was laid to rest on the left side of her husband. Nearly forty years later, when the Empress Chou was buried, it was discovered that in accordance with her orders, the opening between her predecessor's crypt and that of the emperor had been walled up!

Cheng-t'ung also broke with the tradition inherited from the Mongols that a certain number of concubines be forced to accompany the emperor to his grave. He forbade the suicide of concubines, whether voluntary or forced, on the occasion of his death. From this time on, no concubines were buried in the Imperial tombs. Special cemeteries were established for them in the eastern and western areas of the Imperial graveyard.

10

Mao-ling

TOMB 5

BURIED HERE
Emperor Ch'eng-hua, died 1487
Empress Wang, died 1518
Empress Chi, died 1475
Empress Shao, died 1522

Mao-ling gives a clear illustration of the principles established in the previous reign governing the right to be buried in the Imperial tomb. Of the three empresses, the first was the emperor's second wife, who had no son. (He had dethroned his first wife one month after their marriage because she had his favourite concubine, Wan Kuei-fei, beaten.) The second, a concubine who died thirteen years before the emperor, was moved from the concubine cemetery to Mao-ling when her son became emperor in 1487. The third, the Empress Shao, was the direct ancestress of the later half of Ming rulers. She was a concubine who bore the emperor his fourth son. When the Emperor Cheng-te died in 1521 without an heir, the Throne of Heaven passed to the nearest surviving direct descendant, the son of this fourth son. The new emperor then raised his father, mother, and grandmother to the Imperial rank and his grandmother was moved to the Imperial tomb. At the time of building, no provision was made for later additions, so the funeral mound must have been opened at least twice after the emperor died.[1]

Mao-ling, which is built on a nearly due north-south axis, lies to the right of the main road about a quarter of a kilometre beyond the turn-off to Yü-ling. The tortoise stele is in excellent condition, complete with small steps and surrounding wall and standing on a stone base carved with waves and snail-like coils in the four corners. Between the stele and the entrance to the tomb is an unpaved track which runs along the east side of the enclosure. Horse-drawn carts and donkeys, old men and children carrying baskets of wood or leaves, pass continually to and fro. It is common to find several peasants resting on the low wall around the stele or on the edge of the entrance terrace. Just below the road on the other side is a village. Unlike Yü-ling, this tomb is very much part of the life of the people.

The original triple door had already disappeared in 1920. At that time there was what Bouillard calls "a pitiable caricature" built in its place—a small brick wall with a little wooden door and yellow tiled roof in the centre.[2] Today that has been cleared

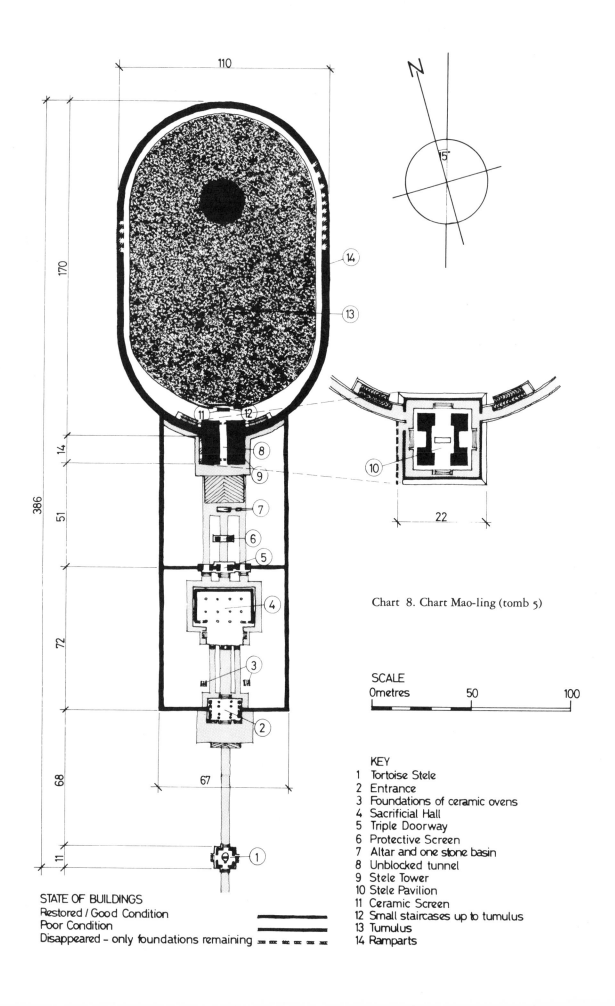

110

170

386

51

14

72

68

11

67

22

Chart 8. Chart Mao-ling (tomb 5)

① 14
① 13
① 11 ① 12
① 8
① 9
① 7
① 6
① 5
① 4
① 3
① 2
① 1
① 10

SCALE
0 metres   50   100

KEY
1 Tortoise Stele
2 Entrance
3 Foundations of ceramic ovens
4 Sacrificial Hall
5 Triple Doorway
6 Protective Screen
7 Altar and one stone basin
8 Unblocked tunnel
9 Stele Tower
10 Stele Pavilion
11 Ceramic Screen
12 Small staircases up to tumulus
13 Tumulus
14 Ramparts

STATE OF BUILDINGS
Restored / Good Condition
Poor Condition
Disappeared - only foundations remaining

away, and the original door foundations can be seen in the opening between the precinct walls. These walls are in a good state, still painted red with yellow tiled roofs.

Whether due to the exigencies of feng-shui or simply to a bad architect, there is something wrong with the proportions of this tomb. Whereas Yü-ling produces a feeling of lightness and elegance, here everything looks heavy. The Sacrificial Hall, crowded by thujas and pines, seems too large for the courtyard (fig. 99). The three walls of the hall are fairly complete, and there are two wooden beams in place. On the outer side of the walls you can see small rectangular holes made to ventilate the beams. Here the basic constructional pattern of Ming funeral buildings is shown very clearly, the beams providing a wooden frame that has been filled in with brick and stone. The paved floor and staircases of the terrace, with the usual central marble slab carved with mountains and clouds, are in a good state; but the marble balustrades, which were still in place in 1920, have gone. To the east and west sides of the paved way leading from the main entrance to the Sacrificial Hall lie the stone foundations of two small rectangular buildings. Bouillard records the eastern one as having been a ceramic oven for burning paper money and silks; the western one, which is not shown on his chart, was presumably its counterpart.

The second courtyard is on a higher level than the first, and originally there was a triple staircase leading up to the triple door. Today the stairs have crumbled away, although the doorway is relatively complete (colourplate 16). The central door has all

99. Stele tower, pavilion, and remains of sacrificial hall

its tiles and the wooden lintel is in place. The two side-doors have lost their decorative tiles and roofs. The courtyard itself gives a thoroughly cramped impression. Here again the proportions seem to be wrong. This courtyard is six metres shorter and seven metres wider than its counterpart in Yü-ling. The stele tower is the same size in both tombs, with the result that here the stele tower seems to dwarf everything around it.

The two marble columns of the protective screen door are in place but all the beams have gone. The altar is the same as in the other tombs and parts of the altar objects are lying around on the ground. There is a very beautiful thuja to the right of the altar growing through a stone basin of the type seen in Yü-ling (fig. 100). The stele tower is a replica of the one in Yü-ling. Here the wide ramp up to the terrace on which the tower stands is in bad condition, and the ramp leading to the stele pavilion up the west side of the tower has completely fallen away. In 1921 the only way up was by ladder. Today the central tunnel through the tower has been opened and cleared (fig. 101). You can therefore see exactly how this tunnel was designed, with a double closure—first a wooden door and then a brick wall—at each end. The roof of the inner section of the tunnel, between the two brick walls, is at least one and a half metres lower than the height at the two entrances.

If you walk through the tunnel, you come to the best part of the tomb. The tumulus of Mao-ling is rather low and the rampart walls and tower loom high behind you. The facing of these walls is more or less intact and the two long ramps that run down from the stele tower are very beautiful (fig. 102). Directly opposite the tunnel exit is a ceramic screen completely intact (fig. 103). This screen and the ceramic frieze round the roof of the stele pavilion are good examples of the high development in Ming times of the use of coloured tiles for decoration.

Behind the screen are two small staircases leading up to the mound (fig. 104). No other tomb has this arrangement, which is not mentioned in earlier records. A small wall supports the southern end of the tumulus and, similar to that in Yü-ling, ends just around the curve of the mound to the east and west.

The pavilion for the stele is the same as that in Yü-ling, but the roof is, if anything, more ruined, and large areas are denuded of tiles (fig. 105). The frieze below the roof is ceramic. The base of the stele is similar to that in Yü-ling with slight stylistic differences in the form of the dragons on the upper layer. The inscription on the stele says: "Tomb of the pure Emperor Hsien-tsung."

The tumulus enclosure is very beautiful (fig. 61). The trees are once again a mixture of oaks and thujas, but here some of the thujas are very old indeed. Walking between the enormous gnarled trunks, you get a feeling of history that is missing in the courtyards. The crenellated ramparts are more or less complete except for a small hole on the west side and a new-looking, rather large breach on the east. In places, trees are pushing through the stonework (fig. 106). The north end of the enclosure lies very close to the mountains, parts of which have been replanted with pines.

This tomb is not, perhaps, one of the most beautiful. It is, however, well worth

100. Thuja growing through stone basin near altar

101. Unblocked tunnel through stele tower

102. Ramp leading from stele pavilion to back area between stele tower and grave mound

103. Ceramic screen

104. Back area, ceramic screen, and steps up to grave mound

visiting in order to see the walls and staircases behind the stele tower, the ceramic screen, and the very old thujas on the funeral mound.

DRAINAGE.   The general principle seems to be the same as that in Yü-ling: a series of stone ridges built at an angle across the rampart lead rainwater through a hole in the inner rampart wall to a stone spout facing inward. The water then falls into a shallow paved gutter going round the funeral mound. The surface of the ramparts is so covered with soil and debris that it is not possible to count the exact number of ridges. There are two large square drains with spouts at the south end of the ramparts; directly below two large drain holes lead through the walls on each side of the stele tower. Similar exit drains can be seen at each end of the south wall of the first courtyard.

Ch'eng-hua, 1464–87

Ch'eng-hua seems to have been completely dominated by women, first by his mother and then by his mistress. He is said to have been handsome, with "bright eyes and a clipped moustache," but he stammered and it is clear that in matters of state he took no independent action. When his father's first wife, the Empress Ch'ien, died soon after he ascended the throne, he was put in the awkward position of having to decide whether to carry out his father's testament and bury her in the Imperial tomb or to follow his mother, who insisted that her rival be buried elsewhere. It is said that when the ministers pointed out that he must obey his father, the young emperor replied: "I know that well; but my only concern is that nothing should be done to oppose my mother."[3]

His first concubine, Wan Kuei-fei, had been Ch'eng-hua's nurse when he was a child, and it seems that she completely dominated the palace. As already mentioned, Ch'eng-hua put aside his first wife after one month because she had Wan Kuei-fei beaten. His second wife accepted Wan's supremacy, and from then on the latter ran the court with the help of the eunuchs. After it became clear that Wan was responsible for the murder of the sons of other concubines who might be possible heirs to the throne, Ch'eng-hua moved to separate quarters; but he continued to let her run things in her own way. Wan Kuei-fei used her position to make money. The sale of offices, carried out by the chief eunuch, was blatantly run from the Imperial store under the cover of transactions in jewellery. Corruption was rampant; eunuch exactions widened the gulf between the rich and the poor, and Ch'eng-hua profited from the increase in the Imperial treasury. The eunuch secret service tyrannised officials, and torture and murder of critics and opponents were widespread. The only sphere in which Wan seems to have been positively efficient was the military. The Chinese army was slowly built up again after the calamitous defeat by the Mongols in 1449 and Wan, who liked to dress in military uniform, took a personal interest in seeing that the northern frontier was reinforced. Some nine hundred kilometres were added to the Great Wall in the northeast in order to strengthen the defences against the Mongols.

105. East side of roof

While Wan ran the empire, Ch'eng-hua patronised the arts. He seems to have been an excellent calligrapher; he enjoyed the theatre and music and was drawn to spiritualism. Taoist priests and Tibetan mystics specializing in pornography and magic were welcomed at court.

Ch'eng-hua's reign is best known today for its porcelain. During these years the kilns at Ching-te-chen developed *tou ts'ai* ware, in which translucent enamels filled underglaze blue outlines. This porcelain, bearing the reign mark of Ch'eng-hua, was later exported to the West and became famous throughout the world.

106. Trees growing through ramparts

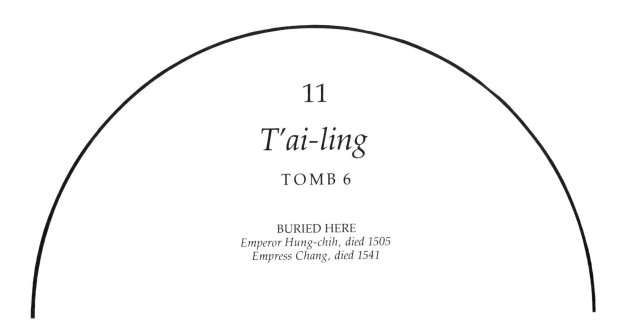

11

T'ai-ling

TOMB 6

BURIED HERE
Emperor Hung-chih, died 1505
Empress Chang, died 1541

T'ai-ling is a sad tomb and only worth visiting for those who wish to see the complete series. Already in 1920 it was in a bad state; by 1931 it had deteriorated still further, and Bouillard wrote: "The whole place is in a deplorable state of decay."[1] The tomb lies at the farthest point to the west that foreigners are allowed to visit on the road past Mao-ling. Since the doorways and large sections of the precinct walls are missing, it has, as it were, been secularised. It is more like a wasteland than an Imperial tomb.

The Emperor Hung-chih seems to have had an uneventful reign. Politically things were quiet, but the decline of the court's prestige and authority which had started under Cheng-t'ung continued. There were the usual troubles on the northern frontier but it was still possible to keep them under control. The emperor had one wife who survived him by thirty-six years and is buried by his side.

The tomb, which is on a nearly due north-south axis, is built on a larger scale than the preceding four. Both courtyards and buildings are larger; the terrace of the Sacrificial Hall is, for example, very nearly double the size of that in Yü-ling. The tortoise stele, which is in good condition but has no surrounding walls, stands in the village street. It is a popular gathering place, and the blank face of the stele is used for contemporary slogans (these had been removed in 1979). The metal road runs between the stele and the entrance to the tomb, continuing along the east side of the precinct. Originally the way crossed a triple bridge; today a modern bridge has replaced this, but you can still see one of the original arches on the western side.

The triple doorway has completely disappeared and the first courtyard opens straight onto the village. Part of the eastern end of the southern wall is missing, and the condition of the roof tiles is very poor. The courtyard, which according to ancient Chinese authors once had more than a hundred trees, is sparsely planted with a few large pines. Unexpectedly, on the right of the paved way there is a small oven for burning paper offerings. Apart from Ch'ang-ling, this is the only tomb in which such an oven has survived. It is a charming building, rather like a miniature doll's house,

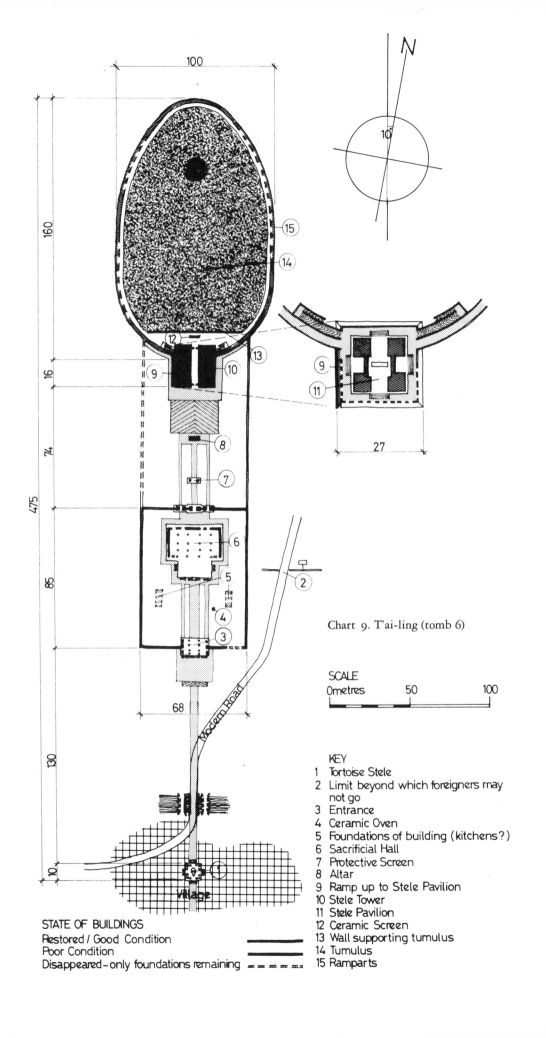

N
10°

100

160

16

74

475

85

130

10

68

27

15
14
12
13
9
10
9
11
8
7
6
5
4
3
2
1

Modern Road

Village

Chart 9. T'ai-ling (tomb 6)

SCALE
0 metres   50   100

KEY
1 Tortoise Stele
2 Limit beyond which foreigners may
  not go
3 Entrance
4 Ceramic Oven
5 Foundations of building (kitchens?)
6 Sacrificial Hall
7 Protective Screen
8 Altar
9 Ramp up to Stele Pavilion
10 Stele Tower
11 Stele Pavilion
12 Ceramic Screen
13 Wall supporting tumulus
14 Tumulus
15 Ramparts

STATE OF BUILDINGS
Restored / Good Condition   ▬▬▬▬
Poor Condition   ▬▬▬▬
Disappeared – only foundations remaining ▬ ▬ ▬ ▬

and apart from having lost most of the tile facing, is complete (fig. 107). To both sides of the paved way there are stone foundations, presumably where the former kitchens and storerooms stood.

The three staircases leading up to the Sacrificial Hall are crumbling, but the marble slab depicting mountains and clouds is unscathed. The walls of the Sacrificial Hall are still standing, although there are several holes on the northern side (fig. 46). The ground is swept clean and all the usual rubble has been cleared away.

Passing behind the Sacrificial Hall and into the second courtyard, you get a shock. Virtually the whole of the western wall of this courtyard is missing. The triple door-way is dilapidated: the roofs have gone, large chunks have fallen from the tops of the door columns, and nearly all the decorative tiles have disappeared. The courtyard, wide open on one side, appears to be more of an annex to the busy agricultural work outside than part of a tomb (fig. 108). The altar is in place and so are the two marble columns of the protective screen. There is also a rather fine upper half of a stone incense burner (fig. 109).

The stele tower is built on exactly the same plan as the preceding two tombs, only it is larger (fig. 110). There is a ramp up to the terrace on which the tower stands; leading off this to the east and west are the two customary narrow walks along the side of the rampart wall until the point where it meets the outer precinct wall. The central tunnel through the tower has been unblocked and is identical to that in Mao-ling. The ramp up the west side of the tower is in a very bad state and does not look as if it will last much longer. The stele pavilion has lost most of its red colour; the parapets on the west and east sides of the little terrace have nearly disappeared; that on the south side has completely gone. The roof is like the curate's egg—good in parts. The two ceramic heads holding the top ridge are in place; the upper ceramic frieze remains, but most of the lower roof and frieze have fallen away and the building is bare to the brickwork (figs. 111 and 112). The inscription on the stele reads: "Tomb of the revered Emperor Hsiao-tsung."

The tumulus at the back is low in relation to the rampart walls. Part of the ceramic screen is still standing, and behind this is a well-preserved low wall supporting the southern end of the mound. If you follow this wall to the east and west, you can see two very specific carved stones that mark where it stops (fig. 113). (This is contrary to Bouillard's description of a supporting wall that goes all round the mound.) The two ramps leading down to the back area from the tower are in a very bad condition; the stone facing on the back of the stele tower is more or less complete.

The funeral mound is large, slightly rounded with a small cone at the northern end, and well wooded with oaks, walnuts, and thujas. Large stretches of the crenellations are missing, especially on the western side. At least half of the inner wall has gone. This has the advantage of providing a clear view of the stone-carved waterspouts pointing inward from the ramparts (fig. 114).

Apart from the oven and the unusually clear wall and end stones supporting the southern end of the tumulus, there is not much in T'ai-ling to attract the visitor.

107. TOP LEFT: Oven for burning paper and silk offerings

108. TOP RIGHT: Stele tower and pavilion seen through missing wall on southwest side

109. CENTRE: Upper half of stone incense burner

110. LEFT: Stele pavilion seen across grave tumulus

111. RIGHT: Roof seen from ramparts on west side

112. CENTRE RIGHT: Corner of roof

113. BELOW: Carved stone marking end of supporting wall at south end of grave mound

114, 115. Ramparts showing stone drain spouts where inner wall has fallen away; detail of stone drain spout

DRAINAGE.   In keeping with its larger size, there is a definite development in the drainage system of this tomb. The basic principle of diagonal ridges to lead the rainwater off the ramparts through the inner wall and down to an open gutter running round the tumulus is the same. Here, however, for the first time, each ridge ends in a specially carved stone spout (fig. 115). On the inner side of the rampart this is formed like a small catchment basin; it then opens out into a long spout leading through the rampart wall and out on the other side. The whole is in one piece. The large drains at the south end of the ramparts are made in exactly the same pattern but are more than twice as large. At ground level, to the east and west of the stele tower at the back, and halfway along both sides of the south wall of the first courtyard, there are the same large, square stone drains as in Yü-ling and Mao-ling.

Hung-chih, 1487–1505

Hung-chih was the third son of the Emperor Ch'eng-hua. His two elder brothers died in infancy, almost certainly murdered by order of his father's powerful mistress, Wan Kuei-fei. Hung-chih's mother was a maid in charge of the palace storeroom and is said to have been taken prisoner from one of the minority tribes on a military expedition. When she became pregnant, the emperor's first wife, who had been dethroned for having Wan Kuei-fei beaten, hid the girl. Hung-chih's birth was kept secret, and not until he was five years old was his father told of his existence. The emperor was delighted to learn that he had an heir and when, within a month of the news being made public, the child's mother died mysteriously, he ordered that the boy be brought up by the empress dowager to ensure his safety.

Hung-chih grew up a strict Confucian. He adored his wife and is the only example of a monogamous emperor in Chinese history. He fulfilled his Imperial duties punctiliously, was humane, and forbade the public flogging of officials, but he does not seem to have been particularly intelligent. Otherwise abstemious, he showered his wife and her family with favours and placed his trust in the eunuchs, thus tacitly allowing the corruption of the previous reign to continue. During his reign period, the general economic condition of the country declined; the rich increased their estates and hoarded wealth, while more and more of the peasants were dispossessed.

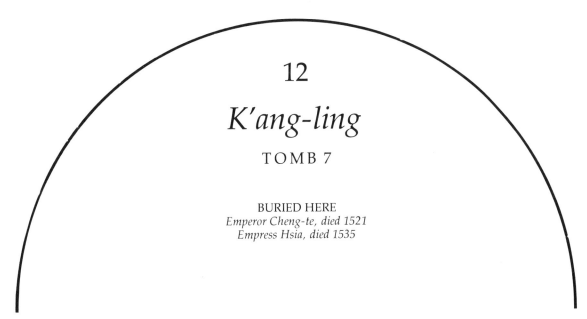

12

K'ang-ling

TOMB 7

BURIED HERE
Emperor Cheng-te, died 1521
Empress Hsia, died 1535

The Emperor Cheng-te was Hung-chih's son and the last in the direct line of Ming emperors. Although he married, he had no surviving son, and after his death the Throne of Heaven passed to a collateral descendant of his grandfather, Ch'eng-hua. Cheng-te seems to have been a complete profligate. He loved women and wine and his great delight was to disguise himself and slip out of the palace into the streets of Peking. Unlike Haroun-al-Raschid, he did not use these sorties to learn more about the opinions of his people. The already tarnished reputation of the court was brought to a new low by the frequent visits of an ill-disguised Son of Heaven to the brothels in the southern part of the city.

His tomb, K'ang-ling, is in one of the most beautiful sites in the valley. Its location shows that the rules of feng-shui were in fact flexible and governed by common sense. His father's tomb, T'ai-ling, stands at the northern end of the valley. For Cheng-te to be buried near his father it was necessary to place his tomb farther south. Since the hills sweep down in a southwesterly direction, this involved a conflict between two cardinal principles of feng-shui—that the tomb be protected from the wind and that it face south. Common sense won and K'ang-ling lies in the foothills in a corner of the valley southwest of T'ai-ling. The tomb is almost encircled by hills, with the grave mound sheltered by the highest point of the mountains and the tomb and tortoise stele facing in the only open direction—nearly due east.

Because of this sheltered site, you cannot see K'ang-ling until you are some way up the valley. It is a good four kilometres from Ch'ang-ling and much the nicest way to approach it is on foot. Just past Mao-ling, the road goes over a modern bridge. Very shortly after this there is a small unpaved road off to the left. This track is in fact just passable for cars but it is much more agreeable to take the rare chance of a country walk. The first part of the way goes through a large orchard of persimmon trees usually filled with Great and Willow Tits. Then you come down to the wide stony bed of the main river in the Ming Valley. In summer, you can ford this on stepping-stones; in

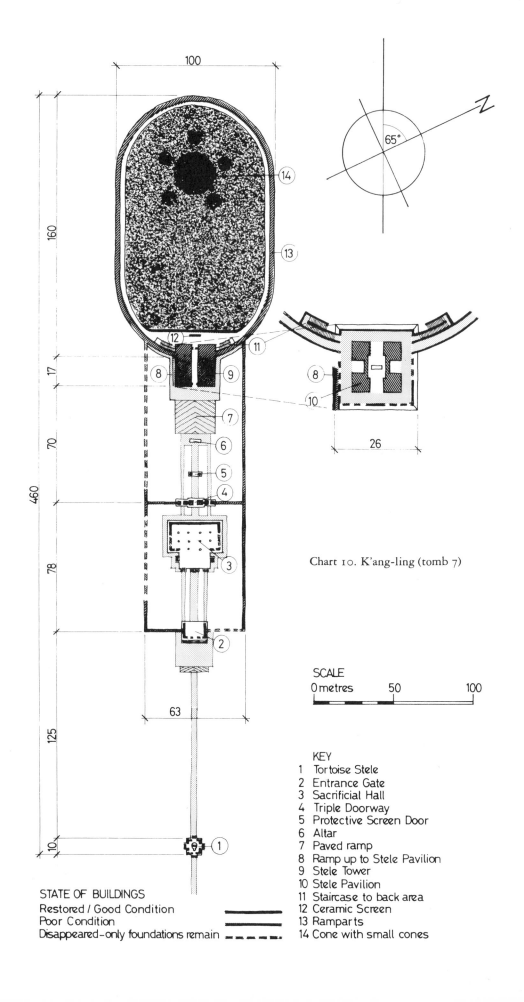

100

160

17

70

460

78

125

10

63

65°

N

26

Chart 10. K'ang-ling (tomb 7)

(14)
(13)
(12)
(11)
(8)
(9)
(7)
(6)
(5)
(4)
(3)
(2)
(1)
(8)
(10)

SCALE
0 metres   50   100

KEY
1 Tortoise Stele
2 Entrance Gate
3 Sacrificial Hall
4 Triple Doorway
5 Protective Screen Door
6 Altar
7 Paved ramp
8 Ramp up to Stele Pavilion
9 Stele Tower
10 Stele Pavilion
11 Staircase to back area
12 Ceramic Screen
13 Ramparts
14 Cone with small cones

STATE OF BUILDINGS
Restored / Good Condition
Poor Condition
Disappeared—only foundations remain

winter it is frozen and you cross on the ice (fig. 116). The riverbanks are usually filled with activity—peasants collecting stones or clearing channels, small boys watering donkeys. To the right, higher up the river in a village, is a pretty walled enclosure with a lot of small conical buildings, silos for storing grain. Across the river the road goes up a steep gulley, then opens out and crosses an old three-arched bridge. The river must have changed course since this was built some four hundred years ago; today the bed is dry and you can climb down to look at the stone foundations. Here in spring are a mass of wild flowers and the sweet, mintlike Artemissia. By now, if you look up the valley, you can see K'ang-ling. In the sharp North China light, the mountain behind it is so clear that you can distinguish each stone, each small grazing goat. The tomb looks down on you, serene in a dark patch of thujas and pines.

From here the path, fenced on both sides, winds uphill between fields. Soon, on the left, you pass another village with high stone walls. Judging from the walls and several very large and beautiful trees, it seems probable that this was once the house of an important dignitary, possibly one of the officials in charge of the upkeep of the Valley of the Thirteen Tombs. Behind the village are thujas and pines, usually the sign of a cemetery.

116. Fording the river on the way to the tomb

Not many foreigners come this way and the small village children usually run out to have a look as you pass by. In front of the village, in an orchard, stands the tortoise stele, and from there, in a straight line up the mountainside, the old paved way leads to the tomb. The stele is a beautiful one and in good condition. Looking back from the entrance gate in winter, it looks particularly lovely against the bare branches of the fruit trees (fig. 117).

The ramp up to the entrance gate is overgrown and unpaved. Most of the "south" wall and all the door posts and roofs are missing. This tomb is in fact far more ruined than T'ai-ling. In a curious way, however, it has retained its dignity and atmosphere. It is not too near the village and is placed so high in the foothills that there is a beautiful view from wherever you look. The "east" side of the doorway stands romantically alone beside an enormous and very old pine tree (colourplate 17 and fig. 118); the rest of the "south" wall on that side has gone. On the "west," the wall extends around the corner and then stops, leaving a large part of the first courtyard open (fig. 119). Even where the wall is standing, it has lost most of its red colour and all of its roof. The base of the Sacrificial Hall, the staircases up to the terrace, and the marble slab carved with mountains and clouds, are all covered with debris; the back walls and a very short part of the two side walls of the hall stand about one metre high. Six or seven very large pine trees are growing in the courtyard, but no young trees.

The second courtyard is, if anything, even more ruined. Practically the whole length of the "west" wall has gone and the little that is left has lost its red plaster, revealing the bricks (fig. 120). The two marble columns of the protective screen, the altar, and the scattered altar objects stand among a lot of old and decorative pines. The central part of the wide ramp leading up to the terrace on which the stele tower stands, is paved; the rest is rough earth with stone slabs along the edge (fig. 121). The terrace extends to both sides of the stele tower in the same narrow walks along the rampart walls as in the previous tombs (fig. 122). These walks and the rampart walls are thickly overgrown with pine trees. The usual way up to the tower, the ramp up the "west" side, has completely broken away a few metres from the top, and the only way into the grave mound enclosure is through the central tunnel, which has been unblocked.

The area between the back of the stele tower and the funeral mound is generally decayed. There are remnants of paving stones and two very fine examples of square drain holes going under the rampart walls on both sides of the tower. The ceramic screen has lost its roof but is otherwise in good condition; the two staircases leading down from the tower and the facing on the back wall of the tower are crumbling.

The stele pavilion is the same as in the previous tombs; the two sides are blocked and the stele is level with the little terrace, in other words, without steps. The inscription reads: "Tomb of the intrepid Emperor Wu-tsung." Very little is left of the parapet around the little terrace.

This stele pavilion was destroyed in 1644 when the Ming Tombs were pillaged by the rebel leader Li Tzu-ch'eng on his way to capture Peking. It was he who defeated the last Ming emperor, but when he declared himself emperor, the Chinese general in

117. Tortoise stele in winter
118. View through entrance to the tortoise stele

119. LEFT: "West" side of entrance
door and steps, seen from the "south"

120. LOWER LEFT: View over courtyards from stele pavilion
showing the missing walls

121. BELOW: Ramp up to the terrace on which the
stele tower stands, seen from the "east"

122. OPPOSITE: Stele tower and pavilion from the "southeast"

123. FAR BELOW: Ramparts overgrown with trees

charge of the troops on the northern frontier refused to accept him. Instead, this general opened the gates to the Manchus, who swept Li Tzu-ch'eng away and established the Ch'ing dynasty. Apart from the destruction of this building and the pavilion in Chao-ling (tomb 9), it is not known how much damage the rebels did to the tombs. What is certain, however, is that the following dynasty went to considerable expense to restore the damage, reckoning that by showing respect to the tombs of these Chinese emperors, the local population could be assuaged.

The walk around the ramparts of K'ang-ling is one of the most beautiful in the valley. The mound is thickly planted with oak, mostly young, and a few large pines. The ramparts are very dilapidated; roots are pushing the stones out of place and tree trunks grow across the wall (fig. 123). To the left you can see an enticing valley leading into the heart of the mountains. Toward the far end of the mound there is a cone similar to that seen in earlier tombs, but here it is as if the cone had pupped—it is surrounded by smaller cones. De Groot says that in ancient times it was the custom to build a large central mound for the head of the family with small mounds around it for the younger members, but the records do not mention whether children were ever buried in Ming Imperial graves.[1]

Despite its advanced state of decay, this tomb is well worth visiting. The walk there is lovely; it has a beautiful site and is a good place for watching birds. From the stele tower we have seen Broad-billed Rollers and on the mound, Rock Thrush. Red-footed Falcons nest in the tall courtyard pines.

Architecturally, K'ang-ling has no great interest. Just as Hsien-ling and Ching-ling form a pair, so this tomb and its three predecessors should be considered together as a group. They lie next to each other up the northwest side of the valley: first Yü-ling, the tomb of Cheng-te's great-grandfather; then Mao-ling, tomb of his grandfather; next, T'ai-ling, where his father was buried; and finally his own tomb, last of the direct line. All four were buried within a period of fifty-seven years, so it is hardly surprising that architecturally their tombs are practically identical.

DRAINAGE.   The ramparts are so overgrown that it is impossible to check the drainage pattern. K'ang-ling is smaller than T'ai-ling but otherwise an almost exact replica, and what traces of drainage I have been able to find, support the view that the system is the same as in the previous tomb. Here and there it is possible to find a diagonal catchment ridge on the ramparts and a stone spout carved in one piece as in T'ai-ling. In the back area behind the stele tower, two drains carrying water away from the funeral mound and under the rampart walls are in very good condition. It is not possible to find any traces of drains in the two courtyards.

Cheng-te, 1506–21

Cheng-te reacted strongly against the demure Confucianism of his father. Even by Ming standards he seems to have been unusually debauched. Affairs of state, official-dom, and palace life bored him. He was always on the lookout for amusement. As we have seen, he liked to escape from the Forbidden City in disguise and seek pleasure in the streets of Peking. He was a heavy drinker and demanded a steady flow of young girls for his harem. At times he was attracted by Lamaism, wearing Lamaist robes and initiating some of the palace women as nuns. He is said to have loved lanterns. When, during a pageant with several hundred lanterns a palace caught fire, the young emperor commented, "What a magnificent display of fireworks!"

Incurably extravagant, Cheng-te resented any attempt to curb him. Military pomp took his fancy and it became fashionable at court to wear yellow, meshlike armour. Another time, officers were all issued new ornate hats—a sort of sunshade adorned with large goose plumes. On one military expedition to the North he ordered one hundred and sixty-two luxury yurts for camping and when, on the grounds of expense, senior officials petitioned against a second expedition, he had them flogged so severely that several died.

It was natural for such an emperor to give power to the attentive eunuchs. During the first four years of his reign, an uneducated eunuch, Liu Chin, ran the government. Liu was so blatantly corrupt that finally even the emperor was forced to take notice. This he did by having Liu assassinated and confiscating his fortune for the Imperial treasury. According to the Official Records, this fortune consisted of 251,583,600 taels (ounces) of gold and silver, 24 pounds of precious stones, two suits of solid gold armour, five hundred gold plates, three thousand gold rings and brooches, and four thousand belts adorned with gems. In addition to all this there was a large house in Peking, said to be as luxurious as a royal palace. The astounding thing about this inventory is that Liu Chin came from a poor family and had only held office for a few years. Eunuch extortion from office holders both in the capital and the provinces had reached a new and shameless level; the peasantry and the countryside were being steadily impoverished in order to fill the eunuchs' pockets and the Imperial coffers. Through their secret service, the eunuchs strangled the administration; through their trading agencies in silk, porcelain, and other precious commodities they strangled the economy. Not surprisingly, rebellions and banditry became rife in the provinces. The history of the Han dynasty was repeating itself and the dominance of eunuchs at court was leading to the break-up of the empire.

Halfway through Cheng-te's reign, in 1514, the first Portuguese arrived in South China. This was an event of great importance, since the nature of these first contacts determined the future policy of both the Ming and the Ch'ing dynasties toward Europeans. The Chinese were long used to foreign traders. In T'ang, Sung, and Yüan times, foreign merchants—mostly Arabs, Indians, and Persians—were allowed to travel and reside in Chinese ports and cities in the interior, including the various dynastic capitals. When the first Portuguese arrived, the Chinese treated them the same way they did the Arabs and Moslems they were used to. Unfortunately the Portuguese, brought up in a world in which religion, the sword, and trade were inseparable, and accustomed to treating all infidels like the pirates of the Barbary Coast, quickly distinguished themselves from their fellow traders. The pagan world was to be conquered and plundered; trade was a useful first step in achieving these aims. The first Portuguese ship came and went in peace. In the following year, however, four Portuguese ships arrived together in Canton. They were received in the traditional peaceful manner and a delegation bearing "tribute" to the emperor was allowed to go to Peking. While the delegation was away, the Portuguese ships began to harass the coast. Their aggressive and piratical behaviour confirmed reports that were reaching Peking of Portuguese actions in other parts of Southeast Asia. The Chinese were already being plagued by pirates from the Japanese islands. Henceforth the Portuguese were categorised as pirates, and later, when other European traders arrived, the Chinese regarded them in the same light. The pattern of hostility toward Europeans was set. The closed-door principle that strictly controlled and limited foreign traders to the port of Canton, and then only for part of the year, lasted until it was blown open by British gunboats in 1840.

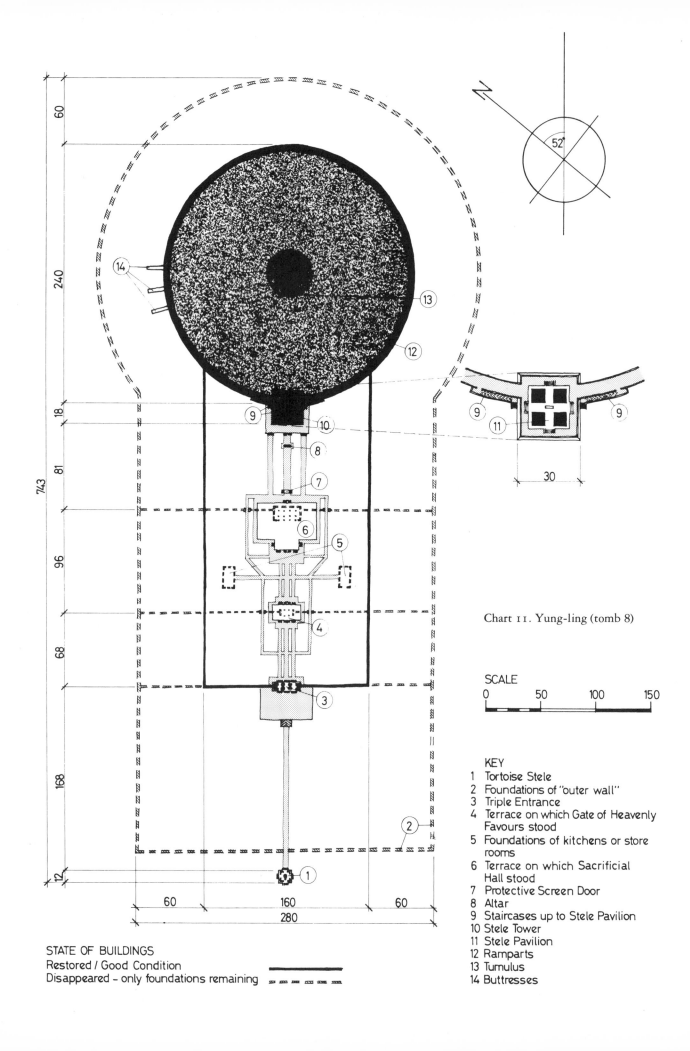

52°

Chart 11. Yung-ling (tomb 8)

SCALE
0   50   100   150

KEY
1 Tortoise Stele
2 Foundations of "outer wall"
3 Triple Entrance
4 Terrace on which Gate of Heavenly
   Favours stood
5 Foundations of kitchens or store
   rooms
6 Terrace on which Sacrificial
   Hall stood
7 Protective Screen Door
8 Altar
9 Staircases up to Stele Pavilion
10 Stele Tower
11 Stele Pavilion
12 Ramparts
13 Tumulus
14 Buttresses

STATE OF BUILDINGS
Restored / Good Condition
Disappeared – only foundations remaining

743
60
240
18
81
96
68
168
12
60   160   60
280
30

13

Yung-ling

TOMB 8

BURIED HERE
Emperor Chia-ching, died 1567
Empress Ch'en, died 1528
Empress Fang, died 1547
Empress Tu, died 1554

The Emperor Chia-ching brought new life into the stagnating Ming dynasty. His predecessor died without an heir and it was necessary to go back two generations to the line stemming from the Emperor Ch'eng-hua and his concubine, the Lady Shao, in order to find the new Son of Heaven. All the later Ming emperors descend from him, and his tomb reflects this position of honour. Yung-ling is a grand tomb, rivaled only by Ch'ang-ling (tomb 1). Here we are back in the palatial style—a far cry from the more modest and somewhat stereotyped tombs of his immediate predecessors.

Three empresses are buried with Chia-ching. His first wife, the Empress Ch'en, died in 1528 before the tomb was built. Both she and the concubine Tu, who died in 1554 and was posthumously created empress when her son became emperor in 1567, were transferred to the Imperial tomb in that year. His second wife, the Empress Fang, was buried in Yung-ling in 1547, showing that work on the tomb must already have been far advanced at that time.

The tomb is of great interest. It is beautiful, in a good state of repair, and shows a unique attention to detail and building materials. The Emperor Chia-ching took an active part in its design and the tomb reflects the artistic vitality which returned to Peking during his long and crowded reign. Work was started on the tomb thirty years before the emperor's death, and it is said that he visited it many times during construction. In general the tomb is based on Ch'ang-ling, but it has some important refinements both in structure and decoration. While the tomb was being built, the emperor also added to the grandeur of the valley as a whole by building the P'ai-lou, one of the most impressive monuments in the whole necropolis. He inspected the tombs of the earlier emperors and, as we have seen in Ching-ling, ordered repairs and alterations where these were deemed necessary.

Yung-ling lies on a nearly east-west axis, one and a half kilometres to the southeast of Ch'ang-ling; its situation is similar to that of the latter, with soft hills rising behind the grave mound. You can approach the tomb in two ways—either by taking the road from Ch'ang-ling eastward or by following the original and much more beautiful "spirit way" which branches off the first road to the right off the main road just after the reservoir. Quite long stretches of this old road are still paved with large stone cobbles or slabs; after crossing first a single- and then a triple-arched bridge, it leads uphill to the tortoise stele. The stele is in good condition and stands on a square terrace with four small staircases in the middle of each side (fig. 13). The tortoise is highly decorated and the stone base is carved to represent the sea. On the four corners of the base are a shrimp, a turtle, a fish, and a crab. Like all sea creatures, these denoted wealth, harmony, and connubial bliss.

Between the stele and what today is the "south" wall of the precinct, you can see the foundations of another wall. Originally there was an outer wall extending the whole way around Yung-ling, and the area inside this outer wall is larger than the whole area of Ch'ang-ling. The precincts proper and the buildings of Yung-ling are, however, somewhat smaller. This outer wall, which is found only in this tomb and Ting-ling (tomb 10), had already disappeared when Bouillard examined the site in 1920. (Such a wall was fairly common in smaller non-Imperial tombs and can, for example, be seen round one or two of the concubine cemeteries in the Ming Valley.)

The triple entrance gate stands on a stone platform and has clearly been restored fairly recently (fig. 124). Not only are the walls and tiled roofs intact, but the wooden doors have been replaced and the tomb is locked at dusk. If you should arrive before the gates are open in the morning, a passerby will quickly find the elderly guardian who lives in the village below the tomb on the right.

Yung-ling, like Ch'ang-ling, has three courtyards. The triple entrance leads into a forecourt, on the far side of which is the Gate of Heavenly Favours. Through the Gate of Heavenly Favours is the second courtyard with the Sacrificial Hall, and beyond that, the third courtyard culminating in the altar and the stele tower.

Today the courtyard of Yung-ling is unique. In the course of restoration, the remains of the two separating walls, the Gate of Heavenly Favours, and the Sacrificial Hall have all been cleared away. What is left is an open and extremely beautiful enclosure with first a small and then a large white terrace standing amid trees and wild flowers (colourplate 18 and fig. 125). Here the trees are mixed. A very tall lace-barked pine, "*Pinus bungeana*," is growing just in front of the right-hand corner of the first terrace; to the left is a large oak tree, a "*Quercus acutissima*," and on the terrace itself are thujas and other small bushes. Farther on are pines, more thujas, and apple trees. For most of the year the courtyard is filled with wild flowers. The first to appear in the spring are violets, wild iris, and anemones; then come bluebells, a sort of orange lily, honeysuckle, wild raspberries, delphiniums, and an occasional fritillary. In the autumn it is thick with wild pink crysanthemums and pale mauve asters.[1] In winter Hawfinches, Bramblings, and Rosefinches abound in the grass, in spring Willow Warblers in the trees. The terraces, just over two metres high, are approached by finely carved marble staircases. The general effect of green grass and dazzling white stone reminds one a little of a ruined Greek temple.

124. Triple entrance gate with wooden doors in place

125. Corner of terrace of Gate of Heavenly Favours with lace-bark pine

126. Stele pavilion with steps and marble slab in foreground; note the first appearance of the phoenix on such a slab

127. Altar and incense burner with wood gatherer in foreground

128. Ch'i-lin on protective screen door

The original Gate of Heavenly Favours, a triple doorway in the usual form, stood in the centre of the first terrace. Three marble staircases lead up to the terrace on both sides. The central marble slab is unusually fine (fig. 126). The lower half shows the sea and the mountains; above this, among clouds, a dragon and a phoenix with a pearl between them symbolise the emperor and empress moving through the heavens. This is the first time the phoenix, symbol of the empress, appears in the mausoleum. Along the walls and at each corner of the terrace are stone gargoyles in the form of the head of a mythical animal, no doubt a dragon. The animal's upper lip curves back rather like a short trunk of an elephant and there is an outlet for water between its teeth. It has elaborately curled hair like a Chinese lion and two scaly four-clawed feet tucked under its head.[2] As in Ch'ang-ling, the gargoyles at the corner are considerably larger than those on the side.

As may be seen from the plan, the pattern of paved paths leading through the courtyards is much more complicated here than in the other tombs. To the "east" and "west" of the first terrace you can see the stone foundations of the wall that joined the terrace to the outer wall of the precinct. On each side of the terrace, some seven and a half metres along this wall, were two side doors; the stone bases of the doorposts and the steps leading up to the doors are still visible. If you follow the network of paths between the Gate of Heavenly Favours and the Sacrificial Hall, you can see the stone foundations of two fairly large buildings, no doubt the former kitchens.

The second terrace is very large (58m × 28m) in relation to the Sacrificial Hall. Its decoration is similar to that of the first terrace but is even more ornate. Here there are five staircases to the "south," three central and two side "service" staircases. The balustrades of these have gone, but the steps, the marble dragon and phoenix slab, the decorations on the side of the terrace wall, and the gargoyles are all in excellent condition. On the "north" side of the terrace there is a single staircase with a marble slab similar to the three we have already seen. The curious thing about this staircase is that it can only have been built for symbolic reasons since there was no exit from the hall to this side. The back and side walls of the hall were blank, and the wall separating the second and third courtyards joined the hall on both sides.

Instead of the usual triple ceramic-covered doorway into the third courtyard, there were two single doors, one on each side of the hall about halfway along the transverse wall. Today two thujas and a large pine grow up on the terrace, looking almost as if they had been planted there deliberately. Just beyond are a very large Chinese oak (*Quercus dentata* Thunb.) and some fruit trees. This last courtyard is long, spacious, and well planted. From the terrace you get a lovely view of the stele tower and pavilion with the white altar standing in front (fig. 127). The protective screen door is complete with its wooden framework, ch'i-wen, and ch'i-lin (fig. 128); one of the five precious objects remains on the altar.

Already from the gargoyle heads and the decorations on the sides of the terrace walls it is clear that this was a luxurious tomb in which great attention was paid to detail. This is even more noticeable when you come to the stele tower. Whereas all the other stele towers are built of rough grey stone, this one is faced with very fine polished stone, pinky-red with yellow and white veins.* The blocks are beautifully cut and aligned. Moreover, the form of the tower is quite distinctive (fig. 129). There is no tunnel through the centre and no ramp up the "west" side. Instead, an elegant staircase followed by a wide ramp leads up each side of the tower (fig. 130). At the foot of these ramps are niches for door hinges. (In 1920 Bouillard noted doors at the foot of similar ramps in Ting-ling, but he does not mention them in connection with Yung-ling). The side wall of the ramparts, the staircase, and the ramp are all finished in the same polished stone. The general effect is one of luxurious sophistication—a far cry from the "defensive tower in a city-wall" aspect of the other stele towers. The tower is 30 metres square; for comparison, that of Ch'ang-ling is 34 metres square while most of the others range between 20 and 22 metres square.

The stele pavilion is similar to that in the other tombs, except that here, for the first time, all four arches are open. The stele stands on a base of four layers carved with waves, mountains, clouds, and finally the Imperial dragon moving through more clouds.[3] The inscription reads: "Tomb of the respected Emperor Shih-tsung."

On top of the stele, among the entwining dragons, the characters for "Great Ming" are engraved in chuan script. The double roof is in excellent condition and the wooden name plaque is in place. From the terrace outside the stele house there is a spectacular view over the trees to the reservoir and the mountains beyond.

The tumulus is completely circular and the rampart walk unusually wide. Here again Yung-ling resembles Ch'ang-ling in that the mound is built right up the circular rampart wall, level with the walk itself. There is thus no need for any ramps down the back of the tower nor is there any paved area at the back or ceramic screen. The mound, which rises gently, is thickly planted with thujas, oaks, and jujube trees with bright red berries (*Zizyphus jujube*); the apricot trees mentioned by Bouillard appear to have died out. In the middle of the mound is a small cone, also covered with trees, similar to that in Yü-ling or Mao-ling.

The outside of the rampart wall is crenellated and has at one time been faced with the same polished stone as the stele tower. Some attempt has been made to restore these crenellations where they have fallen away; from the blocks lying stacked here and there, you can see just how the stones were cut to fit each other. The inner rampart wall is rounded; in places the surface has crumbled away, revealing that the wall was first topped with interlocking tiles and then covered with a hard grey facing (fig. 131). At some time three buttresses have been built at ground level to support the outside of the "southwest" section of the rampart wall (fig. 132). As can be seen below, the drainage system was very elaborate, and it is particularly worthwhile to

*De Groot describes the stairs and ramparts as being made of "white limestone, in large-sized slabs," but this must be a mistake. The most distinctive feature of the masonry in the tower and the ramparts is its pink-veined colouring. Ku Yen-wu refers to "'veined stone' which gives the buildings a grandeur and elegance surpassing that of Hsiao-ling (the tomb at Nanking) and Ch'ang-ling." Bouillard writes of "superbes blocs de pierre, soigneusement taillés à angles droits, et qui sont du plus joli effet par leur couleur sombre et leur régularité" (See De Groot, 3:1233; Bouillard and Vaudescal, pp. 74, 76).

129. Stele tower, pavilion, and altar with incense burner
130. Stairs and ramp up "west" side of stele tower

131. Inner wall of rampart showing construction with tile lining

132. Buttresses outside ramparts on "southwest" side

look for the stone gargoyles on the outer side of the crenellated wall. To the "east" there is a very good view of Te-ling.

This tomb is a delight to visit. The partial restoration has struck the perfect medium between the completely renovated where the present dominates the past, and those few tombs where the decay has gone so far that it gives one a sad feeling that there will soon be nothing left. Although the walls that separated the courtyards have been cleared away, the precinct has lost none of its calm. You can wander for hours examining the fine carving on the white terraces and the endless small details in the decoration of such things as the altar, the tower base, and the drain spouts. The white stone of the terraces, the soft pink of the stele tower and ramparts, and the red precinct walls make a perfect colour pattern with the green grass and wild flowers. Even the trees seem to have an unusual elegance—the white-barked pine towering above the first terrace could not have been better placed by any stage director. The tomb radiates confidence. It is solid, calm, and beautiful, clearly built by an emperor who felt that his reign was a success.

DRAINAGE. The drainage system of this tomb is more sophisticated than any we have seen up to now. At regular intervals around the rampart walk, there are fourteen stone ridges leading to a stone catchment spout similar to those in the last two tombs. Here, however, the ridges run in the opposite direction and the water flows through the *outer* wall of the rampart. On the outer side of the wall, the spout terminates in a stone gargoyle similar to those decorating the corners of the terrace walls.

In addition to this, there is a shallow paved gutter around the mound, just inside the inner wall of the rampart walk. Evenly spaced out, three on each side, are six large drains, about 80 centimetres square. These, which were originally covered with a stone grill, consist of a vertical shaft, now blocked up, but once going straight down through the mound to ground level (fig. 133). If you walk around the outside of the ramparts, you can see correspondingly large square drains (many with the stone grill intact), leading through the rampart wall at ground level (fig. 134). Water from the mound would therefore have run into the gutter and then been carried away down the vertical shaft and through the wall to the outside. No doubt there was, at the time of construction, a channel carrying this water to the nearest stream.

These two systems, which must have been able to deal with all possible rainfall, have been supplemented by a third. This consists of seven holes in the inner rampart wall that connect with a tiled spout through the outer wall. The placing of these is irregular, and compared with the carefully finished carving of the gargoyles and stone grills, the workmanship is shoddy. This points to them having been added at a later time. No doubt the vertical shafts became blocked up during the time when the tombs were neglected and it was necessary to make some other outlet for rainwater falling on the mound.

Similar tile drains can be seen on the two front ramparts on both sides of the stele tower. About two-thirds of the way up the second half of each ramp, there is a tile

133. Square drain shaft leading from gutter around grave tumulus to ground level

134. Exit drain from shaft in figure 133 on outer side of "western" rampart wall

spout corresponding to a small hole at the bottom of the sloping ramp leading down from the stele pavilion to the circular walk. The workmanship of these drains is unfinished, and their placing is not very sensible since it directs the rainwater from the upper walk straight down onto the heads of those who are walking up to the ramparts. It therefore seems probable that they were also a later addition. At the foot of the two front staircases there are two more drain holes with traces of stone spouts which seem to be part of the original building. Similar drain holes can be seen in the "west" and "east" sides of the walls of the terrace around the stele pavilion.

I was not able to find any traces of a drainage system in the large courtyards. It may be that the ground level has gradually risen, blocking any holes there once were. It is worth walking around the outside of the tomb on the "west" side to look at the buttresses, the gargoyles, and the ground drains. In some places you can see the foundations of the original outer wall which encircled the whole precinct.

Chia-ching, 1521–67

It is not for nothing that Yung-ling was built on the lines of Ch'ang-ling. It is quite clear from the records that the Emperor Chia-ching was an ambitious man, anxious to emphasize that he was starting a new line in the Ming dynasty. When the previous emperor died without heir, the state councillors, fearful of dynastic rivalry, tried to pursuade Chia-ching to accept the position of an adopted son. Chia-ching refused and insisted that he be named emperor in his own right, as the eldest surviving direct male descendant of his grandfather, Ch'eng-hua. He elevated both his parents and his grandmother posthumously to Imperial rank, and his grandmother was transferred from the concubine cemetery to the Emperor Ch'eng-hua's grave, Mao-ling. Later this pride in his own family led him to ennoble vast numbers of relatives, increasing the number of court dependants, each with their allowances and tax exemptions, to a new disastrous level.

At the time of Chia-ching's accession the empire was in a parlous state. Misgovernment, corruption, and a hopelessly muddled tax system had ruined the countryside and strangled trade. The early Ming system of graduated taxation based on registers of land and manpower had, with the years, been completely distorted in favour of the gentry. The more the eunuchs exacted from Peking, the more local officials multiplied the taxes on the poor. Eventually the peasants, unable to pay, abandoned their land, and whole villages simply ceased to exist.

During Chia-ching's reign a serious attempt was made to reform the whole tax system. His first Grand Secretary, Yang T'ing-ho, one of the more able administrators of the whole Ming era, started a movement to simplify and amalgamate all the different land and labour levies. With a pun on the Chinese character for "item," the movement "to combine in one item" became known as the "single whip" reform. The spread of this reform and the stability resulting from a reign of forty-five years helped to revive the economy and did something to alleviate the general misery and discontent.

But it was not a peaceful reign. The central government was far from being in control of the Middle Kingdom. In the north, the Mongols continued their raids, and in 1550 the powerful leader of the Eastern Mongols, Altan Khan, broke through the Great Wall and besieged Peking. Large areas in the northeast were terrorised and pillaged before he came to terms with the Chinese and withdrew to found a capital of his own to the northwest of Ta-t'ung. Optimistically, the Chinese then gave him a new name—"Obedient and Righteous Prince" (rather in the same spirit in which they had named his camp under the walls of Peking, "turning toward civilisation"), and allowed him to send tribute and trade horses for textiles.

In the southeast things were no better. Japanese pirates raided the coast and sailed up the Yangtze River, sacking cities and holding hostages for ransom. How little control the central government had in the provinces is shown by the fact that, in 1555, a group of only seventy pirates were able to loot their way to Nanking and back for two and a half months before they were stopped. In 1560 six thousand Japanese landed and ravaged Fukien. The Chinese reaction was to ban all maritime traffic and turn ever more inward.

There was, moreover, also trouble with the Portuguese. The latter, after another abortive attempt to land in Canton in the first year of Chia-ching's reign, returned in 1542 and established themselves farther north in Ningpo. Accepted at first in this new place on the same terms as the Arab traders, they were allowed to settle in the city, and it is said that at one time three thousand Portuguese were resident there.[4] Soon, however, history repeated itself and things began to go wrong. The Portuguese resorted to aggression, bullying, and murder. The local population grew hostile and the settlers tried to build a fort. This was too much even for the trade-loving officials of the province, who led an attack on the Portuguese and killed or expelled them all.

Much the same thing happened again in 1549 in Fukien. Not until 1557 did the Chinese arrive at the brilliant compromise whereby they could enjoy all the benefits of trade with the West without disturbing the peace of the empire. The Portuguese were allowed to trade and live on the peninsula Macao, which the Chinese carefully walled off from the mainland, and this place became the stepping-stone for Western trade with Canton.

As seen from Peking, the reign was no doubt a success. Chia-ching was an extravagant emperor and used the new wealth from the revival in trade to decorate his palaces and patronise the arts. He was an ardent Taoist with a longing for immortality. This led to a search for rare plants and drugs, a belief in the planchette board, and the collection of certain animals, especially white, such as cranes, deer, geese, and turtles, which were believed to encourage long life. This emphasis on longevity also affected the arts, where the most popular subjects were now pine trees, cranes, deer, and "Immortals." It is no wonder that the construction of his tomb played such an important part in Chia-ching's life. If he could not live for ever, his spirit could at least live on in a fitting Imperial residence.

14

Chao-ling

TOMB 9

BURIED HERE
Emperor Lung-ch'ing, died 1572
Empress Li, died 1558
Empress Chen, died 1592
Empress Li-shih, died 1614

There is no road to Chao-ling. It lies about one kilometre to the southwest of Ting-ling (tomb 10), and you can only get there by walking through the fields. A small path leads off to the left from the lower end of the parking place in front of Ting-ling. After walking for a few minutes, you come to a stream; the main path goes over the stream and leads to a village. To get to Chao-ling, instead of crossing the stream you take a small track that runs along the right bank. It is a very pretty walk through persimmon orchards and cultivated fields. The fields are usually intercropped—beans and wheat planted between rows of maize. The stream flows quickly, and although it is full of weeds and insects the water is always clear. You get a very strong feeling of life in the countryside. Women and children chat while they wash clothes in the stream; men drive donkeys heavily laden with wood or soil to terrace new fields; the fruit trees are being pruned or the late maize harvested.

Suddenly through the trees on the right you see the familiar red of the precinct walls. Of all the tombs the approach to this one is the most beautiful (colourplate 19). There is no distracting noise from the road; the village is too far away to intrude, and the silent tomb stands among the corn as if time had passed it by. Each time you come the beauty of the place strikes anew. On the left, the tortoise stele stands in a clearing of fruit trees; just in front of the stele are three lovely arched bridges, and to the right a large ramp leads up to the entrance between the high red walls.

The tortoise stele, complete with surrounding wall, is in very good condition, and the base is carved with snail-like coils in each corner (figs. 135 and 136). The triple bridges are unusually complete, the two side ones still having their walls (fig. 137). The tomb, lying on a north-west south-east axis, is built up the side of a hill so that you cannot see the stele pavilion until you are halfway up the ramp. Then suddenly it appears, framed in the entrance gate and towering above the remains of the Sacrificial Hall (colourplate 20).

The entrance to the tomb is more elaborate than those of the earlier tombs and

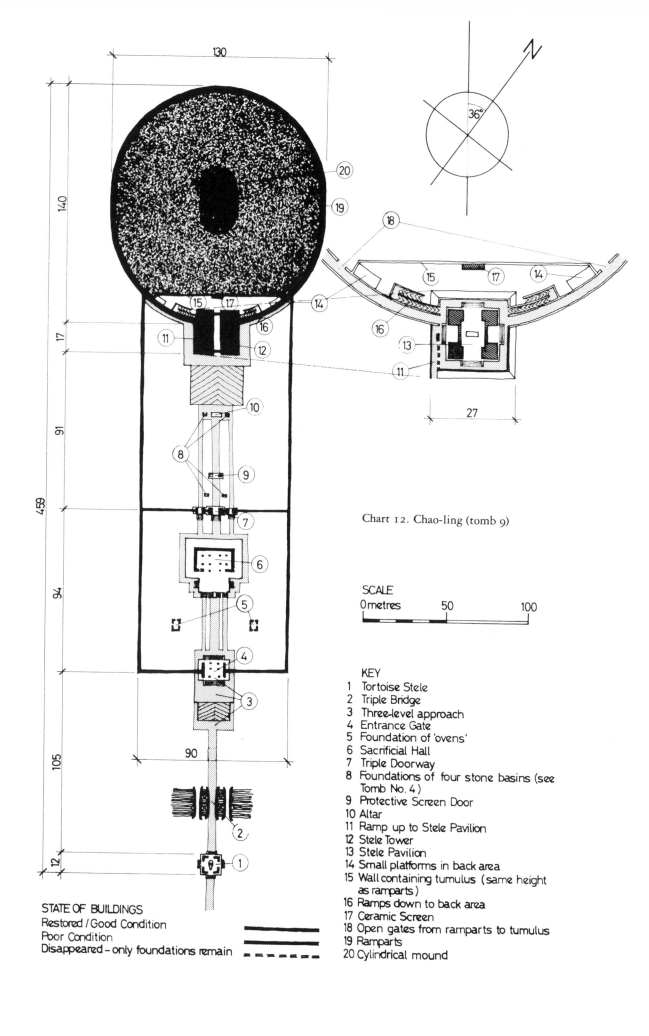

Chart 12. Chao-ling (tomb 9)

SCALE

0 metres   50   100

KEY
1 Tortoise Stele
2 Triple Bridge
3 Three-level approach
4 Entrance Gate
5 Foundation of 'ovens'
6 Sacrificial Hall
7 Triple Doorway
8 Foundations of four stone basins (see Tomb No. 4)
9 Protective Screen Door
10 Altar
11 Ramp up to Stele Pavilion
12 Stele Tower
13 Stele Pavilion
14 Small platforms in back area
15 Wall containing tumulus (same height as ramparts)
16 Ramps down to back area
17 Ceramic Screen
18 Open gates from ramparts to tumulus
19 Ramparts
20 Cylindrical mound

STATE OF BUILDINGS
Restored / Good Condition
Poor Condition
Disappeared - only foundations remain

consists of three levels: first a brick platform, then a wide brick ramp leading up to a stone paved terrace 24 metres wide and 13 metres deep (fig. 138). From there a triple staircase takes you to the open doorway. The "south" walls of the precinct have lost much of their facing but are otherwise in good condition; nothing is left of the triple doorway except the wooden beams in the walls forming the sides of the door entrance.

Large parts of the first courtyard, which is well planted with thujas, are still paved. You can see the foundations of two small buildings to the left and right of the path leading up to the Sacrificial Hall, which were presumably ovens for burning paper offerings. The marble slab in the centre of the triple staircase on the south side of the terrace is carved with mountains and clouds; there are two corner staircases. The back and side walls of the hall are standing but the plaster facing and wooden beams have all gone.

The triple door into the second courtyard is one of the best in the whole valley (fig. 139). The roofs are intact, and nearly all the unusually fine ceramic decorations are in place (fig. 140). A lot of small pines are growing around the rather steep steps that lead up to the doorway on the "south" side (fig. 141). The second courtyard is beautifully proportioned and very peaceful. Among the thujas are a few very large pines where Red-legged Falcons nest. To the left and right of the central paved way are four square stone foundations, two just inside the doorway and two near the altar. The placing of these corresponds exactly to the position of the four stone basins in Yü-ling, and it seems reasonable to suppose that there was a similar arrangement here. The two marble columns of the screen door are in place with their ch'i-lin, and the altar has some fine decoration.

In this tomb, for the first time, there is a well-developed system of drains in the two courtyards. This will be gone into in more detail below, but it is worth looking for the stone coverts with their specially carved drain covers that run parallel to the precinct walls.

According to Ku Yen-wu, the stele tower and pavilion were burnt down in 1644, presumably by the same brigands who pillaged K'ang-ling.[1] It seems likely that the two towers and pavilions were restored at the same time since they are almost identical. A ramp, through which a lot of young pines are growing, leads up to the terrace on which the stele tower stands. To the left and right of this terrace are the same narrow walks found in the earlier tombs. The outer wall of the tunnel through the centre of the tower has gone, but it remains blocked up by bricks. The ramp up to the stele tower on the "west" side is very steep but in quite good order. There are steps up to the four arches in the stele pavilion; the "west" and "east" arches are blind. The grave stele has been broken into many pieces and put together again. It is covered with writing and the inscription: "Tomb of the worthy Emperor Mu-tsung" is hard to read. Most of the plaster facing on the stele pavilion has gone and some of the wall around the little terrace has fallen away. A small tree grows on the roof, which is otherwise in quite good condition (colourplate 21). The wooden frame where the emperor's name would once have hung is still in place, but virtually nothing is left of the ceramic frieze

135. Coil decoration on corner of tortoise stele base   136. Carved coping of wall around tortoise stele

137. BELOW: "Westernmost" of the three bridges, with balustrades in place, leading from tortoise stele to the tomb

138. LEFT: "West" side of three-tiered approach to entrance gate

beneath the roof. From the terrace there is a spectacular view. The tower is high enough for you to see across the valley down the full length of the reservoir.

The area behind the stele tower is quite different from any previous tomb. Here, as in Ch'ang-ling and Yung-ling, the mound has been built up level with the circular rampart walk. The "south" end of the mound has been cut off in a straight line by a wall as high as the outer rampart wall; this wall runs directly "east-west," creating a deep, arc-shaped enclosure between the stele tower and the tumulus (see chart). The whole of this back area is paved, with a short raised platform half a metre high at the two wings of the arch. The ramps down from each side of the tower are in good condition; at the halfway point and the bottom, there are well-carved cornerstones. Opposite the blocked tunnel through the tower there is a ceramic screen which stands right up against the wall and not free as in earlier tombs; the screen roof is complete but most of the tile facing has gone. The high grey walls still have their smooth stone facing, but here and there a pine tree is pushing its roots through and causing cracks.

A similar deep arc-shaped enclosure is to be found in Ching-ling (tomb 11), built some fifty years later, and Te-ling (tomb 12), but not in Ting-ling, the immediately succeeding tomb. It is, of course, possible that the C'hing restorers copied from the later tombs when they rebuilt the damaged tower after 1644. On the whole, however, considering the amount of work needed to excavate such a deep enclosure and the fact that K'ang-ling, which was restored at the same time, does not have a similar arrangement, I am inclined to think that it was part of the original structure. The most likely explanation for this new style of back area seems to me to be purely practical. There was a wish to copy the Yung-ling funeral mound—that is, to fill the mound up to the level of the rampart walk—but this was obviously not practical. Yung-ling's mound could be filled up all the way round because he outlived all his consorts, and once he was buried it was unlikely the tomb would ever have to be opened again. The same situation existed in Ting-ling; when the Emperor Wan-li died, both his wife and the mother of the succeeding emperor were already dead. Lung-ch'ing, on the other hand, died when he was only thirty-four, leaving behind a wife and a young concubine, mother of the new emperor, both of whom would have to be buried in the tomb later. The arc-shaped enclosure provides a compromise whereby the general shape of the mound follows the new pattern but the possibility is left of opening the tomb at a later stage without disturbing the whole mound.

The general arrangement of the funeral mound and ramparts is similar to that of Yung-ling, but there is one innovation. Where the circular walk meets the straight wall at the "southern" end, there is a gateway on each side. Carved stone doors lie on the ground near each of these gateways. These doors must have been very heavy, but a description of a similar arrangement in the Western Tombs of the Ch'ing emperors states quite clearly that they were made to open.[2] I am grateful to Sir John Addis for a photograph taken in the eleventh tomb, Ching-ling, in January 1957, which shows similar doors in place (fig. 171). Just inside each gate, to the right and left, are two large square drain holes connecting with a covered culvert large enough for a man to climb through. The rampart is narrower than in Yung-ling and has the usual crenellations on the outer wall. In the middle of the tumulus is a large, artificial cylindrical mound, some 4 to 5 metres high and twenty-five metres in diameter, made of blocks of packed earth. This mound, like the rest of the tumulus, is planted with thujas and thorn bushes.

Chao-ling is one of the most beautiful of all the tombs. For those who have the time, there is a particular delight in the feeling of seclusion given by the walk. It is the perfect place for a picnic in winter, catching the warmth of the low midday sun. The courtyards are full of charm and quiet; very few visitors come here, and even the militia man has to arrive silently on a bicycle rather than on the more usual motorbike.

Architecturally the tomb is very interesting. In general there is a return to the earlier type of two-courtyard tomb with the traditional grey stone stele tower approached by a ramp up the "west" side. But already, from the elaborate three-tiered approach to the entrance gate, you can see that this tomb is a more sophisticated version of the original plan. The builder has not been content simply to copy but has taken different ideas from different tombs and fitted them, with a few innovations, into the traditional framework. The four stone square bases in the second courtyard hark back to Yü-ling. The funeral mound and rampart walk are like Yung-ling, but the stone gateways from the walk into the mound and the deep arc-shaped back area behind the stele tower are new. The tomb lacks the fine decoration of Yung-ling—here, for example, there are no gargoyles—but from the beautifully finished stonework in the drainage system it seems likely that some of the same craftsmen may have been at work.

DRAINAGE. The development of the drainage system we saw in Yung-ling is carried much further here. This is the first tomb to show a complete system of drainage in both mound and courtyards. Moreover, it is clear that the stonemasons who constructed this system were proud of their work. Whereas up to now we have seen only one type of stone grill to cover a drain, here there are four quite new and decorative types of drain covers. At ground level, at the "southern" end of the "east" and "west" precinct walls, there are two large exit drains with a stone channel covered with large stone slabs leading down to the stream which runs under the triple bridges (fig. 142). The stone grill in these drains is still in place. Inside the first courtyard an underground drain covered with stone slabs runs round the "west," "east," and "south" sides. At regular intervals there are specially carved stones with five holes to catch the water (fig. 143). In the two "southern" corners are two large square drains that lead through the precinct wall to the outside channels mentioned above.

In the second courtyard there is a similar arrangement of an underground stone-covered channel around three walls. Here, however, three different types of carved stone covers are used. In the "west" and "east" corners of the "southern" side, there are two slabs with a large circular hole in the middle and eight small circular holes round the edge (fig. 144). Not far from these, at the "south" end of the "east" and

139. "North" façade of triple doorway

140. Ch'i-wen on roof of triple doorway

141. Steps up to "south" side of triple doorway

142. Covered drain leading out from "southeast" corner of first courtyard.

143. Five-holed drain in first courtyard

144. Nine-holed drain in second courtyard

145. ABOVE: Larger nine-holed drain in second courtyard
146. RIGHT: Two-holed drain in second courtyard

"west" walls, and again halfway along these walls, are stones carved with the same pattern but decidedly larger (fig. 145). Between these, at regular intervals, are small oval slabs in which two small oval holes have been cut (fig. 146). The arrangement is symmetrical, efficient, and shows good workmanship.

Up on the ramparts there has been a return to the system of attracting the rainwater *inward* to the shallow gutter running around the mound, rather than *outward* through the crenellated wall as in Yung-ling. At regular intervals, about 7.5 metres apart, there is a series of diagonal stone ridges leading the water through a decoratively carved hole in the inner wall which culminates in a stone spout. As mentioned above, this gutter leads to four large, square stone holes at the "south" end of the tumulus, one on each side of the two gates where the circular wall meets the straight "southern" wall. Judging from what we could see, these holes opened into large stone-lined conduits leading down through the mound and eventually connecting with the channels at the "south" end of the whole precinct which join the stream.

In each of the raised pavements in the corners of the back area are three drains: two are the two-hole type; the third, the larger nine-hole type. These drains are directly under rainwater spouts from the upper rampart and from halfway down the back ramps.

It was in this tomb that one of the children and a friend, on a New Year's Day, disappeared down a drain in the funeral mound and reappeared, to the surprise of the militia man, outside the precinct walls of the tomb.

Lung-ch'ing, 1567–72

The Emperor Lung-ch'ing was the third son of Chia-ching. He had a secluded and neglected childhood. An older brother, who died young, was expected to succeed to the throne, and so Lung-ch'ing, son of a concubine, received virtually no political education. When at the age of twenty-nine he came to the throne, he was completely unprepared for the task of ruling. He took no interest in affairs of state and seems to have decided that the main point of being emperor was to make up for all the pleasure he had missed as a child.

He must, however, have had some good sense since on acceding to the throne he promoted one of his earlier instructors, Chang Chü-cheng, to the post of Grand Secretary. Chang Chü-cheng is generally regarded as one of the most able of all Ming administrators, and it is no doubt because of him that the Lung-ch'ing era was, on the whole, quiet. The short reign gained some panache from a grand review of the troops held by the emperor in the autumn of 1569. Only three such reviews were held during the Ming dynasty (the other two were in 1429 and 1581), and it seems likely that Chang suggested the review as much to distract and amuse the emperor as to boost the morale of the Imperial Army.

Lung-ch'ing's first wife died before he became emperor and was reburied in Chao-ling at the time of his death. His widow, the Empress Ch'en, was buried in Chao-ling in

1592, and one of his concubines, who was elevated to the rank of empress when her son Wan-li became emperor, was also buried there when she died some forty years later in 1614.

14. Stele tower and pavilion, Yü-ling (tomb 4)

15. Funeral mound and ramparts
in winter, Yü-ling (tomb 4)

16. North façade of triple doorway,
Mao-ling (tomb 5)

17. "East" side of entrance seen from the "north," K'ang-ling (tomb 7)

18. Yung-ling (tomb 8) seen from the "south"

19. LEFT: Approach to Chao-ling (tomb 9) in winter

20. FAR BELOW: General view of Chao-ling (tomb 9) from the "south"

21. BELOW: "South" side of Chao-ling (tomb 9) roof

22. View across fields to Ting-ling (tomb 10)

23. Artificial mound on grave tumulus, Ching-ling (tomb 11)

24. Doorway with ceramic decorations through north wall of first courtyard, Ching-ling (tomb 11)

25. TOP: Stele tower and pavilion, Te-ling (tomb 12)

26. LEFT: View over courtyards toward exit from stele pavilion, Te-ling (tomb 12)

27. ABOVE: Grave stele base with Buddhist symbols, Te-ling (tomb 12)

28. Grave stele and mound, Sze-ling (tomb 13)

29. Stele pavilion from the north, Hsiao-ling (Nanking)

31. President of one of the Six Boards on the
Spirit Road to Hsiao-ling (Nanking)

30. Pair of warriors on the Spirit Road to
Hsiao-ling (Nanking)

15

Ting-ling

TOMB 10

BURIED HERE
Emperor Wan-li, died 1620
Empress Wang, died 1620
Empress Wang, died 1611

The Emperor Wan-li was the last ruler of the Ming dynasty to have a reign of any importance. Ascending the throne in 1572 at the age of nine, he ruled over a united China for forty-eight years, longer than any ruler since the Han Emperor Wu (141–87 B.C.). With him are buried his wife and the concubine Wang, who was raised to the rank of empress when her son became emperor in 1620. Wan-li's tomb, Ting-ling, is the only tomb in the valley that has been excavated. Like Ch'ang-ling, it is usually packed with visitors. The excavations, which lasted from 1956–58, were done with great care and good taste, and today the tomb has become a popular and very interesting museum.

Dr. Hsia Nai, Director of the Peking Institute of Archaeology, led the excavations and has given an account of the work in *China Reconstructs,* March 1959. It was known from excavations in other parts of the country that the main problem was to find the underground entrance to the tomb. The funeral chambers would be strongly built of closely fitting stone, and the only way to get in without spoiling the whole building would be through the door. Buried under an enormous hill of earth, this would be difficult to find. Luck, however, was with the archaeologists. On examining the wall encircling the funeral mound, they noticed that in one place the bricks were weak and falling away. Upon removing some of these bricks they found an archway through the wall. This was clearly the entrance tunnel; it had brick walls but no ceiling and had been filled up with earth when the tomb was closed. They cleared the passage and came to a dead end. Then, entirely by chance, somewhat reminiscent of Alice in Wonderland stumbling across a cake that said "Eat Me," they discovered a small stele saying: "The diamond wall is 16 chang [160 Chinese feet] away and 3.5 chang down."

Here clearly were the instructions the original builders of the tomb had left to guide those who would have to open it when the emperor had to be buried. After his funeral, someone had simply forgotten to remove them. By following the directions, the archaeologists found another corridor with rough stone walls and no ceiling; at the

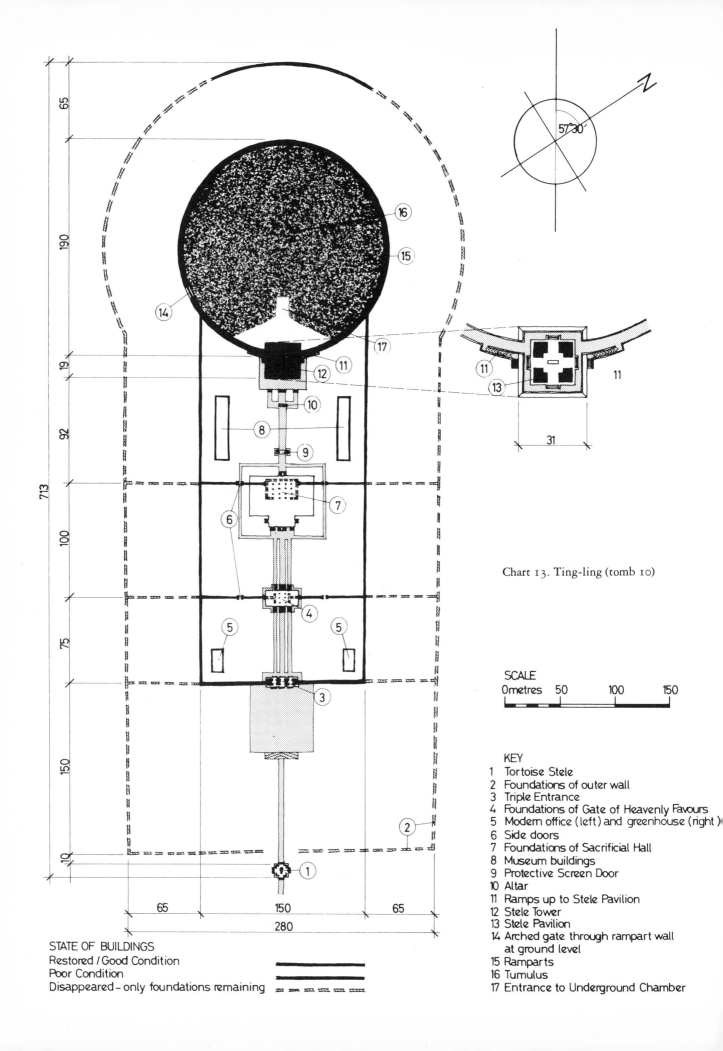

57°30′

Chart 13. Ting-ling (tomb 10)

SCALE

| 0 metres | 50 | 100 | 150 |

KEY
1 Tortoise Stele
2 Foundations of outer wall
3 Triple Entrance
4 Foundations of Gate of Heavenly Favours
5 Modern office (left) and greenhouse (right)
6 Side doors
7 Foundations of Sacrificial Hall
8 Museum buildings
9 Protective Screen Door
10 Altar
11 Ramps up to Stele Pavilion
12 Stele Tower
13 Stele Pavilion
14 Arched gate through rampart wall
    at ground level
15 Ramparts
16 Tumulus
17 Entrance to Underground Chamber

STATE OF BUILDINGS
Restored / Good Condition
Poor Condition
Disappeared – only foundations remaining

end of this was a brick wall—the "diamond" wall—the outer wall of the underground palace.

Once again, a looseness in the brickwork showed the exact point to open. A few bricks were taken out, and then, with the help of a torch, the excavators looked through the hole and saw, at the end of an empty antechamber, two large white marble doors. The suspense must have been almost unbearable, for by now it was clear that the tomb was intact. When they opened those doors they would find things exactly as they had been left after the funeral of the emperor and his wives in 1620.

The doors, each carved from a single enormous slab of marble and decorated with rows of marble studs, fitted tightly. It was known from other graves whose doors had been broken down by grave robbers that they were held closed by a heavy stone buttress. This buttress slipped into a special niche as the door closed so that in theory the door could never again be opened from the outside. The archaeologists ingeniously devised a way of slipping a strong but flexible strip of metal between the doors and then easing it up so that it dislodged the stone slab. The doors then swung back easily on their stone hinges. Aladdin's cave was open! Although it was known from the records that Wan-li was a lover of luxury, the splendour and wealth of the things inside surpassed expectation.

No expense had been spared in building the tomb itself. Work was started when the emperor was sixteen and finished six years later, having cost eight million taels of silver (more than half a million pounds). Every family in the province had to contribute a son to join the work force of 600,000 men. It is said that the bricks were brought from Shantung, the stone from Fengshan and Yenan, the wood from distant Szechuan. In size and general plan, it joins Ch'ang-ling and Yung-ling in the small group of three-courtyard tombs. The ground plan is clearly copied from Yung-ling. Here also there was an outer wall, 65 metres beyond the walls of the precinct proper and encompassing the whole tomb complex. The walls and buildings were damaged by brigands in 1644, restored by the Ch'ing, damaged again in the early part of the twentieth century, and finally tidied up and partially restored at the time of the excavations.

To reach the tomb, you take the first turn to the left off the main road after crossing the bridge at the head of the reservoir. Today the road makes a detour around the original triple bridge with its new balustrades, passes the tortoise stele,* and ends in a large parking place in front of the entrance (colourplate 22). The outer walls of the tomb and the triple entrance doors have been restored; in general, the restoration seems to have been done in the same way as in Yung-ling—the walls and outer doorways have been restored but the ruined buildings inside have simply been cleared away.

The first courtyard is thickly planted with very old thujas; indeed, the whole tomb is as Bouillard noted in 1920, unusually well planted and luxuriant. In places, he re-

*The base on which this stele stands is carved with waves, a turtle, a fish, a crab, and a prawn.

cords, it was difficult to get through the large trees. These must have been planted at the beginning of the Ch'ing dynasty, because Ku Yen-wu writes that at the time the tomb was ravaged, the trees were destroyed.[1] Two new buildings, a storehouse and a greenhouse, flank the "southern" end of the "east" and "west" walls of the courtyard, standing no doubt on the site of the former kitchens.

To enter the second courtyard you cross the marble terrace on which the Gate of Heavenly Favours once stood. The gateway has been cleared away and the adjoining walls finished off just short of where the doorposts would have been. This form of restoration is the same as that found at the entrance gate of Ching-ling (tomb 3). The stone carving on the terrace is very fine. There are three staircases on the "north" and "south" sides with the usual marble slab, carved with dragons and phoenixes playing among clouds above mountains and sea (fig. 147).* Of the gargoyles around the edge of the terrace, all but the corner ones have been broken. These gargoyles are similar to those in Ch'ang-ling and Yung-ling, with curled hair, flat-lying horns, and scaly feet with claws (fig. 148). To both sides of the terrace there are door openings in the dividing wall apparently on the site of original doors.[2] Piles of marble balustrades lie on the ground, presumably waiting to be replaced along the staircase and terrace edge.

As we have already seen, the second courtyard is equally well planted with thujas. The Sacrificial Hall described by Bouillard in 1931 as a "complete ruin,"[3] has been cleared away to reveal the full beauty of the terrace. The side walls have been finished off in the same way as those at the Gate of Heavenly Favours; here also are two side doors through the precinct wall to both sides of the terrace (figs. 149 and 150). On the "south" side of the terrace are five staircases; on the "north," behind what would have been a closed wall, only one. The marble slabs in the central staircases on both sides are identical to those on the first terrace. From the centre of this terrace you get an excellent view of the altar and massive stele tower and pavilion. In summer there is very much a holiday feeling here, old and young queuing under the brightly striped umbrella of the professional photographer to have their portraits taken with the tower as background, or else, amid much laughter, taking pictures of each other. The balustrades on the "south" side have mostly been replaced and are carved with fine dragons and phoenixes. There are eleven small gargoyles along each side of the terrace and a large one at each corner.

The final courtyard, also thickly planted, is dominated by the stele pavilion. The screen door has been restored and all five precious objects sit on the altar (figs. 151 and 152). Running down each side of the courtyard are two low buildings housing copies of the objects found in the tomb itself. The terrace on which the tower stands is approached by three staircases, but this innovation seems to be the result of restoration as in 1931 only the usual ramp existed. The approach to the tower is similar to that in Yung-ling, with wide ramps extending up both sides of the tower. (The gates which Bouillard noted at the foot of these ramps have disappeared.) Here, however, the

*This must be a restoration. In 1920 Bouillard notes: "The terrace has three front staircases; the centre one is without a carved slab" (Bouillard and Vaudescal, p. 81).

147. TOP: Marble staircases leading to the terrace of the Gate of Heavenly Favours

148. CENTRE LEFT: Corner of terrace with gargoyle

149. LOWER RIGHT: Decoration on base of door between second and third courtyards

150. CENTRE RIGHT: Decoration on upper corner of door between second and third courtyards

151. Altar with five precious objects,
seen from stele pavilion

152. Stone incense burner

tower and ramparts are built of ordinary grey stone and not the fine, polished pink stone of Yung-ling. As in Yung-ling, there is no tunnel through the tower and no enclosed back area such as we have seen in other tombs.

The stele pavilion is exactly the same as in Yung-ling, with four open arches (fig. 153); the stele stands on the same sort of square stone base with four layers depicting sea, mountains, clouds, and flying dragons (fig. 14). The inscription reads: "Tomb of the glorious Emperor Shen-tsung." The pavilion has been restored and has a good example of a typical Ming palace style double roof (fig. 51). The rampart walls have been rather roughly restored and the only point of interest is that a short way around the wall to the "west" is a large arched gateway under the rampart at ground level (fig. 154). Bouillard mentions a similar opening to the "east," but I could find no trace of that.[4] These gateways would have opened into the enclosure between the outer wall and the tomb. At the "northern" end of the rampart walk, a modern gate has been made, opening into the mound. From here you can see a short stretch of the outer wall on the slopes of the hill. The mound is luxuriant with thujas.

THE INTERIOR OF THE TOMB.   Behind the stele tower a modern path leads to the entrance of the underground tomb (fig. 155). A large modern stairway takes you down to the level of the funeral chambers and to a modern door whose shape reminds one a bit of the "bee-hive" tombs at Mycenae. This was where the "diamond" wall stood, and just across the small antechamber are the first two marble doors, the entrance to the vault itself. These doors are well worth examining. Each gigantic piece of marble weighs between six and seven tons and is a masterpiece of craftsmanship; the lines are completely straight, the rows of nobs symmetrical, the handle delicately carved in the form of an animal head (fig. 156).* Just inside the doors on the right you can see the stone buttress that served as a self-locking mechanism when the doors were closed (fig. 157).

The plan of the underground chamber is rather like a coptic cross. The most remarkable thing about the building is its beautiful stonework. The stones forming the vault are so finely worked that they fit together exactly without any cement or filling material. When the tomb was opened after more than three hundred years it was found completely dry. The main axis consists of a passagelike, vaulted hall (empty when the tomb was opened), which leads through another pair of marble doors into a longer but similarly shaped central hall (fig. 158). This was the Sacrificial Chamber; in it were three marble thrones, one for the emperor, carved with dragons and clouds, the other two carved with phoenixes, for the empresses. Large blue and white Ming

---

*This is another example of the Chinese custom of repeating a well-known decorative theme in different materials. In the P'ai-lou and the small ovens, the intricacies of the classical Chinese roof are copied in stone and ceramic; here the bronze knobs and door handle of the traditional palace door are reproduced in marble. According to tradition, these knobs were introduced by Lu Pan, the god of carpenters and masons. Noticing that a conch shell, when touched, closes itself up and clings tightly to the surface on which it is standing, he decided to reproduce conch shells on all doors as a symbol of tightness and security (see Arlington and Lewisohn, *In Search of Old Peking,* p. 29).

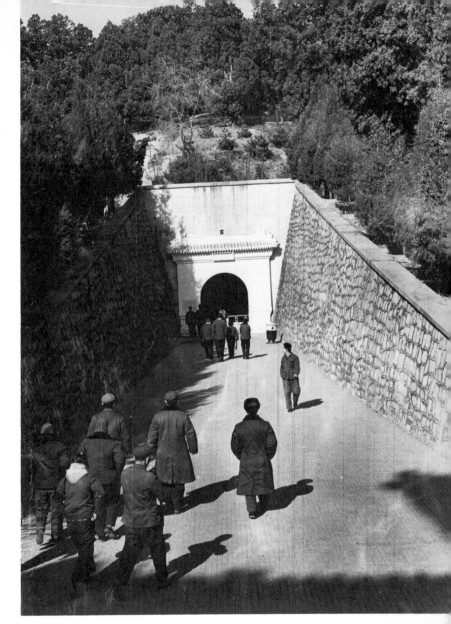

153. OPPOSITE: "North" face of stele pavilion seen from exit of underground chamber

154. ABOVE: Door through "west" side of rampart wall leading from tumulus to former outer enclosure

155. RIGHT: Entrance to underground chamber

vases, nearly a metre high, were found here still filled with sesame oil and wicks; these were "everlasting lamps" that must have gone out for lack of oxygen. As we have seen, the purpose of these lamps was to succour the spirit of the deceased. Weakend by its separation from the body, the spirit was believed to gain strength from the warmth and light of the flame. The thrones, vases, and the stone bases for the set of five altar objects are still in this hall but have been slightly rearranged. The altar objects were made of glazed pottery and are not yet on view.

The third pair of marble doors at the end of this hall lead into the burial chamber, which runs at right angles to the axis. This chamber, considerably larger and higher than the first two halls, is similarly vaulted. On a stone dais opposite the door stood the three red-lacquered coffins of the emperor and his two wives. Around them on the ground was a bewildering quantity of treasure: chests of jewellery, delicate porcelain,

156. Animal head on marble door to underground chamber

157. Marble slab used to lock doors from the inside

158. Underground chamber with marble thrones

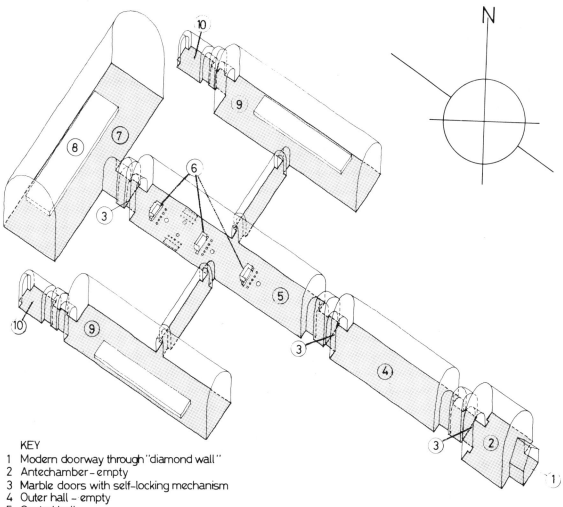

N

KEY
1 Modern doorway through "diamond wall"
2 Antechamber - empty
3 Marble doors with self-locking mechanism
4 Outer hall - empty
5 Central hall
6 Three marble thrones, each with five stone bases for ritual vessels and one "everlasting lamp" (large blue and white vase). Dotted lines show original positions of empresses' tombs
7 Burial chamber
8 Dais with three coffins (copies) and various smaller chests for treasures (copies)
9 Two side chambers, empty, each with dais for coffin
10 Exit corridors from side chambers (not open to visitors)

Chart 14. Underground mausoleum, Ting-ling (tomb 10)

figurines, even stones chosen for their special shapes. Today copies of some of these are on display in the two museum buildings in the third courtyard, and the burial chamber is empty save for replicas of the vast coffins and chests.

Two smaller vaulted chambers, also empty, and joined by vaulted passages to the central hall, form the arms of the cross. Each of these chambers had its own narrow entrance corridor with self-locking doors leading out through blocked doorways to the open air; it is believed that this was in case some wife of the emperor should survive him and have to be buried later, after the emperor's own burial chamber was closed.

DRAINAGE. This is not a good tomb in which to examine the drainage system since the restoration makes it difficult to judge what is new and what is original. Ironically, the only place where Bouillard notes drainage at all is in his description of the first courtyard of this tomb.[5] He mentions gutters and channels running alongside the inner wall, joining in front to form the stream that runs under the triple bridge. From this it would seem there was a system similar to that in the courtyards of Chao-ling.

The drainage system on the ramparts is based on that of Yung-ling. Water from the ramparts is carried *outward* through the crenellations by the same combination of diagonal stone ridge, catchment stone, and gargoyle. Rainwater falling on the mound is collected in the same sort of shallow gutter skirting the inside of the inner wall, with the same large, square drain shafts joining exit drains through the rampart walls at ground level. It is interesting to note how effective this system was; however good the stonework, the interior of the tomb could not have remained dry for so long if water had been continually seeping through the mound.

The drain holes around the stele building appear to be new, but those at the foot of the staircases leading up to the tower are similar to those in Yung-ling.

CONTENTS OF THE TOMB. The official report of the excavations at Ting-ling has not yet been published, although photographs of the various chambers as they were opened have been released and a colour film was made showing the work of excavation. The best account of the excavation remains Dr. Hsia Nai's article, mentioned above. Nagel's *Guide to China* gives a reasonably detailed description of the objects on display in the museum buildings in the Ting-ling precinct. According to Dr. Wang Yeqiu, the only original find on display is the empress's head-dress with blue enamel clouds and pearls, which can be seen in the Palace Museum in the Forbidden City. I gathered that other objects would be shown once the official report was out.

The objects shown in the Ting-ling museum are divided roughly on the "his" and "hers" principle; that is to say, the "western" building houses things that belonged to the emperor while the "eastern" building displays possessions of the two empresses. The most striking items in each are the various forms of head-dress. In the western building, a black iron helmet belonging to the emperor and found in one of the chests in the grave chamber, is decorated with martial figures in gold and has a long red plume. (A sword, not unlike those worn by the stone generals in the alley, with fine clasp and fittings, was found in the same box, along with a piece of iron scale-armour not on display.) Another head-dress, found in the coffin itself, is made entirely of very fine gold thread knitted into a gauze and decorated at the back with two facing dragons pursuing a flaming pearl. It has the form of a round bonnet with wings like horns and a high back part. A black and gold head-dress, worn for official audiences, is flat-topped like a mortar-board, with rows of tassels threaded with beads hanging from the sides and a long jade pin through it. Another black and gold silk hat, rounded and decorated with strings of precious stones, was worn when the emperor made official journeys

159. Emperor's hat, Ting-ling Museum

160. Empress's headdress, Ting-ling Museum

(fig. 159). Some gold and jade vessels and a few of the two hundred–odd miniature pewter vessels found on the dais, each marked with its name, are on display in the central case; there are also wooden models of furniture such as sedan chairs, and some rather rough-looking wooden figurines. A jade ewer with its lid fastened by a chain of jade links appears to have been carved from a single piece of stone.

On the "empress" side there are two flamboyant head-dresses—"phoenix crowns"—richly decorated with dragons and phoenixes (fig. 160). These are a piercing light blue; originally the upper part was made from kingfisher feathers mounted on paper. Part of these crowns consists of overlapping pale blue enamel clouds studded with pearls, and at the back are elaborate pearl-studded streamers, each with three wings. There are also some bejewelled hat pins, jade pendants and belt fastenings, and examples of embroidered silk brocade. Round the walls of both rooms are photographs taken during the excavations and replicas of the steles bearing the instructions that helped the archaeologists find the entrance to the underground chamber.

Among the many articles not yet on display are golden chopsticks, spoons, boxes, washbasins, and a spouted ewer, apparently for ceremonial use; models of coaches, spears, and flagstaffs with banners used in Imperial processions; lacquered toilet articles and a bronze mirror with a wooden frame lacquered in red. There are fine porcelain bowls and cups and many articles in jade, some with golden framework. There is also a unique collection of later Ming textiles—rolls of silk woven in fine patterns, many with golden thread. These bear the date and place of manufacture (usually the Imperial workshops at Nanking and Soochow), as well as the name of the weavers and supervising officials. Many of these articles were in an exceedingly frail condition and have had to be especially treated in order to be preserved.

The Emperor Wan-li is a good example of Lord Acton's dictum: "Power tends to corrupt and absolute power corrupts absolutely." Wan-li's reign started auspiciously. He ascended the throne as a child of nine, and for the first ten years the empire was governed by his mother, the chief eunuch, and the Grand Secretary, Chang Chü-cheng. Chang Chü-cheng, who had held office throughout the previous emperor's reign, was an exceedingly able administrator and dominated the political scene until his death in 1582. It was a time of economic growth. The population of China was reckoned to have doubled since the beginning of the Ming dynasty; new crops from America, such as maize, sweet corn, and groundnuts led to a revival in agriculture; and the tax reforms of the last forty years caused a boom in trade. The revival of the arts in the preceding reign was carried on by the new emperor, who encouraged artistic skills and the manufacture of new products to decorate his palaces. Chang Chü-cheng strove hard to improve administration and extend the "single whip" reform—the movement to simplify and improve the tax system which had begun under the Emperor Chia-ching. He tried to correct abuses whereby certain lands had been exempted from taxation, and he tried even harder to limit the privileges and perquisites of the official classes and the Imperial family.

Chang Chü-cheng had a certain influence over the young emperor, but not enough to counteract the disastrous effects of a purely eunuch education on what must in any case have been a weak character. Growing up in the gilded palaces of the Forbidden City, surrounded by exotic luxuries of every sort, the young man knew that his power was supreme. He had only to ask in order to receive. No one could force him to do anything he did not wish to do. The result was inevitable: a thoroughly degenerate and bloated creature who dissipated his strength in rich living and lost not only the will-power but also the interest to govern. When Chang Chü-cheng died, power slid into the hands of the eunuchs.

The Emperor Wan-li lived on for another thirty-eight years, eventually too fat to stand without support, uncontrollably extravant, and neglecting affairs of state. From 1589 he ceased to give general audiences; from 1591 onward he refused to participate in the great public sacrificial ceremonies; and he did not even attend the funeral of his mother in 1614. The dates of his rare interviews with the Grand Secretaries are illuminating: there were two in 1593, one in 1594, one in 1602, one in 1615, and finally one when he was dying in 1620. Whole generations of ministers came to power without ever having seen the emperor; his orders reached them through the filter of the eunuchs. Imperial audiences were held with visitors kowtowing in the traditional way to an empty throne.

The Imperial coffers were emptied to provide entertainment for Wan-li's jaded palate. Ninety thousand taels (ounces) of silver were spent on one of his marriages; 12 million taels went to invest certain princes, and 9 million taels to rebuild palaces. Taxes increased greatly, corruption abounded, and with it every sort of administrative malpractice. The emperor refused to deal with tax matters and official appointments. By the time he died, it is reckoned that half of all provincial posts were unfilled and most of the more able officials in Peking had retired and withdrawn to the countryside. The dynasty was slowly grinding to a halt. An expensive and unsuccessful war with Japan in Korea was ended by the death of the Japanese shogun, but this was only a short respite. Before the end of the reign, the Manchus had established a kingdom in Kirin and began to take over southern Manchuria.

An interesting light is thrown on the life of the court in Peking during these years by the comments and memoirs of the famous Jesuit, Matteo Ricci.[6] This remarkable man, who early discovered that the only way to influence the Chinese was to meet them on their own ground, had, since his arrival in China in 1582, mastered all the important Chinese classics. In a country where merit was equated with classical ability, he won a position for himself as a wise man; he could cap his Chinese friends' quotations and use arguments from their own philosophers. His formidable memory, which enabled him to read a page of five hundred characters through once and then repeat them either backward or forward, aroused admiration in the official classes. His original training in Rome in the essentials of modern mathematics, geography, astronomy, and music put him far ahead of his Chinese counterparts in those fields and helped him in his finally successful struggle to get to Peking. His aim was to convert the Chinese to Christianity by gaining influence at court. Earlier experience in the provinces had convinced him that piecemeal conversion of the peasantry had no chance of success as long as the official classes remained hostile.

Ricci's first visit to Peking was a complete failure. After the peace in Korea in 1598, tens of thousands of eunuchs, freed from the lucrative task of provisioning the army, swept southward; they set themselves up as petty rulers in the provinces and exacted tolls from the local people. It took Ricci, despite all safe-conducts and passes, two years to battle through their network of red tape and corruption. When eventually he reached Peking, he was quite unable to approach the court, and recognising defeat, he returned to Nanking.

Two years later he set off again, armed with powerful credentials and what he hoped would be powerful presents. En route he was waylaid by Ma T'ang, one of the most independent eunuchs of the time. Ma T'ang lived like an emperor. He traveled in "a large and very elegant boat, suitable even for the Emperor to travel in, with saloons, rooms and numerous cabins, all very wonderful and commodious. The galleries and the window casings were made of an incorruptible wood carved in various designs, shining with a coat of Chinese sandarac [a transparent varnish], and resplendent with gold."

Ricci found himself in a golden cage. He and his party were escorted to Tientsin, where Ma T'ang relieved him of his valuable presents and left him, despite all the Imperial safe-conducts, a virtual prisoner. Several months passed, and then—quite suddenly, presumably because some rival eunuch came to hear of this extraordinary foreigner and his abilities—orders came from Peking that Li Ma-tou (Ricci's Chinese name) was to be brought to the capital. Ma T'ang, with bad grace, returned the presents, and on 28 January 1601, Ricci arrived in Peking.

The careful choice of presents which Ricci had brought show the dual nature of his task. First he had to attract the emperor's attention, then he hoped to convert. Half the presents were religious—a breviary with gold thread, a cross with precious stones and relics of the saints, and the four Gospels. The other half were purely secular and designed to awaken curiosity by their novelty: a big clock worked by weights, a small spring-clock in gold, two crystal prisms, two hourglasses, a clavichord, European cloth, and a rhinoceros horn said to cure diseases. History does not relate how the Gospels were received, but the clocks brought Ricci to the palace. After a week, during which the Board of Rites was advising the emperor against accepting the gifts, the large clock stopped striking. Wan-li was furious, and in desperation the Jesuit was sent for. The first European ever to set foot inside the Forbidden City, he spent three days instructing the members of the Imperial College of Mathematicians in the workings of the two clocks. During these three days he was bombarded with questions from the emperor. Messengers raced to and fro with questions about every aspect of European life. This curiosity on the part of Wan-li seems to have continued in a spasmodic way until the Jesuit's death in 1610. In 1608 the emperor ordered a large copy of Ricci's "Mappa Mundi," which he had made into a screen. He was avid for scraps of knowledge but never appears to have followed up on any one subject. Once the court musicians were sent to Ricci to learn how to play the clavichord. It was assumed that this was also something which could be mastered in a few days. Ricci taught the musicians a simple piece and then wrote eight "Songs for the Clavichord." He made use of the old Chinese idea that "music is an instrument of politics and a means of expressing morality," and the songs illustrated moral concepts with Christian quotations. The emperor became sufficiently interested in Ricci and his companion Pantoja to demand that they be painted, but he never saw them. The audience with the emperor granted to them took place with the usual empty throne.

This, then, was the Peking of Wan-li—a luxurious spiderweb of intriguing eunuchs and frightened cliques of officials; the spider at its centre was all-powerful and thoroughly bored. It is in keeping with his nature that when his tomb was finally finished, Wan-li threw an enormous party in the funeral chambers.

16

Ching-ling

TOMB 11

BURIED HERE
Emperor T'ai-ch'ang, died 1620
Empress Kuo, died 1613
Empress Wang, died 1619
Empress Liu, died 1610

The Emperor T'ai-ch'ang, who lies here, ascended the throne in August 1620 and died before a month was out. With him are buried three empresses: his official wife, the Empress Kuo, who died in 1613 without having borne a son; the Empress Wang, a concubine who died in 1619 and whose son became the next emperor; the Empress Liu, another concubine who died in 1610 but was reburied in Ching-ling in 1628 when her son became the last Ming emperor.

T'ai-ch'ang's death was sudden and unexpected. It presented his successor with an awkward dilemma. T'ai-ch'ang had not had time to prepare a tomb for himself; on the other hand, it would not be seemly to leave him unburied for as long as it would take to build a tomb from scratch. This explains why he was buried in a tomb originally prepared for someone else.

In 1449, when the Emperor Cheng-t'ung was taken prisoner by the Mongols, his brother Ching-t'ai was created emperor. Ching-t'ai prepared a longevity mausoleum, Ching-ling, for himself, but when he died, Cheng-t'ung, who had regained the throne, refused to allow him to be buried in the Imperial cemetery. The unfortunate Ching-t'ai was relegated to a prince's grave and orders were given for Ching-ling to be destroyed. It seems likely that these only applied to the buildings above ground, since one hundred and seventy years later, the problem caused by T'ai-ch'ang's sudden death was solved by building on the earlier substructure. The result is a mixed tomb with an underground chamber and foundations dating from around 1450 and a superstructure built in 1620–21.

Like Hsien-ling, Ching-ling consists of two separate enclosures: one for the Sacrificial Hall and one for the altar and funeral mound. Once again, the reason for this is the presence of a small hill, presumably having an auspicious shape and therefore not to be moved. As a tomb, however, the layout of Ching-ling is much more successful than that of Hsien-ling. Here the open walk between the two courtyards adds to the charm of the tomb.

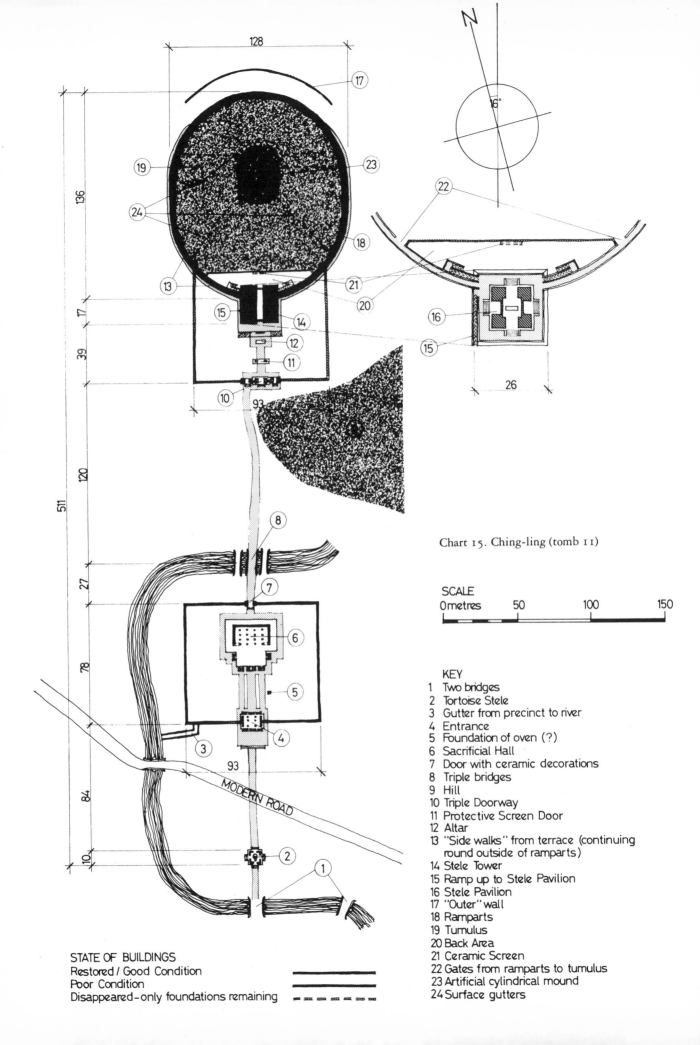

128

17

19

24

23

18

13

15

14

12

11

10

93

136

17

39

511

120

27

8

7

78

6

5

4

3

93

84

10

2

1

MODERN ROAD

N

16°

22

20

21

16

15

26

Chart 15. Ching-ling (tomb 11)

SCALE
0 metres   50   100   150

KEY
1 Two bridges
2 Tortoise Stele
3 Gutter from precinct to river
4 Entrance
5 Foundation of oven (?)
6 Sacrificial Hall
7 Door with ceramic decorations
8 Triple bridges
9 Hill
10 Triple Doorway
11 Protective Screen Door
12 Altar
13 "Side walks" from terrace (continuing
   round outside of ramparts)
14 Stele Tower
15 Ramp up to Stele Pavilion
16 Stele Pavilion
17 "Outer" wall
18 Ramparts
19 Tumulus
20 Back Area
21 Ceramic Screen
22 Gates from ramparts to tumulus
23 Artificial cylindrical mound
24 Surface gutters

STATE OF BUILDINGS
Restored / Good Condition
Poor Condition
Disappeared - only foundations remaining

If you take the road to the west from Ch'ang-ling, Ching-ling is the second tomb on the right. About a hundred metres before the tortoise stele is a small stone bridge just off the road on the left. It is worth stopping there and, if you have time, climbing down into the paved riverbed. The channel is about two metres deep, and in some places the original facing made from large, grey stone blocks is still in place. In others, the stone blocks go halfway up and then phase into smaller grey bricks. The arched bridge is a fine construction; beyond it the river winds, leading to a second, equally picturesque bridge (fig. 161). If you climb up the bank here, you will find yourself beside the tortoise stele of Ching-ling.

161. Bridge over dry riverbed near tortoise stele

The stele is in excellent condition. It stands on a small platform with a low surrounding wall and a staircase on each side. The base of the stele around the tortoise is carved with waves; in the four corners are a crab, a shrimp, a turtle, and a fish. The road passes between the stele and the first courtyard. Just beside the southwest corner of the enclosure it crosses another very beautiful bridge, this one complete with carved stone balustrades. From a square drain at the west end of the wall, a well-built stone gutter leads down into the river (fig. 162). The stele, bridge, and gutter are all in such good condition that it seems likely there has been some recent restoration.

The entrance to the courtyard is on two levels: a couple of steps go up to a paved platform from which staircases lead to the site of the triple door. The doorway has completely gone; the side walls are half crumbled down. You can see the stone column bases and sockets for the doors. On the other side, three sets of stairs lead down into the courtyard (fig. 163). Here there are many pine trees and a great deal of broken stones and rubble. The back and side walls of the Sacrificial Hall are standing but there are no beams, facing, or roof. The staircases up to the hall terrace are intact, without balustrades, and there is a very good marble slab with phoenix and dragon (fig. 164). Behind the hall, in the middle of the north wall, is a single door. This door is the best example in the whole valley of the Ming art of using ceramic tiles to simulate painting as a form of decoration (colourplate 24). The panels on either side of the door are covered with large garlands of flowers made from green and yellow tiles. Except for the central flower in each panel, the tiles are complete.

This door opens onto a very beautiful walk leading slightly uphill to the grave enclosure (fig. 165). First the path crosses three lovely arched bridges over a small river. This is the same river that runs past the tortoise stele, and the particular placing of the tomb may well have been influenced by the way in which it winds in front of the grave area, thus fulfilling the highest demands of feng-shui. In summer you walk between fields of sorghum, Indian corn, and persimmons; in winter, goats graze on the small hill and the red walls of the second courtyard glow through the bare branches of the trees.

The triple doors into the second courtyard are very decayed. The two side doors have lost their roofs and are without tiles or plasterwork; the central door is crumbling fast. It still has a roof, with several small trees growing on it and even a dragon's head holding the ridge, but below that the whole surface has broken away, exposing the bricks. If you look back through the gate, you will see that the two enclosures are not quite aligned. The walls of the enclosure are complete but have lost much of their colour. The courtyard, as in Hsien-ling, the other divided tomb, seems very small in relation to the stele tower. There are a lot of pines and thujas, the usual columns of the screen door, and a finely decorated altar.

The terrace on which the stele tower is built has certain peculiarities. Instead of the usual wide ramp up the front, there are two side ramps that lead to a little landing from which a short staircase goes up to the terrace proper (fig. 166). On each side of the tower, opening off the terrace, run the same narrow walks we have seen in other

162. ABOVE: Drain leading from corner of first courtyard to river

163. RIGHT: North side of entrance with steps into first courtyard

164. BELOW: Triple staircase up to sacrificial hall

165. View of triple bridges and path leading to second courtyard, seen from north doorway of first courtyard

tombs. Here, however, unlike all previous examples, these walks continue beyond the precinct walls, creating a sort of buttress halfway up the outer rampart wall. As the hill rises toward the north, the walks gradually taper away to ground level. The precinct wall is solid and there is no sign that it was ever possible to get from one side of the walk to the other. Behind the mound at the northern end, a second semicircular wall contains the hill, leaving room for a wide stony track round the outside of the ramparts.

The stele tower is built in the traditional manner, with a central tunnel, still half blocked, and a steep ramp up the west side (fig. 167). The west wall of the tower bulges ominously. The stele pavilion has lost its tiled roof and only the wooden beams and interfilling bricks remain, covered with grass and other small plants (fig. 168). The side archways are blocked; those to the north and south are open. The stele inscription reads: "Tomb of the righteous Emperor Kuang-tsung." The crenellations on the three sides of the terrace around the stele house are in good condition.

The layout of the grave mound and the back area between the stele tower and the mound is almost exactly the same as in Chao-ling—that is to say, the mound is built up

166. Altar and ramp up terrace on which stele tower stands

167. Ramp up west side of stele tower

168. Roof of stele pavilion from the northwest

169. TOP LEFT: Corner of ramp from stele pavilion down to back area between stele tower and grave mound

170. ABOVE: Back area between north side of stele tower and wall enclosing south end of grave tumulus

171. LEFT: Stone gate in position, photographed by Sir John Addis in 1957

to the same level as the rampart walk but at the south end a straight wall, running east-west, cuts off an arc-shaped courtyard between the tower and the mound. Ramps lead down into this deep courtyard from both sides of the tower (fig. 169). These were obviously imposing at one time, but today the whole of this back area is rather dismal. The ground is thick with rubble and very little remains of the ceramic screen (fig. 170). There are large, forbidding cracks in the tower and rampart walls, and over wide stretches the stone facing has fallen away.

172. Stone gate lying on the ground in gateway from rampart walk to grave tumulus

It is a relief to get back up onto the ramparts. These are some of the finest in the whole valley. Indeed, this is a curious tomb in that decay has attacked it so irregularly. Whereas some doorways and roofs have suffered badly, the ramparts are almost perfect, and the walk around the mound is a delight. The stone gates, which Sir John Addis photographed in place in 1957 (fig. 171), lie on the ground near the stone gateways at the southern corners of the grave mound (fig. 172). The drainage system is very easy to see and very interesting. It is particularly worth noting that here, for the

173. Ramparts with drain spouts through inner wall to shallow gutter around grave mound

174. Surface drain on grave mound

first time, there are stone gutters running across the surface of the tumulus. The trees here are mostly thujas, very old, and in spring there are always a mass of wild flowers. The tumulus is in the usual hill-shaped form; but here, as in Chao-ling (tomb 9) and Te-ling (tomb 12), there is a large artificial cylindrical mound (6 metres high and 25 metres in diameter) just north of the centre of the grave enclosure (colourplate 23). As far as I could see, these mounds are faced with packed earth rather than any form of stonework or plaster. They are grass-covered, and trees grow freely both on the summit and through the sides. In each of these three tombs the area inside the ramparts has only been filled in enough to form a very gently sloping hill; it seems probable, therefore, that the extra mounds were built for feng-shui purposes to give added protection against harmful influences from the "north."

This tomb is very well worth visiting. The ceramics on the north gate of the first courtyard are unusually fine; the walk between the two courtyards, over the three arched bridges and through the fields, is full of charm and gives one some idea of the exigencies of feng-shui. The ramparts are almost perfect; from the east there is an excellent view of Yü-ling and Mao-ling, from the west, of Ch'ang-ling. For those interested in drains, Ching-ling is unique in having a surface drainage system on the mound.

DRAINAGE.   This tomb has a very well-developed drainage system both in the funeral mound and in the courtyards. Almost the first thing you notice when approaching the tomb is a fine stone channel leading from the southwest corner of the first enclosure to the little river that skirts the tomb. Inside the first courtyard a large, square drain hole can be seen at each corner of the south wall. Similar drains through the east and west corners of the southern wall of the second courtyard are also easy to locate. Unfortunately, both courtyards are so filled with rubble that it is not possible to trace any inner gutter system. The arc-shaped area behind the stele tower was also so filled with debris that I was unable to see the pattern of the drains.

Up on the ramparts there is a return to the system of bringing rainwater through the *inner* wall of the walk to a shallow gutter skirting the mound (fig. 173). Diagonal stone ridges at intervals of 8 to 9 metres lead through the wall to stone spouts of the now familiar type. Most of these spouts are unbroken and still in place. Spaced evenly up each side of the mound are three large, square drain shafts, some of which still have their stone grids. Unfortunately, it is impossible to see where these come out. There appear to be no exit holes at ground level outside the circular wall; it may be that the buttress around this was added later and has covered them up. Alternatively, it is possible that there is an underground channel inside the walls that connects with the two exit points at the south end of the second courtyard.

Ching-ling is the only tomb with surface gutters on the grave mound (fig. 174). One wide stone gutter runs across the tumulus just to the north of the artificial mound, joining the circular gutter at each side, a little above the last of the three drain shafts. Two diagonal gutters, running southeast and southwest from the artificial mound, connect with the circular gutter just above the first pair of drain shafts. Running around the tumulus, rather like contour lines, are a series of brick ridges not to be seen in any of the other tombs. It would be interesting to know whether this system of surface gutters dates from the construction of the original tomb or was added in 1620 or even later.

T'ai-ch'ang, 1620

As has been seen, T'ai-ch'ang reigned for only one month. He was a son of the Emperor Wan-li and the concubine Lady Wang. Wan-li never liked T'ai-ch'ang and tried hard to disinherit him in favour of a son by a later, preferred concubine. The tradition that the eldest son must inherit was, however, too strong, and in 1601, when T'ai-ch'ang was nineteen, he was officially appointed Heir Apparent. From then until his ascension to the throne and sudden death he was surrounded by intrigue. Powerful factions at court opposed him, and this led to what were known as "the three cases." The first occured in 1615, when an unknown commoner with a club invaded T'ai-ch'ang's palace and tried to kill him. The second two cases are connected with his death. T'ai-ch'ang acceded to the throne on 28 August 1620 and immediately started to reorganize the government. This, of course, meant consolidating the position of his own supporters at the expense of rival factions. Nine days later he fell ill. The Chief Minister then brought in an official of the Court of State Ceremonials who claimed to have a wonder-working pill. After the emperor took it, his condition rapidly deteriorated, and on September 26 he died. Before his death, his favourite consort, "Western Li," was banished from court. These cases—"the man with the club," "the red pill," and "the expulsion of Western Li"—were used as examples by the Tung-lin reformers during the next reign in their attacks on the corruption at court.

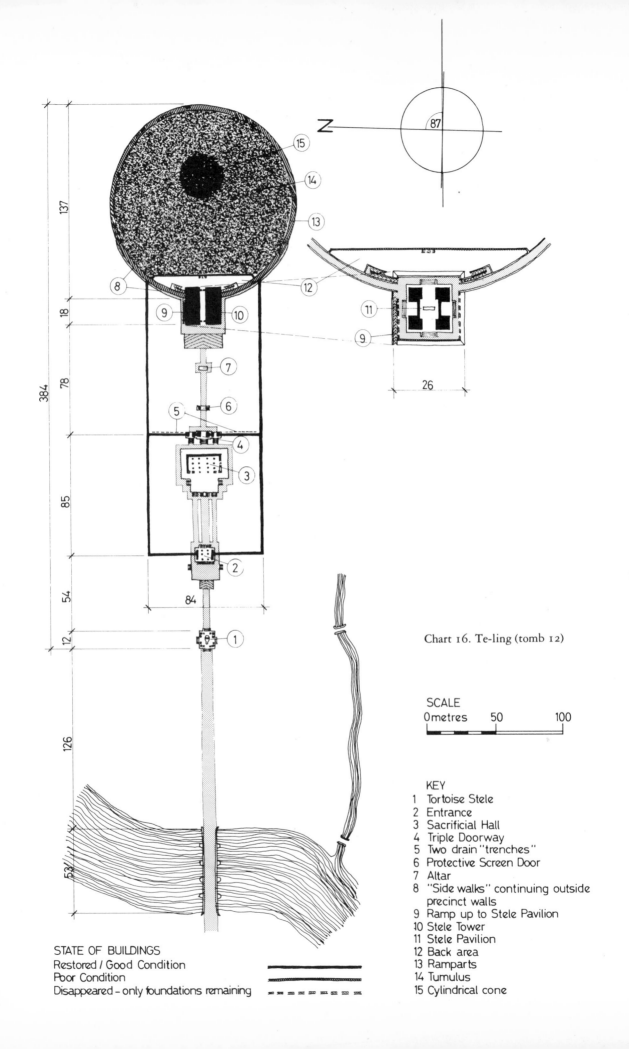

87

Z

137

18

384

78

85

54

12

126

53

84

26

233

Chart 16. Te-ling (tomb 12)

SCALE
0 metres   50   100

KEY
1 Tortoise Stele
2 Entrance
3 Sacrificial Hall
4 Triple Doorway
5 Two drain "trenches"
6 Protective Screen Door
7 Altar
8 "Side walks" continuing outside
   precinct walls
9 Ramp up to Stele Pavilion
10 Stele Tower
11 Stele Pavilion
12 Back area
13 Ramparts
14 Tumulus
15 Cylindrical cone

STATE OF BUILDINGS
Restored / Good Condition
Poor Condition
Disappeared – only foundations remaining

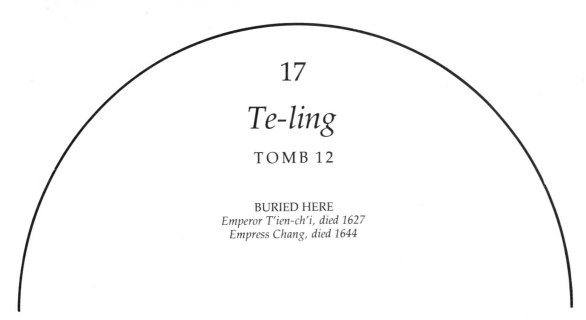

17

Te-ling

TOMB 12

BURIED HERE
Emperor T'ien-ch'i, died 1627
Empress Chang, died 1644

Te-ling lies in the southeastern corner of the Imperial cemetery. Driving to the east from Ch'ang-ling, you pass Yung-ling, and then as you turn the corner, Te-ling comes into sight on the far side of the valley (fig. 175). It is built rather high in the foothills and stands quite alone. The nearest village is down in the valley by the river.* Spanning the river is a fine five-arched bridge, and in places you can see the remains of the original embankments. The road rises gently until you come to the tortoise stele.

It is a very beautiful tomb. Architecturally it is similar to its predecessor, Ching-ling, but it lies on an east-west axis. Although Te-ling is one of the smaller tombs, its courtyards are relatively wide, and this gives it a feeling of spaciousness. Its perfect setting—high enough to afford a view across the valley below and far enough from the village and traffic to be completely quiet—makes it the ideal place for the escapist. The buildings are sufficiently ruined to be romantic but not so ruined as to be depressing.

The tortoise stele is in perfect condition (fig. 176). It stands on a platform with a staircase on each side but no surrounding wall; once again, the base is carved with waves, a fish, a crab, a shrimp, and a turtle (figs. 177–180).

The approach to the tomb is similar to that at Chao-ling. A wide ramp leads up from the paved way to a large terrace; this can also be reached by a small staircase on each side. From the centre of the terrace, more steps lead up the platform on which the triple gateway once stood (fig. 181). Only the side walls and stone column bases of the doorposts are left, but you can clearly see the stone pivots which held the doorjamb. The walls are complete with roof tiles in place; the colour has faded to a soft pink. The first courtyard was once paved but is very overgrown. There are usually a lot of birds here, Tits and Blue Magpies flitting between the large pines and thujas. The back and side walls of the Sacrificial Hall are still standing, although there is quite a large hole in

*This village is worth a visit; it has retained the original high square walls with a single entrance door that were common to most towns and villages before 1949.

the left side. The terrace is covered with rubble and grass, small thujas and wild flowers. Large pieces of marble balustrade lie on and around the five staircases (three in front and two at the side); once again the general effect of marble and flowers in the spring reminds one of Greece (figs. 182 and 183). There is no staircase on the "north" side of the terrace. The marble slab up the central staircase on the "south" side is unusual; here for once, the dragon, playing with the phoenix, has caught the pearl (fig. 184).

Three staircases lead up to the triple doorway into the second courtyard, which is on a considerably higher level than the first. This is a lovely courtyard. The stele tower and pavilion are impressive but not overpowering (colourplate 25). The doorways are in good condition and have obviously been repaired in recent years. The three roofs are more or less complete with tiles and wooden beams in place; the central door still has its ceramic flower decorations on the two doorposts, and one of the ceramic heads holding the top roof ridge is intact. Just inside the door, running along the sides of the "south" wall are two stone trenches ending in a drain hole that goes through the wall at each corner. The marble columns of the protective screen door are very lovely and the ch'i-lin, which is unusual, with an upturned bushy tail, seems to be looking up into the trees (fig. 185). The decorative pattern on the altar is somewhat clearer than that in other tombs; the altar objects are lying about on the ground.

The ramp up to the terrace on which the stele tower stands is overgrown, and the two narrow side walks are falling away. Here, as in Ching-ling, these continue beyond

175. View of tomb from ramparts of Yung-ling (tomb 8)

176. Tortoise stele and guardian's bicycle

177–80. Turtle, prawn, fish, and crab
on corners of tortoise stele base

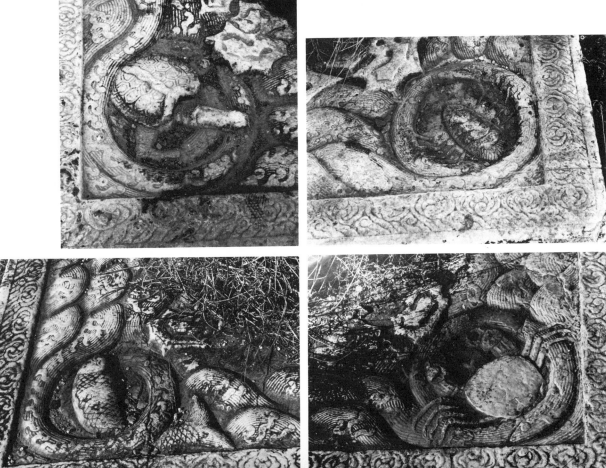

181. "East" side of tiered approach to entrance

the precinct walls but very quickly slope down to ground level. The tunnel through the tower has been opened but is full of stones and difficult to get through. The ramp up the "west" side is in a perilous state; trees are growing through the walls, a large part of which have fallen away.

The stele pavilion is exactly like that of Ching-ling, with side arches blocked. The little terrace around the pavilion is filled with rubble and broken tiles from the roof. Only on the "south" side are the crenellations in good condition; from here there is a lovely view over the courtyards and through the ruined gateway to the tortoise stele (colourplate 26). In the distance you can see the reservoir with hills on the far side. The stele is painted red and green. Ku Yen-wu wrote that the grave stele at Ch'ang-ling was painted red with gilt lettering, and E. Fonssagrives describes a grave stele in the Ch'ing dynasty Western Tombs as being painted red with multicoloured dragons.[1] From these accounts and from the traces of colour on earlier steles in the valley, it seems that it was common practice for them to be painted. The stele base is more ornate than in other tombs; one layer is decorated with the Eight Buddhist Emblems and the Eight Precious Things (colourplate 27). This is the only place where these appear in the mausoleum.[2]

The roof of the building is in a bad state; during the four years we were in Peking a large number of tiles fell down—assisted, we suspect, by eager foreign souvenir-hunters (fig. 186). In one place there is a hole in the wall of the pavilion, showing the internal wooden beams (fig. 187). As has been seen, these beams, like the steel girders

182. Side stairs up to terrace of sacrificial hall

183. LEFT: Fragment of marble balustrade lying on the ground

184. BOTTOM LEFT: Detail of marble slab showing dragon that has caught pearl

185. BELOW: Ch'i-lin with bushy tail on protective screen door

of today, formed the framework of the building. To prevent them from rotting, small ventilation holes were left in the outer wall and then covered with a decorative grill. (You can see the same arrangement in the walls of the Forbidden City.)

The funeral mound is similar to that in Chao-ling and Ching-ling—oval with a straight wall cutting off the "south" end to form a deep, arc-shaped back area (fig. 188). This area is in a very bad state. The two ramps leading down to it are crumbling, the ceramic screen has nearly gone, and more serious, most of the smooth facing of the grey stone wall has fallen away (fig. 189).

The walk around the ramparts is very beautiful. The ramparts are overgrown and large stretches of the crenellations missing, but something, perhaps the proximity of the hills, gives you a feeling of walking around the ramparts of a mediaeval border castle. First you look down on the benign home territory of orchards, and ground-nuts; then, at the back, between steep hills, two valleys wind out of sight and you half expect to see hostile horsemen riding down from the mountain passes. On the "east" side, the hills come very close to the walls, and atop one is some sort of stone ruin—perhaps a remainder of the wall that used to enclose the mausoleum. The mound is well planted with thujas and pines and has the same high, artificial cone 6 or 7 metres high with trees growing on it as Ching-ling.

Although it has no particular architectural interest, Te-ling is beautiful—a beautiful ruin in a beautiful setting. It is a place of utter peace and many birds. Here we have seen several Golden Eagles and, once, Chough. In winter the sun sets across the valley exactly opposite to the entrance of the tomb. As you walk out, the ruined walls form a dramatic foreground to the pink sky and hills beyond.

DRAINAGE. The drainage of Te-ling is similar to that of Chao-ling and Ching-ling, combining some features from each. There is a fine example of an exit drain with stone conduit leading down to a riverbed just around the "southeast" corner of the outer wall of the precinct. Inside the first courtyard there are no signs of drains, but a row of slabs running parallel to the "southern" wall lie differently from the rest of the paving and probably cover a gutter similar to that in the second courtyard.

Just inside the second courtyard an open stone trench runs parallel to the "south" wall on each side (fig. 190). It seems probable that this is the sort of construction which lies beneath the drainage holes circuiting the courtyard walls in Chao-ling. From these it can be seen how much attention was paid to drainage. The work is solid, stones carefully tailored to fit, and the trench is wide enough to cope with any sudden downpour.

There are small stone spouts leading water off both sides of the little terrace around the stele pavilion. The floor of the back area is so filled with rubble that it is impossible to see what sort of exit holes there have been.

The system of directing water off the ramparts is the same as in Chao-ling—diagonal ridges every 7 to 8 metres leading to a catchment stone which goes through the inner wall of the rampart walk and ends in a spout (figs. 191 and 192). The catchment stone

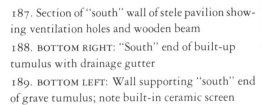

186. Ceramic head on end of roof beam

187. Section of "south" wall of stele pavilion showing ventilation holes and wooden beam

188. BOTTOM RIGHT: "South" end of built-up tumulus with drainage gutter

189. BOTTOM LEFT: Wall supporting "south" end of grave tumulus; note built-in ceramic screen

190. Open drainage trench in "southwest" corner of second courtyard

191. FAR ABOVE: Catchment basin and drain hole through inner rampart wall

192. ABOVE: Drain spout leading from drain hole in figure 191 to gutter around tumulus

is slightly more evolved than earlier ones, the lower edge being definitely raised to make a sort of cup. The carving above the spout on the inner wall is different from that in Chao-ling and Ching-ling. Here, the shallow, paved gutter, which in earlier tombs runs directly along the inner wall, is placed about a metre in from the wall. The drain shafts are not covered with grids but have carved covers with holes reminiscent of those in the courtyards at Chao-ling. The rise in ground level around the outside of the tomb makes it impossible to see if the water flowed straight down and out under the wall as in Chao-ling or was carried underground to the exit at the "southeast" corner.

T'ien-ch'i, 1620–27

The Emperor T'ien-ch'i was a sorry figure. He ascended the throne at the age of fifteen, having grown up in the depraved court of his grandfather, Wan-li. He was good with his hands but illiterate. Chinese sources put it more politely: "He did not have sufficient leisure to learn to write," but once at his workbench, "he forgot cold or heat, hunger or thirst" in his pursuit of carpentry.

The long reign of Wan-li had irrevocably weakened the power of the Imperial government. The sudden death of T'ien-ch'i's predecessor within a month of taking office made confusion worse confounded. The new emperor put his confidence in a close friend of his nurse, the eunuch Wei Chung-hsien (1568–1627). Wei, who had been butler to T'ien-ch'i's mother, was a gangster of the first order. He ran the court with an army of eunuchs; through a network of spies he dominated the provincial governments. Officials were appointed entirely on the basis of their loyalty to him and their ability to exact heavier taxes. Critics were imprisoned, tortured, and killed. In the early years of the reign, Wei's power was counterbalanced by that of a reform party, the Tung-lin, who had gained control of most of the central administration. The Tung-lin, who were campaigning for a moral revival based on pure Confucianism, attacked Wei and, in 1624, bravely presented a petition accusing him of twenty-four serious crimes, including murder and forcing the empress to have an abortion. Wei's response was swift. The Tung-lin leaders, "the six heroes," were tortured and beaten to death; some seven hundred Tung-lin supporters were purged, and the last three years of the reign can only be described as a rule of terror. Wei finally destroyed any moral claim to the throne the Ming dynasty might still have had. In the Chinese view of the world, the Son of Heaven must be righteous. When a dynasty ceased to produce good rulers, it must be changed. With the Emperor T'ien-ch'i's passive acceptance of Wei Chung-hsien the Ming dynasty was doomed.

T'ien-ch'i's official wife, the Empress Chang, is buried with him. She outlived him by nearly twenty years, but when Peking fell to the rebels in 1644, the last Ming emperor ordered all the palace women to commit suicide. The Empress Chang strangled herself and was later buried by the Ch'ing beside her husband in Te-ling. T'ien-ch'i had no sons and was succeeded by a younger brother.

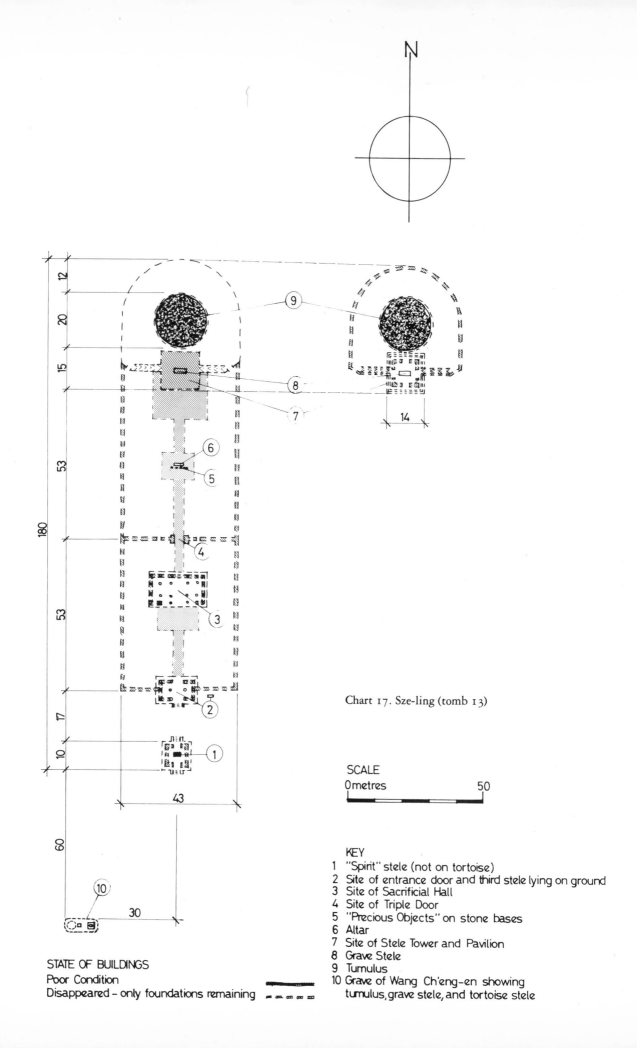

N

⑨

⑧

⑦

14

⑥
⑤

④

③

②

①

Chart 17. Sze-ling (tomb 13)

SCALE
0 metres — 50

⑩

30

STATE OF BUILDINGS
Poor Condition
Disappeared – only foundations remaining

KEY
1 "Spirit" stele (not on tortoise)
2 Site of entrance door and third stele lying on ground
3 Site of Sacrificial Hall
4 Site of Triple Door
5 "Precious Objects" on stone bases
6 Altar
7 Site of Stele Tower and Pavilion
8 Grave Stele
9 Tumulus
10 Grave of Wang Ch'eng-en showing tumulus, grave stele, and tortoise stele

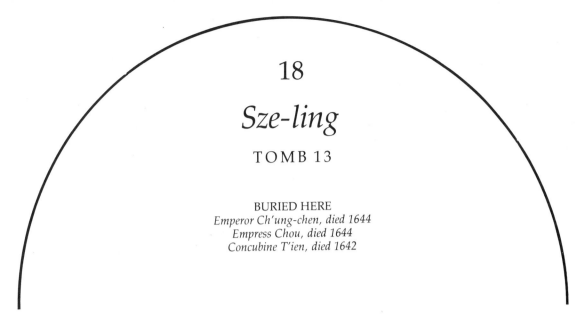

18

Sze-ling

TOMB 13

BURIED HERE
Emperor Ch'ung-chen, died 1644
Empress Chou, died 1644
Concubine T'ien, died 1642

Strictly speaking, the thirteenth tomb, Sze-ling, lies outside the Imperial part of the cemetery, and without explanation it might be difficult to recognise it as an Imperial tomb. It was originally the tomb of one of the emperor's concubines. In the dark days of the fall of Peking and the emperor's suicide, this tomb was opened again to bury both the emperor and his official wife. Later the first Ch'ing emperor ordered the tomb to be repaired and enlarged in a manner reasonably befitting an emperor's grave.

The last emperor, Ch'ung-chen, never had a chance. As we have seen, the last vestiges of respect for the Imperial court had been dissipated by the eunuch Wei. When severe famine struck the northwest in 1628, the central government was powerless to help. Local groups of bandits leapt into the vacuum and the situation was soon very similar to that in 1368, when the first Ming emperor captured the throne. The circle was complete. Once again a corrupt and inefficient dynasty was to be chased out and new rulers would try to reestablish the necessary harmony between Heaven and Earth.

Ironically, the intellectual life of the court seems to have had a revival during these years. Matteo Ricci's successors, Adam Schall Von Bell and John Shreck (Terrentius), had arrived in Peking in 1622 and early in the new reign established their position in a way that reminds one of the drama of Rider Haggard's *King Solomon's Mines.* In Chinese statecraft, astronomy was all-important; a mistaken calculation in the calendar, leading to the rites being performed on the wrong day, could provoke the wrath of Heaven. An eclipse of the sun, long regarded by the Chinese as an omen of great misfortune, was due on 21 June 1629. The Chinese Board of Astronomers predicted that it would start at 10:30 A.M. and last for two hours; Schall and Terrentius held that it would start at 11:30 A.M. and last for two minutes. The whole court assembled to see the result, and it must have been an unpleasant morning for the official astronomers when the Jesuits' prediction was proved to be completely accurate.

One of Ricci's converts, Paul Hsü, was vice-president of the Board of Rites. Three months after the eclipse, he instigated an Imperial edict entrusting the reform of the Imperial calendar to the Jesuits. This was followed by a wide-ranging plan to translate Western scientific works on mathematics, astronomy, and optics. Schall wrote a description of Galileo's telescope in Chinese, stressing its military value: "In the mountains or on the sea...one can see ahead of time incursions of brigands or pirates."[1]

In 1630 the court even resorted to hiring four hundred Portuguese mercenaries under the command of Gansalvo Texeira, hoping that their vastly superior power of firearms would be able to check the Manchus in the north, but this expedition never came to anything, since the merchants of Canton were sufficiently powerful to bribe northern officials to send the Portuguese back to Macao.

At court, the Jesuits made a minute step forward toward their missionary goal. It is reckoned that in the whole of China in 1640 there were several thousand Christians, among whom were fifty palace women, forty eunuchs, and another hundred court followers. In a way, the mere fact that the Jesuits were able to make any headway at all shows how weak the dynasty had become.

The final debacle was due not to the Manchus but to the Chinese rebel Li Tzu-ch'eng, the "Dashing General." He had risen to power in Shensi during a famine; later his troops spread northward, and by the end of 1643 he occupied the whole of western and northwestern China. When he finally swept down on Peking in April 1644, sacking the Ming Tombs en route, he was virtually unopposed.

The last days in the palace have been recorded in detail and are vividly described by Nigel Cameron in *Peking: A Tale of Three Cities.* On the last evening, it is said that the emperor called a council at which "all were silent and many wept." Then he seems to have been abandoned by all his followers except for one eunuch, Wang Ch'eng-en. Outside the palace, eunuch commanders were surrendering and the Imperial troops fled. In the Forbidden City followed a night of horror worthy of a Greek tragedy. The emperor, having helped his two small sons to escape in disguise, got drunk. Summoning the palace women, he told them that they must die. A leading concubine tried to flee but was cut down by the emperor himself. The empress fled and hanged herself in the Pavilion of Feminine Tranquillity. In a frenzy the emperor hacked the arm off one of his daughters and slaughtered another. Rushing through the palace, he found his wife hanging from a beam. He then killed all the other concubines. When the great bell rang at dawn, there was no one left to answer its summons. The emperor, accompanied by the loyal Wang Ch'eng-en, laid his dragon robe aside and, dressed in purple and yellow with one foot bare, walked through the palace and up Coal Hill. There he paused to write a last message on his robe:

> I, feeble and of small virtue, have offended against Heaven; the rebels have seized my capital because my ministers deceived me. Ashamed to face my ancestors, I die. Removing my Imperial cap and with my hair dishevelled about my face, I leave to the rebels the dismemberment of my body. Let them not harm my people!

Then, choosing a locust tree, he hanged himself. The ever-faithful Wang followed suit, and the Ming dynasty was over.[2]

The Sze-ling is hard to find. The map given by Bouillard in 1920 shows a small road branching off to the left by the Great Red Gate and leading to a "Little Red Gate"; from this "Little Red Gate" there was apparently a "spirit road" to the tomb. This "Little Red Gate," of which we were not able to find any trace, must have been the official entrance to the series of concubine cemeteries found in this part of the valley.

We found that the easiest way to go is to turn left at the village after the Dragon and Phoenix Gate; when you come to another village, take a rougher road to the right that skirts the hills. Following this road (which will eventually lead to the river), turn left toward the first village under the hills. It is best to leave the car and walk from there.

The village street ends at a large walled enclosure with a green and yellow tiled doorway. Behind this was one of the Imperial concubine cemeteries. You follow the path to the left, along the cemetery wall and then out into the countryside up a very pretty valley. When I returned to Peking in 1979, a new road was being made which, following the side of the hills, leads almost straight to the tomb.* After nearly half-an-hour's walk, you come to a stream on the far side of which is a wood with pines and thujas, and a village. The path on the near side of this stream turns left, southward, and leads out into open farmland. Slightly to the left, by a very small mound, is the marble grave stele of the Emperor Ch'ung-chen (colourplate 28). On a straight axis farther south, is a second stele. To the southwest is another grave, that of the faithful eunuch, Wang Ch'eng-en. It is well worth the walk. There is something very moving about these stone memorials. Here amidst the ploughed fields lie the last of the dynasty which in its early vigour produced the palatial Ch'ang-ling.

Chinese authors have left us a detailed account of how the emperor and his wife were buried. On 23 March 1644, the rebel leader Li Tzu-ch'eng gave orders that they

*Before this road was built, the path led farther to the north, past four of the old concubine cemeteries. These are worth exploring for those who have the interest and the time. Little is left, so that the walk takes on the nature of a treasure hunt. The first cemetery, which is square, is the largest and best preserved, with most of its outer walls intact. It has clearly been on two levels, and it is possible to trace the site of various buildings from the remaining column bases. Possibly this was one of the two "wells" in which concubines, forced to commit suicide when their emperor died, were buried until this barbaric custom was stopped by the Emperor Cheng-t'ung in 1464.

The second cemetery is smaller, rounded at the northern end with an outer wall, as in Yung-ling and Ting-ling. An altar lies to the south of a small funeral mound. Nearby is a stone stele base, carved with a dragon and phoenix on the long sides and a phoenix chasing a pearl on the short sides. There is also a stone incense burner, complete with top. According to Bouillard, this may have been the grave of Ch'eng-hua's concubine, Wan. The third cemetery, again oval at one end with a double wall, is less well defined and has been partially absorbed by a village. The stone altar can be seen between the houses at the edge of the village (fig. 193). Possibly this is where Ku Yen-wu mentions that four concubines and two sons of the Emperor Chia-ching were buried.

Finally, in the wood beyond the stream—that is to say, after the turning south to Sze-ling—there is another large, square enclosure, thickly planted with thujas. This has a large funeral mound and several smaller ones. Various stone ornaments lie among the trees, and some of the stone column bases can be seen. In general, this cemetery corresponds to the description given by Bouillard of Tao-ling, but he mentions a pond, of which there is now no trace. The Empress Ch'en, wife of Chia-ching, was buried in Tao-ling before being transferred to Yung-ling; three of the emperor's other concubines were buried there later. For a more detailed account of these cemeteries, see Bouillard and Vaudescal, pp. 97–100.

were to be buried in the tomb of the Imperial concubine, T'ien; he insisted that the coffins should reach the valley by April 3, that the burial should take place on April 4, and that his orders were to be obeyed! The poor official to whom the task was entrusted, Chao Yi-kuei, records: "It was not an auspicious moment. The treasury was empty. The officer in charge of the Rites did not know what to do." As we have learned, it was a difficult and lengthy matter to open the subterranean entrance to a grave. In this case, they were pressed for money and time. In the end, Chao and nine other loyal supporters raised 340,000 coins and then, as Chao tells us:

They hired workmen, in order to open and close the underground passage in the grave. It was 13 chang and five feet long, one chang wide, and three chang five feet deep. Under their control the men worked four days and nights, and it was not until the second hour after midnight of the fourth day of the month that they caught a glimpse of the stone door of the crypt. With levers, iron pins, and keys they forced open this stone door of the first compartment, and thus gained access to an incense temple with three divisions, in which some sacrificial implements were arranged. In the middle stood a stone incense table, with five pieces of five-coloured silk stuffs arranged on both sides; objects and dresses such as Palace Dames in attendance on the Emperor are wont to use during life, were placed in large red boxes and in the middle hung two perpetual lamps (lit. of ten thousand years). In the eastern compartment of this temple stood a sleeping-couch of stone, on which was spread a carpet of trimmed velvet, covered with a

193. Altar, probably from a concubine cemetery, preserved on the edge of a village on the way to Sze-ling

pile of blankets, mattresses, pillows stitched with dragons, and other things of this description. They now opened the stone door of the second apartment, and entered a large hall of nine compartments, which contained a stone couch of the same length as the preceding, one foot five inches high, and one chang broad, upon which the outer and the inner coffin of the Imperial Concubine rested.

On the fourth day of the month, the animated remains of the late Emperor arrived shortly after the second hour in the afternoon, and were put up in a sacrificial shed. A pig, a goat, paper documents of gold and silver and sacrificial articles were set out there, and the multitude, crowded together, poured forth lamentations, offering sacrifices and libations. At the burial, the petty official personally took the lead of the workmen, and entered the crypt; they shifted the Concubine T'ien to the right side of the couch, placed the Empress Chou on the left of it, and then respectfully gave the coffin of the late Emperor of the Ch'ung-chen period the place in the middle. The Concubine T'ien having been buried at a time in which no troubles prevailed, an outer coffin had been prepared for her, as well as an inner coffin. An officer with the title of Superintendent of Funerals and the petty official, seeing that their late Master had only an inner coffin and no outer coffin, removed the Concubine out of hers, and used it for him. An incense table with sacrificial implements was then placed in front of each coffin; the petty official with his own hands lighted the perpetual lamp; the two stone doors were shut, and the place immediately covered with earth. The ground was then level, no tumulus having been raised.[3]

Later another hundred workmen were hired to make a tumulus five feet high and surround it with a wall.

Soon after this, Li Tzu-ch'eng was defeated and driven from Peking by the Manchus. Li had been unwise enough to appropriate a beautiful concubine belonging to Wu San-kuei, the Chinese general then guarding the Great Wall. When Li refused to return the girl, Wu retaliated by opening the gates and inviting the Manchus in. Once in, the Manchus stayed, and their young emperor entered Peking in 1644 and became the first Manchu emperor of China.[4] From the beginning the Manchus were anxious to establish that there had not been an alien conquest, merely a change of dynasty in the classical Chinese way. Therefore, in the Chinese tradition, respect must be shown to the Imperial graves of the previous dynasty. The new ruler ordered a proper tomb enclosure to be made for the last emperor. As can be seen from the chart, the plan corresponds roughly to that of the other tombs. The most striking difference is, of course, the size. The tomb was only forty metres wide and one hundred and eighty metres long, one quarter the length of Yung-ling.

So little remains of Sze-ling that it may be worthwhile recapitulating earlier descriptions of the tomb. On the whole, the account given by Bouillard in 1920 corresponds to that of De Groot. The tomb lay on a true north-south axis. The "spirit" stele stood on a square pedestal, not a tortoise. It was housed in a small pavilion with a double roof, similar to the pavilion in the southeast corner of the first courtyard of Ch'ang-ling but much smaller and in very bad condition. The pedestal was carved with dragons painted green on a red background. The stele was made of black stone with white lettering and a crowning border of the usual intertwining "li," or hornless dragons. De Groot says that the stele carried no inscription other than the characters for "Erected by Imperial Command" on the crowning border. Bouillard, on the other hand, says that one side of the tablet carried an account of the misfortunes of the last Ming emperor written by a councillor on the orders of Shih-tsu, the first Ch'ing emperor to reign in Peking.

The precinct walls were painted the usual red and had yellow tile roofs, and the tomb was entered through a simple and unadorned double door. The Sacrificial Hall, a miniature edition of the halls found in the other tombs, stood on a low stone platform; there were no balustrades, ornamental terrace, or staircases. The triple doorway leading into the second courtyard lacked the customary tile decorations. There was no protective screen but a curious duplication of the "five precious objects." Just south of the altar, each object, carved in stone on a much larger scale than usual, stood on a separate square stone socle. On the altar itself the five objects were to be found again in normal size.

The stele tower, only fourteen metres wide and four metres high, had no central tunnel or ramp. Entrance to the grave enclosure was through two doors in the rampart wall to the east and west of the tower. The rampart was a simple brick wall half a metre wide—the width of a single brick—but was crenellated on top. The stele pavilion was reached by two brick footpaths up the side of the rampart wall. The pavilion was in the usual form, with a double roof and open on all sides but not elevated. The stele stood on a square stone base carved with dragons on the front, unicorns on the back, and lions at the two sides. In the centre of the grave enclosure was a small free-standing tumulus sixteen metres wide and four metres high, enclosed by a brick wall one metre high. A Chinese source mentions that the tumulus was whitewashed.[5] In this case, the whole arrangement inside the grave enclosure would correspond to some of the tumuli built in the Ch'ing Imperial cemeteries.

Today all the Ch'ing constructions, buildings and walls, have disappeared; only a miserable little grave hill, the marble steles, altar, and altar objects survive. It is possible to trace the contours of the old walls, many of whose stones are incorporated into the terrace walls of the surrounding fields.

The little mound and the grave stele are not without beauty and charm. A large pine tree grows on the east side of the funeral mound. The grave stele, just to the south, stands in the open on the remains of the stele tower, with small, upright marble slabs marking the four sides. The carving on the base of the stele is unexpected and lovely. Instead of the formal representation of mountains, clouds, and dragons, here are animals at play. It is true that they are not ordinary animals. On the east and west sides small cubs climb over a curiously frowning lion with a new hair style (figs. 194 and 195); on the south face a dragon is surrounded by four small dragons against a background of clouds; on the north side there is a dragon or perhaps a ch'i-lin, flanked by two scaled animals—one looking rather like the hsieh-chai in the spirit alley and the other, a jolly little piglike creature with horns and scales, running fast with its long snout in the air (figs. 196–198). In the lower corners are two more dragonlike figures. The top and sides of the stele are decorated with dragons. For once the inscription reads truthfully: "Tomb of the Emperor Chuang-lieh who inspires compassion."

To the south of the stele, and on a lower level, is the altar (fig. 199). This, too, is a Ch'ing innovation. Instead of the usual rectangular block, the altar is made of two large stone slabs, the lower carved with the legs of a heavy table and the upper, with upturned ends, like a scroll table. The surface of the altar is carved with flower patterns and has five round bases. There are no remnants of any of the habitual five precious objects corresponding to the size of these bases but round about are several stone "pineapples" (fig. 200). These have a diameter of 30 centimetres, 2 centimetres less than the round bases on the altar. Just south of the altar are the five separate socles mentioned by Bouillard, and on the ground nearby lie the remains of the large "precious objects" which once stood on these socles. It is perhaps possible that, in order to avoid duplication, the altar table was—unusually—decorated with the pineapples. Alternatively, they may simply be the heads of some earlier balustrades. The five large socles are square and flamboyantly decorated. The altar pieces are larger than in any other tomb—the candlestick base is one metre high, the flower vase

194. West panel of grave stele base

195. East panel of grave stele base

196. South panel of grave stele base

197, 198. Details of the north panel, showing ch'i-lin and "flying pig"

199. Altar and remains of five precious objects with socles

200. Stone "pineapple"

201. Stone vase

202. Lower half of stone incense burner

203. Stone candlestick

204. Panel from candlestick showing the legendary figure, White Monkey, giving a birthday present to his mother and wishing her a long life

205. Wang Ch'eng-en's grave

(fig. 201) nearly one and a half metres. The style of carving is quite different and the decorative subjects unusual; the incense burner (fig. 202) has a four-clawed dragon and one panel on the candlestick apparently shows the legendary figure, White Monkey, giving a birthday present to his mother and wishing her a long life[6] (figs. 203 and 204); another panel seems to depict a man reading. As far as I know, these are the only examples of carvings of human figures on a relief in the valley.

Walking southward, you cross the brick foundations of a gateway and then a slightly raised rectangle where the Sacrificial Hall has been. Beyond that again is the "spirit" stele. On the whole, this is as described by Bouillard, but it is made of marble and not black stone. Part of the stele is painted black and this may have led to misunderstanding. The inscription on the south face was, as Bouillard recounts, written under the Ch'ing and gives an account of the misfortunes of Ch'ung-chen; the north face is blank and the two sides carved with dragons. The base of the stele is similar to that of the grave stele—exuberantly carved, with north and south panels showing dragons and other fantastic animals, while on the east and west, lions play with their cubs. Lying on the ground between this stele and the base of the former Sacrificial Hall is a third stele, roughly the same size as the other two, with a long inscription from the Ch'ing era. This describes the burial of the last Ming emperor and was apparently erected in the sixteenth year of Shih-tsu on March 15 at noon (1660).

To the southwest of the spirit stele, lying on an east-west axis, is the tomb of the faithful Wang Ch'eng-en (fig. 205). His grave mound is small and unadorned. Just in front of it is a small marble stele surmounted by the usual intertwining dragons. The area between this and the tortoise stele, some 15 metres, is now in cultivation. The tortoise stele is large, rising much higher than the funeral mound; on it is engraved a memorial written by Emperor Shih-tsu in honour of Wang Ch'eng-en, who preferred to commit suicide rather than outlive his master. Nearby on the ground lies another stone slab with the characters "Wang Ch'eng-en" on it, and beside that a beautifully carved square block. One panel of this depicts a deer with a sprig of leaves in its mouth, prancing lightly over mountains while two clouds float overhead.

The atmosphere of these tombs is full of compassion. The emperor may lie modestly, but his only loyal friend rests within sight of the Imperial tomb. The carvings on the memorial slabs seem to have been done with the idea of creating happiness. The racing pig, the playful cubs, seem like a deliberate attempt to obliterate the horror of the black dawn on Coal Hill.

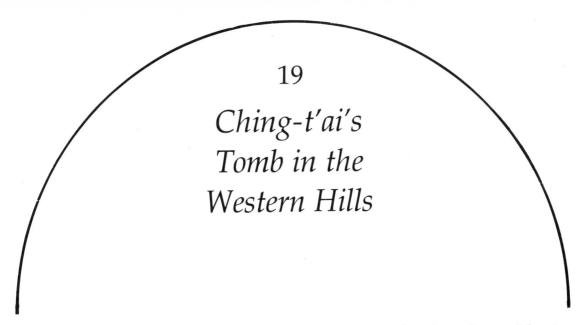

19

*Ching-t'ai's
Tomb in the
Western Hills*

Ching-t'ai's tomb is not hard to find, but it is seldom visited. Taking the road for the Western Hills and the Temple of the Sleeping Buddha, it is exactly four kilometres from the car park at the Summer Palace. On the left is the Jade Fountain Pagoda; on the right, a small village, Niang niang-fu, and a military camp. Behind the village on a rise in the ground is the stele pavilion of the disgraced emperor. The easiest way to get to it is to follow the course of a small stream or ditch running between the village and the camp.

Ching-t'ai's reign had been an interregnum between the two reigns of his elder half-brother, Cheng-t'ung. When the latter was taken prisoner by the Mongolians after the defeat of the Chinese army at Huai-lai in 1449, a group at court prevailed on Ching-t'ai to take the throne in the place of Cheng-t'ung's infant son. One purpose of this manoeuvre was undoubtedly to reduce the importance of the captive emperor as a bargaining counter. Ching-t'ai seems to have been a weak man, much in the hands of his advisors, but once enthroned he was reluctant to give up power. When after a year and a half the Mongolians released Cheng-t'ung, the new emperor hung on to the throne and kept his half-brother more or less a captive. In the eighth year of his reign he fell ill; a rival palace clique deposed him and reinstated Cheng-t'ung as emperor for the second time. There are stories that Ching-t'ai, who died soon afterward, was murdered by one of the palace eunuchs.[1]

As we have seen, Ching-t'ai was denied an Imperial tomb in the Ming Valley. Instead he was buried as a prince of the first class and given the posthumous title Li, "the rebellious one." Later, in 1475, the Emperor Ch'eng-hua re-established his half-uncle's Imperial status and declared that the rites should be performed at his grave in the Imperial manner. Not until the fall of the dynasty, however, was Ching-t'ai given full Imperial status with a temple name of Tai-tsung.

The stele pavilion of this tomb is unique. If you exclude the great stele at the entrance to the Ming mausoleum, it is the only surviving example of a traditional Ming

207. Ceiling of stele pavilion

206. OPPOSITE: Stele pavilion from the north

Imperial "spirit" stele with a roof (fig. 206). Small, square and in almost perfect condition, it answers completely to the description of some of the tortoise stele pavilions in the Ming Valley given by Ku Yen-wu in the 1650s. The pavilion has a double roof of yellow tiles; there is a painted frieze beneath each set of eaves. The walls have a base, about a metre high, of tailored bricks; above this they are made of the usual rough stonework covered with plaster and painted red. There are open arches on all four sides. The building stands on a stone terrace with three steps leading up to the north and south. Unlike the walls around the tortoise steles in the Ming Valley, this wall is not contiguous with the terrace; there is a walk about one and a half metres wide between the two. The marble stele rests not on a tortoise but on a rectangular base with six layers; these are decorated with cloud, lotus, and knot patterns, but the upper layer, where one would have expected to find dragons, is plain. The top of the stele is carved with five-clawed, Imperial hornless dragons, and further recognition is given to Imperial status by the characters *Ta Ming,* ("Great Ming"), in the usual chuan script. The inscription on one side reads: "kung jen k'ang ting Ching huang-ti chih ling," which could be translated as "The tomb of the Emperor Ching of reverent virtue and peace." This was the title given during the rehabilitation of 1475.*

*In the *Dictionary of Ming Biography* the order of these characters is slightly different: "kung-ting k'ang-jen Ching huang-ti" (see p. 297).

On the other side of the stele is an inscription dating from the era of the Ch'ing Emperor Ch'ien-lung, referring to the tomb as Ching-ti ling. Ching-ti was the name by which Ching-t'ai was usually known. There are no signs that this stele was ever painted.

The ceiling is not flat as in other buildings we have seen, but rises in layers of painted panels alternating with beams of decreasing length making an almost tent-shaped form (fig. 207). The whole is painted in brilliant colours, so bright that they must have been restored fairly recently. There are yellow flowers and golden dragons among the general patchwork of scarlet, blue, and green.

The tomb lies on an axis some ten degrees west of due north-south. About fifty metres north of the stele pavilion is the entrance to the tomb precinct (fig. 208). This is a modest building, built in the traditional shape but only three bays wide, the entrance being through the central bay. In design it is exactly like a miniature edition of the Gate of Heavenly Favours at Ch'ang-ling. The walls have been whitewashed and the roof is of grey unglazed tiles with flower patterns on the circular tiles at the edge of the eaves. The columns supporting the roof are painted red, and there is a decorative frieze around the building under the roof which includes a row of silver-coloured swastikas on a pale blue background, and Buddhist "eyes" (fig. 209). Although the structure is being used as a farm building, the walls, roof, and columns are all in good repair. The precinct wall, which joins the entrance on both sides, is also well preserved. It is red with a grey tile roof. To the east and west of the main entrance are two small side doors. There are some good examples of drain holes on both sides of the wall (fig. 210).

The grave enclosure is similar in shape to that shown by Bouillard in his map of the eastern concubine cemetery—that is to say, a rectangle with a rounded north end.[2] Today the area inside the wall is being cultivated as a vegetable garden. It is clear both from the lie of the land and the different levels of the side walls that the precinct was originally on two levels. There is no sign of the Sacrificial Hall, but where the land rises there are many yellow and green tile shards, and a fine white stone drain spout, similar to those in Yü-ling, lies among the crops. In the middle of the northern end of the enclosure is a small, uncultivated cone, obviously the remains of the tumulus above the grave. Unlike the Imperial tombs in the Ming Valley, this tumulus appears to have been in the same enclosure as the Sacrificial Hall; there are no signs of a stele tower or grave stele pavilion and no indications that there have ever been encircling ramparts. It was not possible to map the area accurately, and chart 19 is based on pace-measurements.

Although this tomb has been taken over for agricultural use, it retains an air of peace. In some ways it reminds you of an old-fashioned English walled vegetable garden. The entrance hall has lost its splendour, but the stele pavilion is a delight, particularly as it is unlike any other Ming Tomb building. There is a good view of the beautiful Jade Fountain Pagoda which stands on a hill to the south, rising clearly above the modern buildings of the nearby village (fig. 211). Juliet Bredon records that the

208. Entrance hall from the north

209. Decoration on roof eaves

210. Drain through courtyard wall

211. View southward toward the Jade Fountain Pagoda from the grave mound

penultimate Ch'ing emperor, Kuang Hsü, who was imprisoned by his aunt, the Empress Dowager Tz'u Hsi, "had a melancholy devotion to the memory of Ching-t'ai by reason of their common sorrows. From a window in the Summer Palace he would gaze for hours at the grave of his luckless predecessor and, lamenting its neglected state, he persuaded one of his eunuchs to plant new trees about it and to repair the pillars of the main hall of sacrifice, bidding him at the same time to take care that the Old Buddha should not know by whose orders these things were done, lest she become angry."[3]

Whether the captive emperor could really see the tomb from the Summer Palace is doubtful, since the hills of the Jade Fountain seem to be in the way. Nevertheless, some attention must have been paid to the grave during the late Ch'ing dynasty or it could hardly have survived until today.

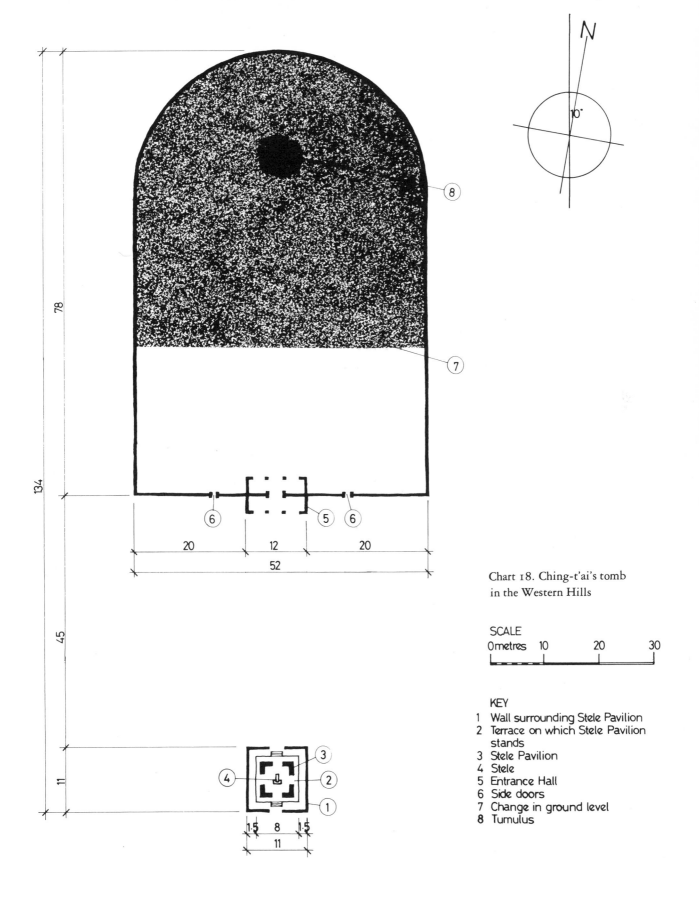

N

10°

78

134

45

11

8

6

5

6

20

12

20

52

3

4

2

1

1·5

8

1·5

11

Chart 18. Ching-t'ai's tomb
in the Western Hills

SCALE

0metres   10   20   30

KEY

1 Wall surrounding Stele Pavilion
2 Terrace on which Stele Pavilion
   stands
3 Stele Pavilion
4 Stele
5 Entrance Hall
6 Side doors
7 Change in ground level
8 Tumulus

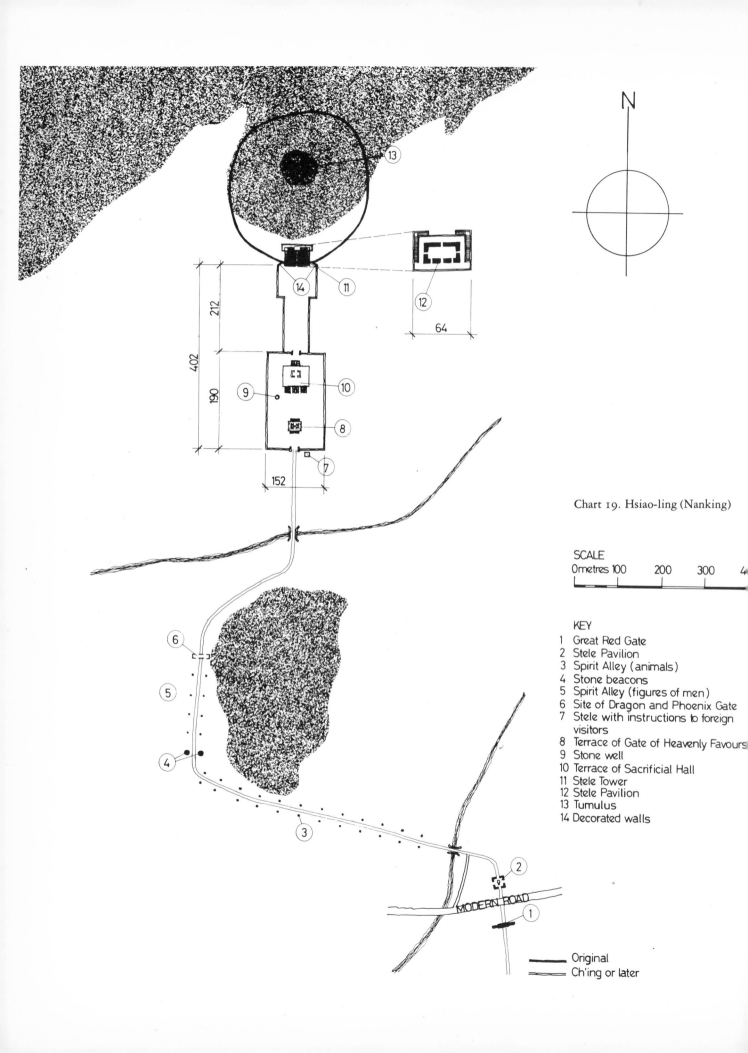

N

212

402

190

152

64

Chart 19. Hsiao-ling (Nanking)

SCALE
0 metres 100   200   300   4

KEY
1 Great Red Gate
2 Stele Pavilion
3 Spirit Alley (animals)
4 Stone beacons
5 Spirit Alley (figures of men)
6 Site of Dragon and Phoenix Gate
7 Stele with instructions to foreign
   visitors
8 Terrace of Gate of Heavenly Favours
9 Stone well
10 Terrace of Sacrificial Hall
11 Stele Tower
12 Stele Pavilion
13 Tumulus
14 Decorated walls

MODERN ROAD

——— Original
=== Ch'ing or later

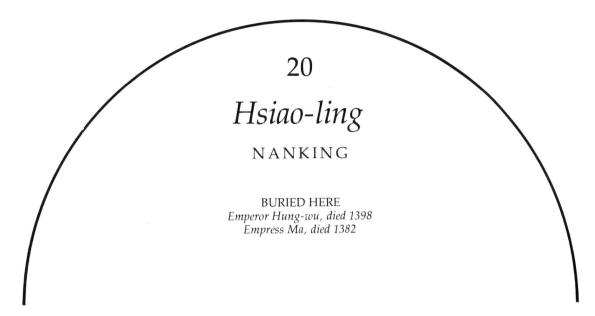

20

Hsiao-ling

NANKING

BURIED HERE
Emperor Hung-wu, died 1398
Empress Ma, died 1382

Hsiao-ling is the tomb of the founder of the Ming dynasty, Chu Yüan-cheng, or as he is more commonly known, Hung-wu. With him is buried his official wife, the Empress Ma. Hung-wu was prolific: in all he had thirty-six sons and sixteen daughters, and when he died, thirty-eight of his forty concubines were forced to commit suicide.

Today the tomb is a popular park and tourist attraction.[1] It lies at the foot of the Eastern Hills on the outskirts of Nanking, an area considered auspicious since earliest times. The principal mountain, the "Purple Golden Mountain" or the "Shining Spirit Mountain" has had many names and been the theme of many poems.* Sun Ch'üan, founder of the Wu dynasty (one of the Three Kingdoms) in the third century A.D., is said to have been buried under a small hill just to the south of Hung-wu's grave. In more recent times, the mausoleum of the founder of the Chinese Republic in 1911, Doctor Sun Yat-sen, was built in the same area.

The tomb is of great interest in the history of architecture as it offers proof of the tenacity of the classical Chinese tradition. As we have seen, Hung-wu was the son of an illiterate peasant. After his father's death, poverty forced him to enter a Buddhist monastery, and there he received some education; but the tenor of his life was far from scholarly and he rose to power as a rebel leader through fighting. The dynasty he ousted was an alien one that had maintained its own funeral customes for the Imperial family. Under these conditions it is remarkable that Hung-wu was able to design a mausoleum which fits so clearly into the traditional pattern of an Imperial tomb.

All the elements of the tomb are taken from the T'ang, but with its practical sense for the lie of the land, the plan of the tomb is less formal than that of either Hung-wu's

---

*According to De Groot, there is a tradition that in A.D. 307 a bell bearing an inscription from the Ch'in dynasty (third century B.C.) fell from the sky into a brook on the mountain, which was thereafter known as "Bell Mountain." The name "Purple Golden" was given by the Chin Emperor Yüan (A.D. 317–323) because of the way the mountain changes colour on bright days. He records that in 1531 the Ming Emperor Chia-ching renamed it "Shining Spirit Mountain." Dr. Feng at the Kiangsu Provincial Museum, however, says that this name was given by Yung-lo in honour of his father Hung-wu. De Groot, *The Religious System of China*, 3:1257.

predecessors or successors. Determined to be buried in a particular place, he adapted the necessary traditions to the geography of the area. The Great Red Gate and the tortoise stele lie on a near north-south axis; the spirit road makes a violent swing—west, north, and east—round a hill, then turns north again toward the tomb buildings. These lie on a north-south axis but are by no means in line with the Great Red Gate and stele pavilion. The hill which causes this asymmetry is said to be where Sun Ch'üan lies buried. Hung-wu's advisors asked for permission to remove it but the emperor refused, saying that Sun Ch'üan had been a hero and a brave man and, if left undisturbed, would act as a powerful guardian to the mausoleum.

The whole tomb area was enclosed by a wall about twenty kilometres long, including the site of both the Sun Yat-sen mausoleum and the Ling Ku Ssu park. The stele ordering officials and others to dismount, which in the Ming Valley stood by the Great Red Gate, was at Hsiao-ling wei, the guardian camp of the tomb some two kilometres to the southeast of the enclosure. Recently this stele had to be moved to make way for a new road, but it is still intact and it is planned to re-erect it shortly. Just beside it stand two other steles relating to the tomb: one from 1641 forbids the quarrying of stone, hewing of wood, or hunting in the tomb area; the other, carved by order of the Emperor Yung-lo, bears the name of the Shining Spirit Mountain (Shen lieh shan) in honour of his father.

When visiting the tomb, you will probably be driven to the beginning of the Spirit Road. To see the Great Red Gate and stele pavilion, you must cross the road by which you came and take a small path through a wood and up a hill to the stele pavilion. Beyond this is a gully through which runs a road; on the hill on the far side of this is the Great Red Gate.

The Great Red Gate is similar to the one in the Ming Valley but smaller. It is in good condition, made of soft pink-coloured brick on a base of white stone decorated at the corners with lotus and knot patterns. The roof, which was once made of yellow tiles, has completely disappeared, and small plants and trees grow on the flat brick surface.

The stele pavilion, surrounded by trees, is a beautiful place; now roofless with high grey walls, it is somehow more impressive than its successor in the Ming Valley (colourplate 29). Light streams down on the stele from the open roof and through the four arches. The tortoise and stele are entirely classical; the centre of the stele top is dominated by a large pearl surrounded by a pattern reminiscent of the Buddhist wheel of life (figs. 212 and 213). On either side are two upright dragons. The south face of the stele carries an inscription from the eleventh year of the Yung-lo era, 1413, commemorating the feats of Hung-wu. Yung-lo, anxious to do honour to his father, first chose an even larger stone for the stele in Yang Shan, some hills about thirty kilometres outside Nanking. Soon, however, it was discovered that this stone was too heavy to be moved. It is apparently possible to see this half-finished stele with inscription in situ. Outside the southern arch of the pavilion are the remnants of a marble slab, similar to those lining the central staircases to the sacrificial halls in the Ming Valley. This is carved with two lions playing with a ball, very like the two lions on the

212. ABOVE: North face of tortoise stele top

213. BELOW: West side of tortoise stele top

214. RIGHT: Patterned stone slab lying on the ground to the south of tortoise stele

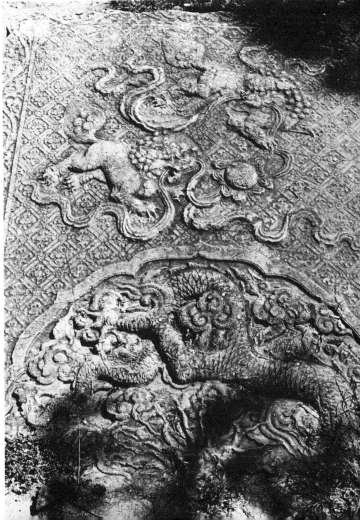

outer panels of the base of the P'ai-lou. Beneath them, in a circular frame, is a dragon twisting around a central flower or plant (fig. 214). Just south of this slab, which lies on the ground, is a short balustrade the posts of which are carved with five-clawed dragons and phoenix. In the grass, a little to the southeast, is a complete corner rainwater spout in the form of a gargoyle. This is exactly the same sort of gargoyle as that found in Ch'ang-ling.

Retracing your steps through the wood and down the hill, you come to the start of the Spirit Road. This is only 3 metres wide—very much narrower than that in the Ming Valley (10 metres) or, to take another example, than that of the T'ang Emperor Kao-tsu. Between the animals, at intervals, are small cloud-patterned posts. These are later additions, probably put up to keep traffic from passing between the figures. Today there is a small road on either side of the alley which is flanked by trees.

The first part of the alley consists of twenty-four animals in pairs, first sitting and then standing. The animals are the same as in the Ming Valley: lions, hsieh-chai, camels, elephants, ch'i-lin, and horses. These figures, like most of the original buildings in the tomb, are made from a hard stone quarried in the Yang Shan known as "Nanking red marble." It has a soft pinky-red colour and gives the figures a somewhat more vital air than their Peking counterparts. The style of carving is distinctive; the animals tend to be smaller and more compact while the faces and heads are broader and heavier, showing, perhaps, traces of Mongol influence (figs. 215–220). The lions are more like those seen in Ta-t'ung and the northeast than in Peking. Both the hsieh-chai and the ch'i-lin differ considerably from the later versions; the elephants are particularly elegant, with their delicately carved ears veined like a flower or leaf.

The alley is never quite straight; it winds up toward the camels and then down again to the horses. Here there is a gap and then, with a ninety-degree swing to the north, the alley begins again with two stone beacons (fig. 221). According to Dr. Feng, the placing of these beacons halfway down the alley is unique (see p. 21). Seen here, they reinforce the theory that part of their purpose was to show the way. Something was necessary to link the two halves of the alley, and the beacons, towering above the stone figures, provided the solution. They are decorated with stylized cloud patterns from top to bottom and there is no dragon in the rounded head (fig. 222).

The second half of the alley consists of eight figures, four warriors and four civilians, in pairs and facing each other. The costume of the warriors differs in several respects from that worn by the figures in the Ming Valley (colourplate 30). All four warriors are alike, both hands holding a baton with a knob. A sword hangs from the belt; its handle is ornate but it lacks the elaborate fittings of the Ming Valley swords. The sleeves are a different shape. Instead of the rather artificial "wing" on the elbow, these hang down in folds, just below the elbow, revealing an armour-clad forearm. There are animal faces on the epaulettes, but it is not possible to see if these are repeated in front, as the belt clasp is covered by the arms and baton. The lower part of the upper garment at the back is embroidered with flower patterns. The most striking difference is the helmet (fig. 223). Obviously intended to represent metal, it is round with a long plume at the

215. Pair of seated lions on the Spirit Road

216. Standing hsieh-chai

217. Standing camel

218. Sitting elephant

219. Standing ch'i-lin

220. Pair of sitting horses

221. Beacons at start of second half of the Spirit Road

222. Details of pattern on beacon shaft

223. Back of warrior's helmet   224. Back view of warrior, with mantle

back; a protective covering hangs down from under the helmet to cover the shoulders. Beneath this, crossed over at the back, is an embroidered mantle (fig. 224). These figures look much more military and less ceremonial than their later counterparts. Dr. Feng referred to them as "palace warriors," presumably members of the "Embroidered-uniform Guard" which came into existence in the 1360s and was formally organized in 1382.[2]

The civilian figures bear a much closer resemblance to their successors in the Ming Valley (colourplate 31). The robe is very similar; it has the same flowing sleeves, but here there is a sort of cummerbund in front. The back of the robe has the same panel with six cranes (fig. 225). The framework of the panel is, however, different, and at the top looks as if it is threaded with a narrow leather thong. The figures stand in the same position with hands clasping a "hu," and their hats are similar to those worn by the statues representing the Presidents of the Six Boards in the fifteenth century. They have no plaque or decoration round the neck and the five ribbons with beads hang from a belt at the back rather than at the side.

The difference in style between these figures and those in the Ming Valley can be explained by the decrees of 1391 governing court dress. When the alley at Hsiao-ling was laid out, these new rules, insisting on a complete return to the T'ang and Sung regulations, had not been made.* What we are seeing, therefore, is what high officials—military and civilian—wore at court during most of the reign of Hung-wu.

The alley ended with a Dragon and Phoenix Gate. Of this nothing remains but the marble foundations (fig. 226). Beyond this, the road swings again, first east and then northward over a bridge and up to the main entrance to the tomb. The tomb buildings were more or less completely destroyed during the recapture of Nanking from the T'ai-ping rebels in 1864. The Ch'ing Imperial forces had their camp in the guardian village outside the precinct wall; as a result, the battle raged over the whole tomb area. Roughly speaking, what is left are the terraces on which the Gate of Heavenly Favours and the Sacrificial Hall once stood, the stele tower and pavilion and parts of the side wall joining the tower to the precinct wall. The precinct walls are all restorations, and the two small buildings on the terraces are Ch'ing constructions.

To the right of a plain unadorned doorway is a stone tablet from 1900 with requests in various European languages that visitors respect the tomb. The wall that would have divided the first two courtyards has gone. On the terrace of the original Gate of Heavenly Favours is a modest building with red walls and grey tile roof and a single door in the north and south walls. On the south side, three staircases, with the usual central marble slab carved with dragons, lead up to the terrace. The inside of the hall has obviously been changed rather recently; it does not correspond to Nagel's 1968 description. Earlier there were five steles here; the central one, on a tortoise, was erected by order of the Ch'ing Emperor K'ang-hsi and carried the inscription: "His

---

*Hung-wu's wife, the Empress Ma, was buried in Hsiao-ling in 1382, so the grave chamber and tumulus must have been finished then. De Groot quotes the Official Annals' statement that the temple buildings were finished in 1383 (3:1265).

225. LEFT: Back of robe, with cranes, President of one of the Six Boards

226. ABOVE: Remains of Dragon and Phoenix Gate with pair of stone civilian figures

227. BELOW: Base of stele in Ch'ing hall on site of Gate of Heavenly Favours

228. RIGHT: Ch'ing pavilion on site of sacrificial hall with original Ming triple marble slab

229. FAR BELOW: Stele tower and pavilion from the south

reign was as glorious as that of the T'ang and the Sung." Behind this were two smaller steles, also from the K'ang-hsi era, one dated 1684 when he offered sacrifices at Hsiao-ling, and the other from 1699 commemorating a visit to Nanking after serious floods. The remaining two steles with bases were so damaged as to be illegible.[3] Today the central stele has been incorporated into a wall which runs east-west, nearly dividing the hall in two. The tortoise protrudes rather curiously from the wall on both sides. On the ground in front of the wall are four stele bases carved with dragons playing with a pearl (fig. 227); two other steles lie on the ground at the back.

The terrace on which the Sacrificial Hall stood is larger and is approached by a triple staircase of three flights as in Ch'ang-ling (fig. 228). According to Dr. Feng, the Sacrificial Hall at Ch'ang-ling was an exact copy on a larger scale of the one in Hsiao-ling. Certainly the marble slab, in three sections up the central stairway, shows the same decoration: horses flying over mountains on the lowest level, then two dragons with a pearl and mountains, and finally dragons disporting among clouds. The small Ch'ing hall is without interest except for the roof. The ch'i-wen holding the upper ridge are in the old southern style, with swinging fish tails. Under the four corner eaves are highly painted wooden lion figures alternately with a ball or cub. On the north side of the terrace there is a single staircase with a marble slab similar to that on the south. To the southwest of the terrace is an old stone well.

The whole of this courtyard with the two terraces is laid out as a park, well planted and supplied with stone benches. Through the modern door at the north end you come to a second courtyard with a wide paved way leading straight to the stele tower and pavilion (fig. 229). These buildings are quite different from those at Ch'ang-ling. They are much larger and rectangular, not square. For comparison, the Hsiao-ling tower is 64 metres by 36 metres at ground level, tapering to 60 metres by 34 metres at the top, and 15 metres high. The pavilion is 40 metres by 20 metres and 7.5 metres high. The Ch'ang-ling tower is only 34 metres square at ground level, tapering to 31 metres and 13 metres high, with a pavilion 18 metres square. The stele tower is made of large blocks of pink stone. Through the centre is a fine vaulted passage with steps leading up to a paved area between the tower and the tumulus. The walls of this passage are original but the steps are new and replace a ramp. The arched doorways at each end show the same double-arch construction as the tunnels through the stele towers in the Ming Valley. Two small staircases at each end of the back area lead to the corners of the tower; a ramp then leads up the east and west walls to the terrace on which the pavilion stands. The pavilion, built of the same pinky-red brick as the Great Red Gate, is, as we have seen, rectangular. It has three arched doorways on the southern side; one each on the north, west, and east sides. The proportions of the building are pleasing, but it seems very large if its only purpose was to house a grave stele. The stele and roof seem to have been victims of the general destruction of battle, and I have not been able to find any description of the pavilion before 1864.

The grave tumulus is oval, well planted, and rising steeply toward the north; from its highest point there is an excellent view over Nanking and the surrounding country-

230. Original Ming decorations on wall adjoining southeast corner of stele tower

side. From the southwest and southeast corners of the stele tower, two short diagonal walls lead outward to join the modern precinct walls. These are original and have some very beautiful decorations in the corners and above the stone base, which are similar to the ceramic decorations on the triple doors in the Ming Valley except that here they are made of polished red stone (fig. 230). This form of decoration was apparently a speciality of Nanking.

Hsiao-ling as a whole is a good deal simpler than Ch'ang-ling. The approach to the mausoleum in the Ming Valley and Ch'ang-ling itself are imbued with a feeling of ceremony. Hsiao-ling, or at least the first and original half of it, strikes one as more personal. This may be due to the fact that it served only one emperor and never had time to grow into an institution. Here, for example, no later emperor came to add a P'ai-lou. Whether or not there were ever a protective screen door and a stone altar in Hsiao-ling is not clear. The paved way between the Sacrificial Hall and the stele tower is certainly long enough to have allowed for both, and it may well be that they were swept away in 1864.

It is perhaps of interest that the first reference by a Westerner to an Imperial Ming tomb is to Hsiao-ling. In a letter dated 18 October 1607, Matteo Ricci mentions a plot to kill some Nanking officials en route to the ceremonies of the winter solstice to be held at the tomb of Hung-wu.[4]

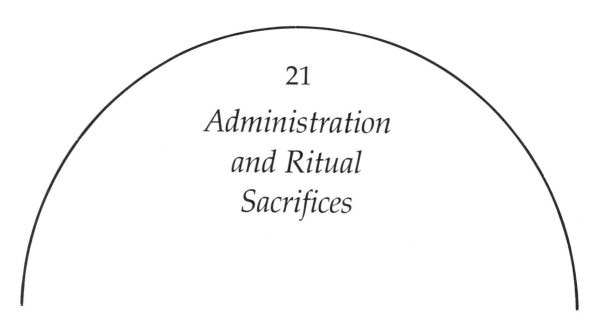

21

Administration and Ritual Sacrifices

The administration of the tombs was complicated. As we have seen, it was believed that the prosperity of the dynasty depended on keeping the ancestral spirits happy, but an essential part of this philosophy was that these spirits could not flourish without the body to which they had belonged. This imposed a double task on the adminisration: it must protect the grave from physical depredations; it must also satisfy the spirits with the rites and sacrifices they expected.[1]

The former task was entrusted to the military. A large military headquarters was set up in the village of Ch'ang-p'ing, to the southeast of the cemetery. By the middle of the sixteenth century it was reckoned that the ramparts of Ch'ang-p'ing were sixteen kilometres long and that the general there commanded some seven thousand troops. It was his duty to provide a garrison for each tomb, to guard the Imperial lands surrounding the cemetery from trespassers, and finally to protect the valley as a whole from marauders. Ku Yen-wu records: "When these troops had nothing else to do, they were trained in the drill ground of the chief city of the department, but whenever there was something alarming abroad, they hastened to all the passes and exits of the valley, to obstruct and defend them."[2]

Whereas the military ensured the physical safety of the tombs, their civil administration fell under the Imperial Ministry of Works and the Board of Rites. Here red tape abounded, and the rank and number of officials responsible for each aspect of administration were specified in detail by Imperial edicts. The inspectorate for each tomb stood just outside the entrance gate of the tomb on the east; the main office for the whole necropolis was next to Ch'ang-ling. It was the responsibility of the civil administrators to see that the tombs were kept in good repair, to cultivate the orchard attached to each tomb and protect the forest, and to provide all the necessary appurtenances to the ritual sacrifices.

This was no mean task. An Imperial edict of 1664 specified that to the tomb of the first Ch'ing emperor alone should be appointed:

24 chair-bearers	2 millers
1 messenger	2 makers of vermicelli
2 farm managers	2 producers of spices
2 chief gardeners	2 wine-distillers
2 Mongolian milkers	4 falconers
12 butchers	40 grass-cutters
4 bird-snarers	17 sweepers
4 fruit gardeners	15 cowherds and goatherds
2 oil-producers	120 general workers
2 sugar-makers	

All this labour was provided by families who were moved to the necropolis and appointed its hereditary guardians.* A small walled village, bearing the same name as the tomb to which it was attached, was built for these "guardian families." (These names have persisted, and in the Ming Valley the village nearest to each tomb bears the name of that tomb.) The life of the guardians was hard. They were not allowed to gather fuel or hunt within the Imperial grounds. Foresters were only paid for a tree they had planted after three years, when it was certain that the tree would survive. Worst of all, neither they nor any member of their families might be buried near their homes. When they died, their bodies were carried out of the cemetery through a special side-door and buried outside the boundaries of the necropolis.

The timing of the sacrifices was fixed by Imperial edict. Generally speaking, they were held on the anniversary of the birth and death of each emperor and empress buried in the cemetery, at the end of the year, and on three festival days consecrated to the dead. Originally these were: (1) Ch'ing-ming, the Festival of Pure Brightness, April 4; (2) July 15, the Lantern Festival, when children carried lanterns through the streets to guide wandering spirits home; (3) the winter solstice. Later, in 1536, the Emperor Chia-ching abolished the second, which fell in the middle of the rainy season, and substituted October 23, the "Day of Frost's Descent," or the "time of sending winter clothes to the ancestors." This was the day when people throughout the empire made paper models of clothes and burnt them before the graves of their ancestors so that the latter could keep warm during the winter.[3] In addition to these, minor rites were held at the full and new moon of each month. These minor ceremonies were carried out by the local staff, but for the major festivals, senior court officials led by a prince of the first rank or an Imperial son-in-law traveled from Peking. In 1538, for example, Emperor Chia-ching performed the rites himself three times. As might be expected, these frequent delegations imposed a great burden on

*The practice of forcibly moving families to Imperial cemeteries dates back at least as far as the Han dynasty. It is recorded that 10,000 families were resettled on the graves of the first two Han emperors and 5,000 on those of the succeeding five. The eighth Han emperor is said to have protested against these mass movements, arguing that they would only breed dissatisfaction among the people. It seems clear, however, that the custom persisted throughout the following dynasties as the only effective method of providing adequate manpower for the tombs (see De Groot, 2: 428).

the local population, who were obliged to feed them; and in the annals of the time there are numerous requests for exemptions from taxes and subsidies for the poor inhabitants of the neighbourhood.

The sacrifices were performed between three and five o'clock in the morning. The visitors from Peking would change into their ceremonial robes in the building just inside the Great Red Gate. A little farther on, by the Dragon and Phoenix Gate, temporary barracks of rushes were put up for the porters who had accompanied the delegation. On arrival at the tomb, there was another chance to rest in one of the side buildings inside the first courtyard. Here it should be noted that in addition to the principal buildings described earlier, there were originally various smaller buildings in the outer courtyards that served entirely practical purposes. These buildings, similar to those which house the museum in Ting-ling, ran along the side walls of the court-yards, facing east and west. Their size was established by law, and those for Imperial graves were allowed "five compartments." In the Ch'ing tombs, it seems that a typical arrangement would have been for the kitchen to have been outside the main gate; in the first courtyard there would have been a pair of waiting rooms and in the second courtyard, a pair of storerooms for utensils used in the rites. Ku Yen-wu, however, states quite clearly that in Ch'ang-ling, for example, the kitchen was on the east side of the first courtyard. The kitchen was said to have consisted of a "main apartment with five divisions, two side rows with three divisions each, and one pavilion (for butchering) containing a pit for the blood."[4] By the end of the last century all such buildings had disappeared from the Ming Tombs, although they were still to be found in places of Imperial worship by the Ch'ing dynasty.

The rites were performed in the Sacrificial Hall. On the far side of the hall, opposite the central doorway, stood the shrine. According to Ku Yen-wu, the four columns surrounding the shrine were decorated with golden lotus leaves while all the other columns were pure red.[5] The shrine stood on a small dais approached by steps and surrounded by a balustrade; all these were made of wood and painted red. Above the shrine hung a wooden canopy and under this was the tablet bearing the name of the deceased emperor. This tablet was the heart of the temple. For the purposes of the sacrificial rites it embodied the spirit of the emperor. On the shrine, in wood or cloisonné, were the "five precious objects" that we have seen copied in stone on the altar in the courtyard: an incense burner flanked by two flower vases filled with paper flowers and two candlesticks. The rest of the hall was usually bare, but outside on the terrace were two incense burners, two cranes symbolizing longevity, and two deer— all in bronze. The latter were sometimes replaced by stone sundials, but the incense burners were obligatory.

For a description of the sacrificial ceremony itself we are indebted to Colonel Fonssagrives, who was stationed with the French troops of occupation in the Western Tombs of the Ch'ing dynasty after the Boxer Rising. In 1901 he had the rare chance for a European of being present at rites held on the Festival of Pure Brightness (April 4). Since the Ch'ing dynasty proved itself extremely conservative in all matters relating to the treatment of the dead, we can reasonably assume that the ceremonies Fonssagrives saw were closely related to those carried out during the Ming dynasty. Manchu influence can be seen in some of the ritual foods he mentions, but it is interesting to note that the bowls used in the ceremonies were archaic copies of early Chinese bronze vessels used for sacrificial rites.

The preparation of the sacrifices followed strict rules. For major occasions, an ox and two sheep were slaughtered. Bishop Favier mentions that animals selected for sacrifice were first tested by having wine poured into their ears. If the animals shook their heads, it showed that they were healthy and suitable.[6] After being butchered, the animals were cleaned, had their hair removed without cutting the skin, and were then boiled whole. (With typical Chinese common sense, this last condition was waived if there was no available pot large enough for a whole ox.) When the meat was cooked, it was carried into the Sacrificial Hall and placed on a special serving table in front of the shrine, the ox in the middle with two platters of mutton on either side. This table was already laden with the following dishes prepared by the responsible officials:

a bowl of soup
a bowl of rice
a bowl of sour milk
a bowl of mutton cut into long thin ribbons
a bowl of pheasant prepared in the same way
a roast pheasant
a dish of dried fish from an island near Ta-lien (Port Arthur)
a dish of saffron
a dish of mushrooms
one dish each of pickling brine, pickled cabbage, cucumbers, celeriac, and
    vegetable marrow
a carp
two legs of beef
two legs of mutton.

Other officials placed special drinks on a small side table inlaid with gold, while yet others brought in twenty different sorts of biscuits and five cakes. The biscuits were mainly distinguished by their colour—white, red, green, and yellow, and by certain decorations; the cakes are described as being white, red, made from dried pears, cherries, and surrounded by fat. Not surprisingly, the right to eat these various delicacies was strictly regulated according to rank. Finally there were bowls of apples, yellow and red pears, nuts, lychees, and various kinds of sweets and candied fruits.

When all this was ready, a senior official entered the hall, kowtowed to the tablet, and then returned to tell the Imperial envoy that all was in order. The latter, wearing the richly embroidered ceremonial robes, approached the hall and stopped, with his entourage, outside the western door of the hall, facing east. The ceremony which now began consisted of three parts. First came a ritual presentation of tea in a silver cup to the spirit of the deceased emperor. This was followed by the ceremonial placing of incense in the large incense burner on the shrine by the prince or chief envoy; at the same time, another high official poured rice-wine into a silver goblet for libations and placed this on the table in front of the shrine. (Fonssagrives gives us a picture of this goblet, which is an archaistic copy of the Shang dynasty ritual "chieh," or cup for offering sacrificial wine.)[7] Finally came the sending of the visiting card. If the proper benefits were to accrue from the sacrifices, it was obviously important that the spirit should know who was looking after him and be reminded of the names of his deserving descendants. Here it is perhaps worth quoting Fonssagrives in full:

> Another Mandarin of the sixth class stands in front of the central door. He carries a small placard, serving the role of a visiting card, on which are written the names of the ruling Emperor, the Empresses and the Prince sent to preside over the ceremony; he faces the interior of the temple and kneels down; the Prince kneels also; an Official of the Board of Rites, carrying a lighted torch kneels beside them; the Mandarin reads aloud what is written on the placard, puts it on the table which is near the temple door, kneels again and kowtows three times, after which he goes to the eastern door.
>
> A Mandarin of the Board of Rites now enters the temple with two cups of wine and makes an offering of these while the Prince again kneels three times and kowtows nine times. The Mandarin who carried the visiting card now takes it up again and goes out to the sacrificial oven, accompanied by another Mandarin carrying a long narrow box in which there is a piece of silk. The placard and silk are burnt, and the Prince, leaving by the western door, returns (to his residence) with his entourage and rests a while before returning to Peking.
>
> The Mandarin who offered the wine returns to the temple, kneels three times and kowtows three times; then he takes the commemorative tablet and replaces it in its alcove, genuflects again three times and goes out. The central and western doors are closed, the eastern door remains open for service.
>
> The waiters then carry out all the dishes which have been offered to the Imperial spirit and distribute them among those present at the ceremony.

Fonssagrives adds that the ceremony was the same for all seasons of the year, except that on the twenty-ninth day of the twelfth month, the paper flowers on the shrine were also burnt and replaced by new ones.

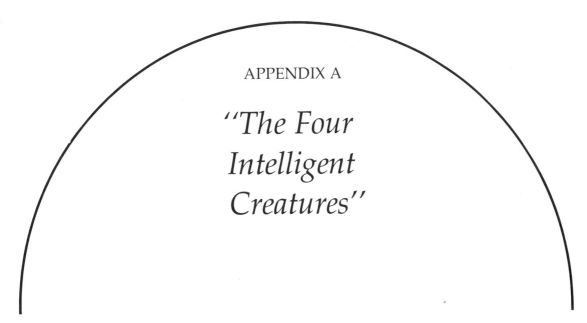

APPENDIX A

"The Four Intelligent Creatures"

"What are the four intelligent creatures? They are the Unicorn, the Phoenix, the Tortoise and the Dragon" ("Book of Rites," or *Li Ki*).[1] The "Book of Rites" was a compilation, made in the second century B.C., of established rites and usages, many of which dated back to the Chou dynasty. It stemmed from the Confucian tradition, and the above quotation therefore gives these four creatures pride of place in the vast repertoire of Chinese mythological animals. This position is clearly reflected in the Ming mausoleum. The dragon, the tortoise, and the unicorn (or ch'i-lin) play an important part in the ceremonial approach; they are also present in each of the thirteen tombs. The phoenix, although less noticeable, still appears more than any other mythical creature, including the usually popular lion.

The Dragon

The dragon has a complex origin. According to legend, a dragon was one of the emblems of the earliest royal house in China, the Hsia, one of whose ancestors transformed himself into a dragon while in a holy place. In early times, the terms for dragon and serpent were practically synonymous, and there is no doubt that the Chinese dragon owes much to the Indian *naga*, or water demon. Edward T. C. Werner reckons that the Chinese name for the Imperial dragon or "lung" is a sinification of the Sanskrit word *naga*. He points out that "the worship of 'nagas' (i.e. dragons or serpents) is indigenous in China . . . dragons being represented as mountain spirits, as tutelary deities of the five regions (i.e. the four points of the compass and the centre), and as guardians of the five lakes and four oceans (i.e. all lakes and seas)."[2] The "green dragon" symbolized the east and spring, and hence fertility and growth. For the Taoists, the dragon symbolized the Way—the ultimate source of all energy.

In European mythology the dragon stands for evil—Saint George is a hero because he slew the dragon. For the Chinese the opposite was true: without the dragon there would be no rain, and without rain, no food. The dragon was therefore necessary to man and was the supreme deity. In the spring he rose into the sky, where he moved between the rain-giving clouds; in the autumn he descended into the seas (fig. 231). Dominant in the world of mythology, it was only natural that the dragon should become the symbol of Imperial power.

Descriptions of the dragon are myriad. Sometimes the dragon family is divided into three subspecies: the "lung," the most powerful, lived in the sky; the "li" was hornless and lived in the sea; and the "chiao" was a scaly animal of the mountain regions.[3] (The "li" is commonly found entwined on the top of memorial steles to those of high birth. See page 16). Others classify dragons by the number of their claws: the Imperial dragon of the T'ang was three-clawed; in Ming times the five-clawed dragon or "lung" was reserved for Imperial use while high officials had to be content with a four-clawed variety, the "mang."[4] An early description refers to the "nine resemblances"—"the head of a camel, the horns of a deer, eyes of a rabbit, ears of a cow, neck of a snake, belly of a frog, scales of a carp, claws of a hawk, and palm of a tiger." But this by no means exhausts all the possibilities. As Schuyler Cammann has pointed out, there were fashions in dragons just as there were fashions in clothes. The Ming dynasty was particularly inventive in animal and bird symbolism, and new varieties such as the "flying fish dragon" appeared along with the "dipper ox" (of Yüan origin), which, contrary to its name, was dragonlike, with downturned horns, stubby toes, and a split tail.[5]

The dragon had numerous progeny, two of which can be seen in the Ming Tombs. The ceramic animal holding the roof ridge in its mouth is a ch'i-wen, one of the recognized descendants of the dragon, and the head carved on the marble doors of the underground chamber is, according to some sources, a "chiao-t'u," another of the dragon offspring (figs. 50 and 156).

The Tortoise

In early Chinese cosmology, the tortoise presided over the northern regions and symbolized winter. The long life of the tortoise is proverbial, and from earliest times it was taken as a symbol for longevity, strength, and endurance. Its dome-shaped back was said to represent the vault of the sky; its belly, the earth which moves upon the waters. According to tradition, the tortoise had the head of a snake and the neck of a dragon (figs. 232 and 233).

As has been seen, the privilege of erecting a memorial stele on the back of a tortoise, thus ensuring long life for the family of the deceased, was reserved for the higher ranks of nobility and officials. The tortoise carrying these steles in the Ming cemetery is clearly based on a water-tortoise or turtle, and is therefore shown on a stone base carved with waves; sometimes the four corners of this slab are decorated with other sea creatures. The tortoise carrying the stele in the first courtyard in Ch'ang-ling differs from its counterparts in the other tombs. Although it is still a water

231. "Watery dragon" in stone basin, Pei Hai Park, Peking

232. Tortoise head from stele in Te-ling (tomb 12)

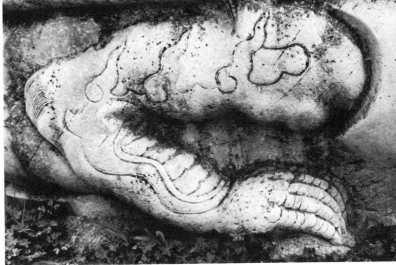

233. ABOVE: Tortoise claw from stele in Te-ling (tomb 12)

234. LEFT: Tortoise head with flowing locks from stele pavilion in first courtyard of Ch'ang-ling (tomb 1)

creature with scales, it has no shell but a spinal ridge like a dragon and a fanciful head with a large bulbous nose, two soft horns, and long flowing locks, reminiscent of the gargoyles on the marble terraces in Ch'ang-ling, Yung-ling, and Ting-ling (fig. 234). Tortoise shells were used for divining; the Emperor Yung-lo consulted a tortoise shell about the placing of the Imperial cemetery.

The Phoenix

The phoenix was believed to preside over the southern regions; it symbolized sun and warmth for summer and harvest. Representing perfect beauty and goodness, it appeared only in times of prosperity and peace. As the dragon became the symbol of Imperial power and hence of the emperor, so the phoenix became the symbol for the empress. It is carved on the posts of the balustrades surrounding the terrace of the Sacrificial Hall in Ch'ang-ling and Ting-ling; the marble staircase slabs in four of the later tombs show a phoenix and a dragon, and two of the thrones in the underground chamber of Ting-ling are decorated with phoenixes to show that these were for an empress (figs. 73, 126, and 158).

Unlike the Arabian phoenix, which was a sort of eagle, the Chinese phoenix is based on the Argus pheasant, and early representations of the bird show a hybrid between an Argus and a peacock. Later, fantasy played a larger role, and the Ming variety seen here has the long neck and wide wing-span of a swan, while the tail consists of long, streaming feathers (figs. 235 and 236).

The Ch'i-lin

The ch'i-lin is more difficult to describe. Perhaps the best definition is that given by Margaret Medley: "It may be leonine, with scales and horns, or it may be an elegant cloven-footed beast, with or without scales, with a bushy mane and tail, and a horn, or a pair of horns. Variations are extremely numerous and impossible to classify."[6] Confusion has been increased by early translations of the name as a "unicorn." Most Westerners have a clear picture of a unicorn and would, if they met an elegant white horse with a single corkscrew horn in the middle of its forehead, recognize it as such. No such clear prototype exists for the ch'i-lin. As we have seen above, animal symbolism flourished in the Ming dynasty. Imagination was fired by descriptions of the strange beasts seen during the great naval expeditions to India and Africa. Among the menagerie of fabulous beasts new figures appeared; some were completely novel inventions, others bore traditional names while taking new forms. The ch'i-lin, with an obscure but ancient origin, belongs to the latter group.

The earliest descriptions quoted by De Groot date from the first century, and they already show doubt as to whether the animal had one horn or two. One writer states: "The ch'i-lin is an animal possessed of humanity. It has the body of a horse, a tail like an ox and horns of flesh."[7] Another writes: "It has the body of an antelope, a tail like an

235. Phoenix, Pei Hai Park, Peking

236. Balustrade column with phoenix from Hall of
Heavenly Favours, Ch'ang-ling (tomb 1)

ox and one horn."[8] By the fourteenth century the ch'i-lin had definitely acquired two horns, although its Japanese counterpart, the "kirin" was still single-horned.[9] Ch'i-lin painted on late Yüan or very early blue and white Ming porcelain were cloven-hoofed, scaly animals with a stag's head, two antlers, and a large bushy tail like that of a horse. Later the Ming ch'i-lin settled into being a creature with the hoofs, legs, and body of a deer, a bushy Chinese lion's tail, and a dragon's head with two horns. This is the version most familiar to Westerners; it persisted into the Ch'ing dynasty, and there is a fine example of such a beast in the Summer Palace (fig. 237).

From all this it can be seen that the artist or craftsman was allowed a great deal of latitude. The distinguishing characteristics of a ch'i-lin were not physical but spiritual. Here, perhaps, one can draw an analogy with the Western idea of a fairy. It is not necessary for a fairy to wear a white ballet skirt and carry a wand; she can also appear in rags as an ugly old woman. What makes her a fairy is the power she has to appear and disappear at will and to influence human lives. The physical characteristics of the ch'i-lin may be vague, but there is a remarkable consistency about its spiritual qualities. The ch'i-lin is above all benevolent. Its gentle and peaceful nature is shown by the fact that its horn or horns are made of flesh. It personifies goodness, this quality being taken to include good government. The ch'i-lin was said to appear when a perfect ruler sat on the Throne of Heaven realizing the Chinese idea of harmony between Heaven and Earth and thus ensuring the well-being of all his subjects. A ch'i-lin was said to have been seen just before the birth of Confucius, and its appearance was therefore taken to augur the coming of a sage.

These qualities made it an eminently suitable guardian for an Imperial tomb, and four types of ch'i-lin can be seen in the Ming cemetery: those shown on the column bases of the P'ai-lou, those standing on the "columns supporting the sky" around the great Stele Pavilion, those in the "Spirit Road," and those guarding the Dragon and Phoenix Gate. All have scaly bodies, cloven hoofs, and horns that are nearly invisible. The ch'i-lin on the P'ai-lou and in the alley are closely related. Both clearly have the body of a dragon with a stiff spinal ridge. The tail is subdued, twining round the back legs. In general, the face resembles that of a Chinese lion, but the back of the head has a very distinctive form: two small horns merge into a large peak of hair which seems to be blown back by the wind. The difference between them is found in the nose. The ch'i-lin in the alley have an unobtrusive nose and the line of the head runs straight from the peak of the hair to the very heavy jowl. On the P'ai-lou ch'i-lin, the nose is accentuated, turning upward into a piglike snout (figs. 5 and 27).

The third type, on the columns around the stele pavilion, is also found on the pair of columns holding the protective screen door just south of the altar in each tomb enclosure. In this beast the dragon has given way to the lion. The body is still scaly and the feet cloven, but the upright spine is barely noticeable; the forelegs are longer and it sits up like a dog waiting for a biscuit. The tail has developed, and in Te-ling, curls up to join the mane. The nose resembles that of its P'ai-lou brethren, but the back of the head, no longer peaked, is lionlike. Whereas the ch'i-lin in the alley are ground animals, looking as if they would be equally at home in water, this creature prefers height. Little wonder that it is commonly referred to in Chinese as "roaring toward the sky" (figs. 17, 128, and 185).

In the last type, on the Dragon and Phoenix Gate, the mixture of dragon and lion is different. The body is dragonlike, scaly, and sinuous, with a long twisting neck, but the animal sits like a dog; the face and head are leonine with a long mane of hair extending right down its back. The tail curls upright, almost reaching the head, like that of a squirrel. This is a regal creature, stern in expression and gazing resolutely forward (fig. 238).

The popularity of and belief in the existence of this fabulous beast were so widespread during the Ming dynasty that when, in 1414, an African giraffe was sent from Bengal to the emperor as a gift, it was taken for a ch'i-lin. Court officials used the

237. Typical Ch'ing ch'i-lin from the Summer Palace, Peking

occasion to congratulate the emperor, reminding him that such creatures were only seen when the empire was being ruled by a sage. Yung-lo resisted this flattery and replied that since he was not a sage, the animal could not be a ch'i-lin. But the following year he seems to have weakened, and when another giraffe arrived, the emperor received it at the Palace Gate in full state. A contemporary Chinese painting of the first giraffe portrays the markings on its body as tortoise scales.

238. Ch'i-lin on Dragon and Phoenix Gate on the Spirit Road in the Ming Valley

APPENDIX B

Birds of the Ming Valley

This is not a list of the birds that may theoretically be seen at the tombs. For this purpose a number of handbooks are listed below. The birds listed are those we have actually seen at or around the tombs and the reservoir and—in the case of a few species—on the road between Peking and the Ming Valley. The list is therefore an indication of what visitors may reasonably hope to see, depending on the time of year they are there. The North Chinese plain is comparatively poor in breeding and wintering birds but rich in passing migrants.

Red-throated Diver (*Gavia stellata*), winter
Great Crested Grebe (*Podiceps cristatus*), winter
Little Grebe (*Podiceps ruficollis*), summer
Dalmatian Pelican (*Pelecanus crispus*), migrant
Common Cormorant (*Phalacrocorax carbo*), migrant
Grey Heron (*Ardea cinerea*), migrant
Purple Heron (*Ardea purpurea*), migrant
Great White Egret (*Egretta alba*), all year
Chinese Pond Heron (*Ardeola bacchus*), summer
Little Green Heron (*Butorides striatus*), summer
Whooper Swan (*Cygnus cygnus*), winter
Swan Goose (*Anser cygnoides*), migrant, rare

Bean Goose (*Anser fabalis*), migrant
Ruddy Shelduck (*Tadorna ferruginea*), migrant
Common Shelduck (*Tadorna tadorna*), migrant
Mallard (*Anas platyrhynchos*), all year
Spot-billed Duck (*Anas poecilorhyncha*), winter
Falcated Duck (*Anas falcata*), migrant
Gadwall (*Anas strepera*), migrant
Green-winged Teal (*Anas crecca*), migrant
Wigeon (*Anas penelope*), migrant
Pintail (*Anas acuta*), migrant
Garganey (*Anas querquedula*), migrant
Shoveler (*Anas clypeata*), migrant
Pochard (*Aythya ferina*), winter
Baer's Pochard (*Aythya baeri*), winter
Tufted Duck (*Aythya fuligula*), winter
Goldeneye (*Bucephala clangula*), winter

Smew (*Mergus albellus*), winter
Goosander (*Mergus merganser*), winter
Osprey (*Pandion haliaetus*), migrant
Black Kite (*Milvus migrans*), all year
Hen Harrier (*Circus cyaneus*), migrant
Sparrow Hawk (*Accipiter nisus*), all year
Goshawk (*Accipiter gentilis*), winter; the
    Siberian, very pale race, *albidus,* can be
    seen
Rough-legged Buzzard (*Buteo lagopus*),
    migrant
Golden Eagle (*Aquila chrysaetos*), migrant
White-tailed Sea-eagle (*Haliaeetus
    albicilla*), migrant
Merlin (*Falco columbarius*), migrant
Kestrel (*Falco tinnunculus*), all year
Red-footed Falcon (*Falco vespertinus*),
    summer, frequent breeder in pines in
    several tombs
Quail (*Coturnix coturnix*), migrant
Common Crane (*Grus grus*), migrant
Moorhen (*Gallinula chloropa*), summer
Coot (*Fulica atra*), migrant
Little Ringed Plover (*Charadrius dubius*),
    summer
Common Sandpiper (*Tringa hypoleucos*),
    migrant
Herring Gull (*Larus argentatus*), all year
Black-headed Gull (*Larus ridibundus*),
    migrant
Bar-tailed Rock Pigeon (*Columba
    rupestris*), all year, frequent breeder on
    stele houses in the tombs
Eastern Turtle Dove (*Streptopelia
    orientalis*), summer
Indian Cuckoo (*Cuculus micropterus*),
    summer, parasites on the Azure-
    winged Magpie
Short-eared Owl (*Asio flammeus*), all year
Common Swift (*Apus apus*), summer,
    breeds on some buildings in
    the tombs

Common Kingfisher (*Alcedo atthis*),
    summer
Pied Kingfisher (*Ceryle lugubris*), summer
Black-capped Kingfisher (*Halcyon
    pileata*), summer
Broad-billed Roller (*Eurystomus
    orientalis*), summer, bred at K'ang-ling
    (tomb 7)
Hoopoe (*Upupa epops*), summer,
    common breeder in most tombs
Grey-headed Woodpecker (*Picus canus*),
    all year
Great spotted Woodpecker (*Dendrocopus
    major*), all year
Grey-crowned Pigmy Woodpecker
    (*Dendrocopus canicapillus*), all year
Skylark (*Alauda arvensis*), all year
Barn Swallow (*Hirundo rustica*), summer
Red-rumped Swallow (*Hirundo daurica*),
    summer, common at the village
    next to Chao-ling (tomb 9).
White Wagtail (*Motacilla alba*), all year
Yellow Wagtail (*Motacilla flava*), migrant
Grey Wagtail (*Motacilla cinerea*), migrant
Richard's Pipit (*Anthus novaeseelandia*),
    migrant
Chestnut-eared Bulbul (*Hypsipetes
    amaurotis*), migrant
Great Grey Shrike (*Lanius excubitor*),
    winter
Black-naped Oriole (*Oriolus chinensis*),
    summer
Black Drongo (*Dicrurus macrocercus*),
    summer, found breeding in
    the tombs
Red-billed Blue Magpie (*Cissa
    erythrorhyncha*), all year, a
    conspicuous and characteristic bird of
    the tombs
Azure-winged Magpie (*Cyanopica cyana*),
    all year, more common in the Western

Hills, the Summer Palace, and the Peking Zoo

Common Magpie (*Pica pica*), all year

Chough (*Pyrrhocorax pyrrhocorax*), all year, bred on Te-ling (tomb 12).

Rook (*Corvus frugilegus*), all year

Collared Crow (*Corvus torquatus*), all year

Daurian or Pied Jackdaw (*Corvus dauuricus*), winter

Japanese Robin (*Luscinia akahige*), migrant

Siberian Blue Robin (*Luscinia cyane*), migrant

Red-flanked Bluetail (*Tarsiger cyanurus*), migrant

Daurian Redstart (*Phoenicurus auroreus*), migrant

Rock Thrush (*Monticola saxatilis*), summer, suspected breeding at K'ang-ling (tomb 7)

Grey-backed Thrush (*Turdus hortulorum*), migrant

Red-throated Thrush (*Turdus ruficollis*), migrant

Dusky Thrush (*Turdus naumanni*), migrant

White's Thrush (*Zoothera dauma*), migrant

White-browed Chinese Bush Dweller or Warbler or Babbler (*Rhopophilus pekinensis*), all year, a charming bird found in pairs, which the learned have great difficulty in placing

Pallas's Willow Warbler (*Phylloscopus proregulus*), migrant, the easiest to identify of this difficult genus, of which

many other species pass through the area

Red-throated Flycatcher (*Ficedula parva*), migrant

Great Tit (*Parus major*), all year, much paler than the western races

Coal Tit (*Parus ater*), all year

Marsh Tit (*Parus palustris*), all year

Nuthatch (*Sitta europaea*), all year

Tree Creeper (*Certhia familiaris*), all year

Tree Sparrow (*Passer montanus*), all year, replaces the House Sparrow in Eastern Asia

Brambling (*Fringilla montifringilla*), winter

Oriental Greenfinch (*Carduelis sinica*), all year, much browner than the western species *chloris*

Pallas's Rosefinch (*Carpodacus roseus*), winter; Yung-ling (tomb 8) is excellent for watching finches in winter

Hawfinch (*Coccothrautes coccothrautes*), migrant

Pine Bunting (*Emberiza leucocephala*), winter

Yellow-throated Bunting (*Emberiza elegans*), winter

Grey-headed Bunting (*Emberiza fucata*), migrant

Little Bunting (*Emberiza pusilla*), winter

Tristram's Bunting (*Emberiza tristrami*), migrant

Reed Bunting (*Emberiza schoeniclus*), summer

Meadow Bunting (*Emberiza cioides*), winter

Bibliography for Birds of the Ming Valley

Cheng, Dr. Tso-Hsin. *Distributional List of Chinese Birds*. Peking: Academia Sinica, 1976. (List with distributional maps, Chinese Text with English and Latin names)

Dement'ev, G. P. et al. *Birds of the Soviet Union*. 6 vols. Jerusalem: Israel Program for Scientific Translation for the Smithsonian Institute and the National Science Foundation, Washington, D.C.

Gore, M. E. J., and Pyong-Oh, Won. *The Birds of Korea.* Seoul: Royal Asiatic Society, Korea Branch, Tokyo and Rutland: Charles E. Tuttle and Co., 1971.

Heinzel, Hermann; Fitter, Richard; and Parslow, John. *The Birds of Britain and Europe.* London: Collins, 1972.

Kobayashi, Keisuke, *Birds of Japan in Natural Colours.* Osaka: Hoikusha Publishing Co., 1965. (Japanese text with English and Latin names and excellent illustrations)

Shaw, Tsen-Hwang. *The Birds of Hopei Province.* 2 vols. Peking: Fan Memorial Institute of Biology, 1936. (Rare)

Wilder, George, D., and Hubbard, Hugh W. *Birds of Northeastern China.* Peking: Peking Natural History Bulletin, April 1938. (Rare)

Notes

Introduction

1 Camille Imbault-Huart, "Les Tombeaux des Ming près de Pékin," *T'oung Pao* (Leyden), no. 4 (1893), pp. 391–401.

2 Ku Yen-wu (1613–82) was a leading scholar in the early Ch'ing era. He remained steadfastly loyal to the Ming dynasty and visited the Ming Tombs frequently between 1657 and 1677 to pay his respects to the deceased emperors. After his first two visits, he wrote *Ch'ang p'ing shan shui chi* [A description of the landscape around Ch'ang-p'ing], and it is from this work that both De Groot and Bouillard quote. See Arthur W. Hummel, ed., *Eminent Chinese of the Ch'ing Period* (Washington, D.C., 1943), 1: 421–26 (hereafter cited as *ECCP*).

3 Sun Kuo-mi, *Yen-tu yu-lan chi* [A visit to the Capital of Yen], 1622. See Paul Pelliot's "Obituary of G. Bouillard," *T'oung Pao* (Leyden), no. 27 (1930), pp. 454–57, and his "Bulletin critique: les sepultures impériales des Ming," ibid., no. 21 (1922), pp. 57–66, for further information.

Chapter One: The Ming Dynasty

1 Here Hung-wu followed the example of the Yüan in choosing a name with a particular meaning for the dynasty rather than one derived from a particular region. It is possible that Hung-wu was influenced in his choice by Manichaeism, a religion which spread from western Asia to China in the seventh century. This doctrine emphasized the fundamental nature of the clash between Dark and Light, and one of its names was "Ming-chiao" (Religion of Light).

2 Chu Ti was Yung-lo's fourth son.

3 Posthumous name, Jen-hsiao.

4 Jan Jakob Maria De Groot, *The Religious System of China* (Taipeh, 1967), 3: 1010.

5 Ibid., 3:1018.

6 Yeh Sheng (1420–74), *Shui tung jih-chi,* quoted in ibid., 3:1182, and in George Bouillard and Commandant Vaudescal, "Les Sepultures impériales des Ming (Che-San Ling)," *Bulletin de l'Ecole Française d'Extrême-Orient* (Hanoi), vol. 20, no. 3 (1920), p. 6.

7 Hsü Hsueh-mo (1522–74), *Shih miao shih yu lu,* quoted in De Groot, 3:1183, and in Bouillard and Vaudescal, p. 7.

Chapter Two: The Approach to the Tombs

1 There are many conflicting opinions about this "ball": while some hold that it represents the Buddhist "night-shining pearl," others claim that it is the sun, or even the symbol of rolling thunder. Margaret Medley points out that the Buddhist guardian lion is often shown "playing with a brocaded ball to which ribbons are attached"; she includes the "flaming pearl" as a separate motif associated with dragons. While these two are distinguishable in their pure forms, it seems likely that, with time, they have become more or less interchangeable. C. A. S. Williams refers to a "pearl entwined with a fillet" as an auspicious symbol. Whether the lions on the P'ai-lou are playing with such a pearl or with a brocaded ball seems in the end to be a question of semantics.

What is certain is that a pearl or ball has been a popular decorative symbol since the Han dynasty. It is frequently found between pairs of lions, pairs of dragons, or between a dragon and a phoenix. In these cases, it is nearly always ornamented and is usually shown as a plaything: on the marble slab at the Ming tomb Te-ling (tomb 12), the dragon has caught the pearl in one of its claws. It can, however, be shown in the mouth or under the paw of a dragon, lion, or tiger. A stone "winged tiger" from the Later Han period, found at Lu-shan-hsien in Szechuan, has a ball in its mouth, and Victor Segalen gives the following description of another "winged tiger" found nearby, at the tomb of Kao I (209 A.D.): "The animal is chewing a sort of ball, held by the front canines; I do not know what its symbolic value is, but I find its sculptural effect deplorable." Both the stone animals encircling the base of a stone column from the tomb of Liang Hsiao Ching hold a ball in their mouths, and to take a much later example, one of the dragons on the dragon wall in the Yu garden at Shanghai (Ming and Ch'ing) holds a "flaming pearl" between its giant fangs. Finally, it is perhaps worth noting that the famous "lion dance" as shown today always includes some play with a ball. Margaret Medley, *A Handbook of Chinese Art*, pp. 92, 95; Charles Alfred Speed Williams, *Outlines of Chinese Symbolism and Art Motives* (New York, 1976), p. 319; Victor Segalen, *The Great Statuary of China*, trans. Eleanor Levieux (Chicago and London, 1978), pp. 45, 47, 109.

2 Two examples of central Indian makara in terracotta from the sixth to eighth centuries A.D. can be seen in the British Museum. See also Stephen Darian, "The Other Face of the Makara," *Artibus Asiae*, no. 38 (1976), pp. 29–34.

3 It is not clear whether the wall was continuous or was confined to the passes and low areas not naturally protected by mountains. De Groot quotes a description by Ku Yen-wu of the extra fortifications and gates at the ten passes round the valley; the latter does not specifically mention a continuous wall, but it may be that he took this for granted, since there seems to be little doubt that earlier cemeteries in Han and T'ang times were completely enclosed, as was the tomb of the first Ming emperor at Nanking. On the other hand, Fonssagrives describes the Western Tombs of the Ch'ing dynasty as being enclosed by a wall except where mountains and hills provided a natural defence for feng-shui purposes. The land outside the wall was delineated by three concentric rings of posts; the innermost were red, the middle blue, and the outer, white. Penalties for trespassing, hewing wood, or infringing any of the multitude of decrees affecting Imperial land varied in severity according to the zone in which they were committed. (See De Groot, 3: 1196, 1243–45, 1331–33; Fonssagrives, passim.)

4 De Groot, 3: 1146.

5 Quoted in ibid., 3: 1160–61.

6 Bouillard and Vaudescal, p. 26.

7 De Groot, 3: 1225–26.

8 According to Ku Yen-wu, there was once an Imperial resting place to the east of the stele pavilion. Ibid., 3:1206.

Chapter Three: The Spirit Road

1 Quoted by De Groot, 2: 814.

2 Ibid., 3:1089.

3 Western authors have frequently described these figures as being carved from marble; De Groot, however, states that analysis of a small particle of stone taken from a crack in one of the elephants showed it to be magnesium limestone (3 Ca CO_3 2 Mg CO_3). Ibid., 2:818.

4 A lion in the sixth-century Buddhist P'in-yang cave at Lungmen near Loyang wears an almost identical neckband with a round pendant. See Segalen, *Great Statuary of China*, plate 41, opposite p. 135.

5 De Groot, 3: 977.

6 Michael Sullivan, *A Short History of Chinese Art* (London, 1967), pp. 228, 229.

7 L. Carrington Goodrich and Chaoying Fang, eds., *Dictionary of Ming Biography* (New York and London, 1976), pp. 362 (hereafter cited as *DMB*). The description was written by Hafiz-i Abru, son of Timur and envoy of Shahrukkh, who had an audience with the emperor early in the morning on 14 December 1420.

8 For identification of the rank and office of these stone figures, I am grateful to Dr. Wang Yeqiu, Chairman of the State Bureau of Museums and Archaeological Data in Peking, and to Sheng Congwen from the Palace Museum, who is a specialist in Ming costumes. While entirely specific about the civilian figures, Mr. Sheng identified the military simply as "generals." In the Kiangsu Provincial Museum in Nanking, they were referred to as "Palace Warriors." Given the meticulous attention to detail in the uniform, it seems likely that the two pairs belonged to different branches of the military establishment.

9 Chinese silk damask panels from the sixteenth century in the Victoria and Albert Museum show the same lotus patterns as those on these uniforms. See Arts Council of Great Britain, "*The Arts of the Ming Dynasty*," (London, 1958), plates 78, 79, 80.

10 Quoted by De Groot, 2:820. The measurements given are equivalent to 76 cms. and 7 ½ cms., respectively; the "one-sixth" presumably refers to the width of the "hu." There is a clear identification of a "hu" in L. Carrington Goodrich, *Fifteenth Century Illustrated Chinese Primer* (Hong Kong, 1967).
11 Reproduced in Oriental Art, n.s. 22 (1976): 380.
12 Bouillard and Vaudescal, p. 31.
13 De Groot, 3:1205.

Chapter Four: Chinese Architecture
  1 The standard books on Chinese architecture are: Andrew Boyd, *Chinese Architecture and Town Planning, 1500 B.C.–A.D. 1911* (Chicago, 1963); Michele Pirazzoli t'Serstevens, *Chine: Architecture Universelle* (Fribourg, 1970); Lawrence Sickman and Alexander Soper, *The Art and Architecture of China* (Harmondsworth, 1956); Thomas Thilo, *Klassische chinesische Baukunst: Strukturprinzipien und Funktion* (Vienna, 1977); and Nelson I. Wu, *Chinese and Indian Architecture* (New York, 1963; London, 1963). The classical Chinese work on the subject is *Ying-tsao fa-shih* [Method of architecture] from the Sung dynasty, 1103 A.D. Manuscript copies of this edition made in 1145 are still extant, and the history of this treatise is discussed by Walter Percival Yetts, "A Chinese Treatise on Architecture," *Bulletin of the School of Oriental and African Studies* (London), no. 4 (1926–28); and by Else Glahn, "On the Transmission of the Ying-tsao fa-shih," *T'oung Pao* (Leyden) 61, nos. 4–5 (1975): 232–65.
  2 De Groot, 3: 1177.
  3 Boyd, p. 5.
  4 According to Glahn, there are at least thirty known pre-Ming buildings, all belonging to the classical Chinese tradition. These date from the ninth to the thirteenth centuries A.D. and rank among the earliest wooden constructions preserved in the world. See also Pirazzoli t'Serstevens, p. 3.
  5 Nigel Cameron and Brian Brake, *Peking: A Tale of Three Cities* (Tokyo and London, 1971), p. 116.
  6 L. Carrington Goodrich's introduction to Cameron and Brake, *Peking*.
  7 Sickman and Soper, p. 422.
  8 Ibid., p. 420.
  9 Williams, p. 137.
10 Mo Tsung-chiang, "Architectural Decoration," *China Reconstructs* (Peking) 4, no. 9 (1955): 15–17.

Chapter Five: Tomb Architecture
  1 Boyd, p. 122.
  2 De Groot, 2: 437.
  3 Quoted in ibid.
  4 A. Boyd suggests that the Ming dynasty was the first to build surface buildings on Imperial graves. This, I think, is mistaken. De Groot gives numerous quotations from Chinese authors referring to such buildings on Imperial graves from Han times onward. One of the first edicts of the Ming decreed that henceforth no more sacrificial halls might be built on the tombs of officials of merit. The reason given was that the custom had been widely abused, leading to extravagance. Moreover, a recent biography of the T'ang Empress Wu, relying on Chinese sources, describes her tomb in this way: "There were temples and sacrificial halls with marble terraces and exquisitely carved railings. Colossal stone columns and giant statues of men, horses and quaint birds stood sentinel along the wide avenue leading to the grave and huge lions guarded the wall gates and 'temple doors'" (see A. Boyd, *Chinese Architecture and Town Planning*, 1500 B.C.–A.D. 1911, pp. 142, 144, and *I Am Heaven* by Jin Sie Chun). According to Dr. Feng, the main difference between the surface buildings on T'ang and Ming tombs is that the former were frequently inhabited by the tomb guardians, whereas Ming buildings were normally empty, being used only for the rites.
  5 Quoted by De Groot, 2: 388.
  6 Ibid.
  7 See William Watson, "On Some Categories of Archaism in Chinese Bronzes," *Ars Orientalis* 9 (1973): 1–13, and Jessica Rawson, "The Development of Archaistic Styles in Chinese Ceramics," paper given at a symposium on Chinese ceramics held at Seattle Art Museum, July 1977.
  8 De Groot, plate 48, 3: 1222.
  9 Ibid., p. 1105.
10 The art of stone vaulting, known already in Han times, was generally reserved for bridges, arches, and doorways in city and palace walls and for underground funeral chambers. There is a vaulted "beamless hall" in the Ling ku ssu (temple) at Nanking which the Danish writer on architecture, J. Prip-Møller reckons was built under the influence of a French monk during the Mongol dynasty. During the last years of the Ming dynasty several temple halls were built and tunnel-vaulted in brick, including one in T'ai-yüan-fu and another in

Soochow. These "beamless halls" were the work of the architect Fu-teng (1540–1613) or craftsmen trained by him, and appear to have had no successors. L. Sickman and A. Soper, p. 463; Nagel's *Guide to China* (Geneva, 1968), p. 996; s.v. "Fu-teng" in the *DMB*, pp. 462–65; and Johans Prip-Møller, "The Hall of Ling Ku Ssu, Nanking," *Artes* (Copenhagen) 3 (1935): 172–211.

11 Quoted in De Groot, 2: 401.
12 Quoted in ibid., 1: 290, 291.
13 Quoted in ibid., 2: 440.
14 Ibid., 3: 902.
15 Ibid., 3: 905.
16 Quoted in ibid., 3: 1206.

Chapter Six: Ch'ang-ling

1 Quoted by De Groot, 3:1212.
2 This attitude was maintained throughout most of the Ch'ing dynasty. C. Imbault-Huart quotes a decree of the Emperor Ch'ien-lung in 1788 which shows that the latter had visited the Ming Tombs himself to perform the rites: "Mais, depuis plusieurs dizaines d'années, les autorités locales n'ont fait l'inspection avec tout le soin désirable, et il en est résulté que, dans beaucoup d'endroits, les constructions ont été endommagées et que les murailles ont penché. Lors qu'il y a deux ans je suis venu faire des libations vers les tombes, j'ai pensé à ces vestiges des dynasties passées, et j'en ai eu le coeur déchiré. Aussi ai-je donné de l'argent et délégué un Inspecteur pour surveiller les travaux de réparation. A présent ces travaux sont terminés; les tombeaux se trouvant sur mon chemin j'ai constaté qu'ils brillaient du plus vif éclat et que les arbres étaient comme au temps jadis. . . . Afin de montré ma pensée intime d'honorer les dynasties passères en protégeant less tombeaux des anciens empereurs, j'ordonne qu'on se conforme à ces ordres. Respectez ceci!" (C. Imbault-Huart, *Tombeaux des Ming près de Pékin*, p. 398).
3 E. Fonssagrives, Si-ling: *Etude sur les tombeaux de l'Ouest de la dynastie des Ts'ing* (Paris, 1907), p. 39.
4 Boyd, p. 27. Other authors have described it as "Persia nanmu," a sort of teak. The characters *nan mu* simply mean "south wood."
5 Vincent Cronin, *The Wise Man from the West* (New York; 1955), p. 131.
6 Reginald F. Johnston, *Twilight in the Forbidden City* (London, 1934), p. 349.

Chapter Seven: Hsien-ling

1 Bouillard and Vaudescal, p. 50.
2 Ibid., p. 53.

Chapter Eight: Ching-ling

1 Bouillard and Vaudescal, p. 55.
2 Sickman and Soper, p. 312.
3 See Edwin O. Reischauer and Jonathan K. Fairbank, *A History of East Asian Civilization*, p. 315.
4 *DMB*, p. 287.

Chapter Nine: Yü-ling

1 George Bouillard, *Les Tombeaux impériaux Ming et Ts'ing* (Peking, 1931), pp. 7–9.
2 Bouillard and Vaudescal, p. 62.
3 Reischauer and Fairbank, *A History of East Asian Civilization*, p. 315.
4 Charles Patrick FitzGerald, *China: A Short Cultural History* (London, 1965), p. 469.
5 The following account is quoted from "History of the Ming Dynasty," chaps. 176 and 177, in De Groot, 3: 1227–29.

Chapter Ten: Mao-ling

1 Bouillard and Vaudescal, p. 65.
2 Ibid., p. 66.
3 Ibid., p. 59.

Chapter Eleven: T'ai-ling

1 Bouillard, *Les Tombeaux impériaux Ming et Ts'ing*, p. 120.

Chapter Twelve: K'ang-ling

1 De Groot, 2: 376.

Chapter Thirteen: Yung-ling

1 These are only the most common. See H. S. D. Garvard, "Wild Flowers of Northern China and Southern Manchuria," *Peking Natural History Bulletin* (1937), for better information.
2 These gargoyles are remarkably similar in form to a grey-green jade "dragon's head finial" in the Arthur Sackler Collection in New York. Desmond Gure attributed this jade head to the ninth/tenth century on grounds of specific features and sculptural analogies. See *Transactions of the Oriental Ceramic Society, 1973–75*, item 257, p. 84.
3 Curiously enough, Bouillard describes this pedestal as being undecorated. Bouillard and Vaudescal, p. 77.
4 FitzGerald, *China*, p. 479.

Chapter Fourteen: Chao-ling

1 Bouillard and Vaudescal, p. 78.
2 Fonssagrives, p. 74.

Chapter Fifteen: Ting-ling

1 Bouillard and Vaudescal, p. 81.
2 There is a definite discrepancy between the present situation and that described by Bouillard. Bouillard mentions blocked side doors in the "south" wall of the first courtyard some ten metres to the left and right of the Triple Entrance Gate. He then specifically states that no such side doors exist in the next transversal wall and that the only way into the second courtyard is through the Gate of Heavenly Favours. I could find no trace of blocked doors in the outer wall. On the other hand, the present openings in the wall between the first and second courtyard stand exactly over stone foundations showing the familiar pattern of stone column bases and niches for door hinges, and the pattern of side doors in this and the next transversal wall corresponds to that in Yung-ling. Moreover, Ku Yen-wu notes that there are doors in the wall on both sides of the Gate of Heavenly Favours and the Sacrificial Hall. The only explanation I can find is that what Bouillard saw must have been due to an erroneous restoration that was corrected in 1958. About the side doors in the wall adjoining the Sacrificial Hall there is no confusion (see Bouillard and Vaudescal, p. 81–83).
3 Bouillard, *Les Tombeaux impériaux Ming et Ts'ing*, p. 127.
4 Bouillard and Vaudescal, p. 84.
5 Ibid., p. 82.
6 The following account of Ricci's experiences in China is largely based on Nigel Cameron's *Barbarians and Mandarins*, pp. 149–94.

Chapter Seventeen: Te-ling

1 Bouillard and Vaudescal, p. 37; Fonssagrives, p. 99.
2 See Medley, *Handbook of Chinese Art*, p. 92, on the Eight Buddhist Emblems: "The emblems are the Chakra or Wheel, the Conch Shell, the Umbrella, the Canopy, the Lotus, the Vase, the Paired Fish, and the Entrails or Endless Knot. A bell is occasionally substituted for the Chakra. At times some of these emblems may be mixed up with some of the Eight Taoist Emblems, but as long as only eight emblems appeared in the decoration, it does not seem to have been very important which ones they were that made up the correct number."

The Eight Precious Things are: "the Jewel; the Cash, a circle enclosing a square; the Open Lozenge, with ribbons; the Solid Lozenge, also with ribbons; the Musical Stone, a roughly L-shaped object suspended from the angle; the Pair of Books; the Pair of Horns; and the Artemisia leaf" (ibid., p. 95).

Chapter Eighteen: Sze-ling

1 See Cameron, *Barbarians and Mandarins*, p. 203, quoting d'Elia's *Galileo*.
2 Cameron, *Peking, A Tale of Three Cities*, pp. 111–12. In his *Emperor of China: Self-Portrait of K'ang-hsi*, (London, 1977), Jonathan Spence gives a different version. K'ang-hsi, commenting on the historians, says: "Others described the death of the last Ming emperor: how, when the bandits entered Peking, he disguised himself as a commoner and went with some eunuchs to his uncle's house, but the uncle had locked the gates in order to watch theatricals and the Emperor couldn't get in. And then, though the Emperor wanted to flee, the eunuch Wang Ch'eng-en said that that could only lead to further humiliations, and so the Emperor committed suicide" (p. 87).
3 Quoted by De Groot, 3: 1235–37; Bouillard and Vaudescal, pp. 91–93; *ECCP*, 1: 192.
4 In 1636, in Manchuria, Abahai had declared himself emperor and changed the name of his dynasty to Ch'ing. After Abahai's death, his ninth son, Fu-lin ascended the throne (8 October 1643) and thus entered Peking as an emperor. See *ECCP*, 1: 2, 225–26.

5 The rest of this author's description in the *Su Song lu,* quoted by Bouillard and Vaudescal on p. 95, is dismissed by the latter as "confused and not according to reality."

6 According to the Ming Tombs Administration Office in Peking, this scene is based on the opera *The White Monkey Presents Longevity,* adapted from a Chinese folktale. The peach motif at the top, symbolizing long life, indicates that the White Monkey, who is celebrating his mother's birthday, is wishing her longevity. Behind the mother is a servant.

Chapter Nineteen: Ching-t'ai's Tomb in the Western Hills

1 *DMB,* p. 297.

2 Bouillard and Vaudescal, plan no. 14.

3 Juliet Bredon, *Peking* (Shanghai, 1922), p. 235.

Chapter Twenty: Hsiao-ling

1 For much of the information in this chapter, I am grateful to Dr. Feng Cangyuan of the Kiangsu Provincial Museum at Nanking. The second half of the tomb with the temple buildings has changed greatly since Bouillard's description of it in 1920; even Nagel's description from 1968 no longer entirely fits. The whole temple area has been tidied up into a sort of municipal park; it was therefore particularly helpful to learn from Dr. Feng which parts of the walls and buildings have survived from the original construction. For a more detailed description of the tomb site between the destruction in 1864 and the latest alterations, see De Groot, 3: 1256–66, Bouillard and Vaudescal, pp. 117–21, and Nagel's *Guide,* pp. 993–95.

2 *DMB,* p. 386.

3 De Groot believes that these tablets may well have commemorated similar Imperial visits, since K'ang-hsi visited Nanking six times. In 1684 and 1689 he performed the rites at Hsiao-ling in person; in 1699 and 1703 he sent a Grand Secretary from the town. In 1705 and 1707 he visited the mausoleum himself. De Groot, 3: 1262, 1263.

4 Quoted from Tacchi-Venturi, *Opere storiche del P. Matteo Ricci,* 1: 587, 2: 320, by Pelliot in his "Obituary of G. Bouillard," *T'oung Pao* (Leyden), no. 27 (1930), p. 454.

Chapter Twenty-one: Administration and the Ritual Sacrifices

1 Further information on this subject can be found in Fonssagrives, pp. 148–56, and Bouillard, *Les Tombeaux impériaux Ming et Ts'ing,* pp. 41–58. Bouillard gives his main sources for this section as Fonssagrives and De Groot.

2 Quoted by De Groot, 3: 1248.

3 The exact dates of these festivals are difficult to establish because of the different ways of calculating the calendar. The above dates are taken from Tun Li-chen, *Annual Customs and Festivals in Peking,* trans. Derek Bodde (Hong Kong, 1965), passim.

4 Quoted by De Groot, 3: 1213.

5 Ibid., p. 1216.

6 Alphonse Favier, *Peking: histoire et description* (Lille, 1900), p. 169.

7 An example of such a goblet dating from the eleventh century B.C. was found in Shansi in 1901. See William Watson, *China before the Han Dynasty* (London, 1966), plate 23.

Appendix A: "The Four Intelligent Creatures"

1 James Legge, trans., *The Li-ki,* 1–10, p. 384, §10, in *The Sacred Books of China—The Texts of Confucianism,* vol. 27, pt. 3 (Delhi: Varanasi, Patna: Motilal Banarsidass, 1966; first published by Clarendon Press, Oxford, 1885).

2 Edward Theodore Chalmers Werner, *A Dictionary of Chinese Mythology* (Shanghai, 1932), p. 284.

3 Williams, p. 133.

4 There are exceptions to this: as John Addis points out, the dragons on the crown of the tortoise stele at Hung-wu's tomb in Nanking have only four claws. John M. Addis, *Chinese Ceramics from Dateable Tombs* (London and New York, 1978), p. 168.

5 Schuyler Cammann, "Some Strange Ming Beasts," *Oriental Art,* n.s. 3 (1956): 94–102.

6 Medley, p. 91.

7 De Groot, 2: 823.

8 Ibid.

9 See Cammann, "Some Strange Ming Beasts," pp. 94–102.

Glossary

Principal Chinese Authors and Works Quoted by De Groot and Bouillard

Hsü Hsüeh-mo　徐學謨, *Shih miao shih yu lu* 世廟識餘錄
Ku Yen-wu　顧炎武, *Ch'ang p'ing shan shui chi* 昌平山水記
Sun Kuo-mi　孫國敉, *Yen-tu yu-lan chi* 燕都游覽志
Yeh Sheng　葉盛, *Shui tung jih-chi* 水東日記

Inscriptions on Grave Steles

Ch'ang-ling: 成祖交皇帝之陵
Hsien-ling: 仁宗昭皇帝之陵
Ching-ling: 宣宗章皇帝之陵
Yü-ling: 英宗睿皇帝之陵
Mao-ling: 憲宗純皇帝之陵
T'ai-ling: 孝宗敬皇帝之陵
K'ang-ling: 武宗毅皇帝之陵

Yung-ling: 世宗肅皇帝之陵
Chao-ling: 穆宗莊皇帝之陵
Ting-ling: 神宗顯皇帝之陵
Ching-ling: 光宗貞皇帝之陵
Te-ling: 熹宗哲皇帝之陵
Sze-ling: 莊烈愍皇帝之陵
Ching-t'ai's tomb: 恭仁康定景皇帝之陵

Principal Parts of the Mausoleum and Tomb Buildings

Archway through stele tower 門洞
"Beacons" 望柱
Ceramic screen 琉璃影壁
"Columns supporting the sky" 擎天柱
Dragon and Phoenix Gate 龍鳳門
"Five precious objects" 石台五供
"Flowery columns" 華表
Gate of Heavenly Favours 稜恩門

"Grave stele" 墓碑
Great Red Gate 大紅門
Linteled Star Gate 欞星門
P'ai-lou 牌樓
Ramparts 寶城
Sacrificial hall (Hall of Heavenly Favours) 稜恩殿
Spirit Road 神道
Stele pavilion 明樓

Stele pavilion or stele house 碑亭

Stele tower 方城

"Tortoise stele" (Spirit Road stele) 神道碑

Triple doorway 陵寢門

Underground chamber 地宮

Mythical Creatures

Ch'i-lin 麒麟

Hsieh-chai 獬豸

"Roaring toward the sky" 望天吼

Bibliography

(References in the text are taken from the latest edition cited in the Bibliography.)

Abbate, Francesco, ed. *Chinese Art.* Translated by P. L. Phillips. London, New York, Sydney, and Hong Kong: Octopus Books, 1972.

Addis, John M. *Chinese Ceramics from Dateable Tombs.* London and New York: Sotheby Parke Bernet, 1978.

L'Architecture d'Aujourd'hui. Chine, 1949–79 (Paris), no. 201 (February 1979).

Arlington, Lewis Charles, and Lewisohn, William. *In Search of Old Peking.* Peking: Vetch, 1935. Reprinted New York: Paragon Book Reprint Corp., 1967.

Arts Council of Great Britain and the Oriental Ceramic Society. "The Arts of the Ming Dynasty." Exhibition, November 15–December 14, 1957. London: Arts Council of Great Britain, 1958.

Barrett, Douglas. "The Buddhist Art of Tibet and Nepal." *Oriental Art,* n.s. 3 (1957): 91–95.

Birch, John Grant. *Travels in Northern and Central China.* London: Hurst and Blackett, 1902.

Bouillard, Georges. *Les Tombeaux impériaux Ming et Ts'ing.* Peking: Nachbauer, 1931.

―――, and Vaudescal, Commandant. "Les Sépultures impériales des Ming (Che-San Ling)." *Bulletin de l'Ecole Française d'Extrême-Orient* (Hanoi), vol. 20, no. 3 (1920).

Boyd, Andrew. *Chinese Architecture and Town Planning, 1500 B.C.–A.D. 1911.* London: Tiranti, 1962.

Boyer, Martha. *Kina før Kejsertid* [Pre-Imperial China]. Copenhagen: Gyldendal, 1973.

Bredon, Juliet. *Peking.* Shanghai: Kelly and Walsh, 1922.

Bretschneider, Emil V. *Recherches archéologiques et historiques sur Pékin et ses environs.* Paris: Ernest Leroux, 1879.

Bulling, A. "Notes on Two Unicorns." *Oriental Art,* n.s. 12 (1966).

Bushell, Stephen Woolton. *Chinese Art.* 2 vols. London: Victoria and Albert Museum, 1904.

Cameron, Nigel. *Barbarians and Mandarins.* New York and Tokyo: Weatherhill, 1970.

―――, and Brake, Brian. *Peking: A Tale of Three Cities.* 2d ed. Tokyo and London: Weatherhill, 1971.

Cammann, Schuyler. *China's Dragon Robes.* New York: Ronald Press Co., 1952.

―――. "Notes on the Development of Mandarin Squares." *Bulletin of the Needle and Bobbin Club* (New York) 26, no. 1 (1942): p. 2–28.

―――. *Chinese Mandarin Squares: A Brief Catalogue of the Letcher Collection.* Philadelphia: University of Pennsylvania Press, 1962.

―――. "Some Strange Ming Beasts." *Oriental Art,* n.s. 2 (1956): 94–102.

―――. *Substance and Symbol in Chinese Toggles.* Philadelphia: University of Pennsylvania Press, 1962.

―――. "Two Rare Ming Textiles." *Oriental Art,* n.s. 10 (1964): 175–80.

Carter, Dagny. *Four Thousand Years of China's Art.* New York: The Ronald Press Co., 1948.

Chalfant, Frank H. "Early Chinese Writing." Reprinted from *Memoirs of the Carnegie Museum*, vol. 4, no. 1 (1906).

Chavannes, Edouard. *De l'expression de voeux dans l'art populaire Chinois*. Paris: Editions Bossard, 1922. Translated by Atwood, Elaine Spalding—*The Five Happinesses: Symbolism in Chinese Popular Art*. New York: Weatherhill, 1973.

————. *Mission archéologique dans la Chine septentrionale*. 3 vols. Paris: Ernest Leroux, 1909–15.

————. *La Sculpture sur pierre en Chine au temps des deux dynasties Han*. Paris: Ernest Leroux, 1893.

Ch'en Yüan. *Westerners and Central Asians in China under the Mongols*. Translated by Ch'ien Hsing-hai and L. Carrington Goodrich. Los Angeles: Monumenta Serica, Monograph 15, 1966.

Chiang, Yee. *Chinese Calligraphy* (1938). 3d ed. Cambridge, Mass.: Harvard University Press, 1973.

Chow, H. F. "The Familiar Trees of Hopei." *Peking Natural History Bulletin*. Peking, 1934.

Christie, Anthony. *Chinese Mythology*. London: Hamlyn, 1968.

Chun, Jin Sie. *I Am Heaven*. Philadelphia: Macrae Smith and Co., 1973.

Cohen, Jerome Alan, and Cohen, Joan Lebold. *China Today and Her Ancient Treasures*. New York: Harry N. Abrams, 1975.

Cohn, William. *Chinese Painting*. London: Phaidon Press, 1948.

Combaz, Gisbert. *Sépultures impériales de la Chine*. Brussels: Presses de Vromant, 1907.

Cronin, Vincent. *The Wise Man from the West*. London: Hart-Davis, 1955.

Couling, Samuel. *The Encyclopaedia Sinica*. Shanghai: Kelly and Walsh, 1917.

Darian, Stephen. "The Other Face of the Makara." *Artibus Asiae*, no. 38 (1976): 29–34.

De Groot, Jan Jakob Maria. *The Religious System of China*. 6 vols. Leyden, 1892–1910. Reprint of 1892 ed. Taipeh: Ch'eng-wen Publishing Co., 1967.

Dennys, Nicholas Belfield. *The Folklore of China* (1876). Amsterdam: Oriental Press, 1968.

Destenay, Anne L. *See* Nagel.

Dixey, Annie Coath. *The Lion Dog of Peking*. London: Davies, 1931.

Dorn, Frank. *Peking, The Forbidden City*. New York: Scribner's Sons, 1970.

Dubs, Homer Hasenpflug. *History of the Former Han Dynasty*. 3 vols. Washington, D.C.: Kegan Paul, French Trübner and Co., 1938, 1944, 1955.

Dunn, J. Li. *The Essence of Chinese Civilisation*. Princeton, N.J.: Princeton University Press, 1967.

Dunne, George Harold. *Generation of Giants: The Story of the Jesuits in China in the Last Decades of the Ming Dynasty*. London: Burnes and Oates, 1962.

Dye, Daniel Sheets. *A Grammar of Chinese Lattice*. Cambridge, Mass.: Harvard University Press, 1949.

Eitel, Rev. E. J. *Feng shui*. London: Trübner & Co., 1873. Reprinted 3d ed. paperback. Bristol: Pentacle Books, 1979.

Elvin, Mark. *The Pattern of the Chinese Past*. London: Methuen, 1973.

Faber, Tobias. "Kinas Arkitektur" [Chinese architecture] (Copenhagen). *Arkitekten* 3 (1978): 53–65.

————. "Soochow's Haver" [The gardens of Soochow]. (Copenhagen). *Arkitekten* 4 (1978): 88–94.

Fang, Wen-pei. *Icones Plantarum Omiensium*. 2 vols. Cheng-tu: National Szechuan University, 1942.

Favier, Alphonse. *Péking: histoire et description*. Imprimeurs des Facultés Catholiques de Lille: Desclée, de Brouwer et Cie., 1900.

Fernald, Helen E. *Chinese Court Costumes*. Toronto: Royal Ontario Museum of Archaeology, 1946.

FitzGerald, Charles Patrick. *China: A Short Cultural History*. London: Cressett Press, 1935; 1st paperback ed., 1965.

————. *A Concise History of Asia*. Australia: Heinemann, 1966. London: Pelican Books, 1974.

————. *The Empress Wu*. London: Cressett Press, 1956.

Fonssagrives, E. *Si-ling, Etude sur les Tombeaux de l'Ouest de la Dynastie des Ts'ing*. Paris: Leroux, 1907.

Fugl-Meyer, H. *Chinese Bridges*. Shanghai: Kelly and Walsh, 1937.

Fullard, H. *China in Maps*. London; Philip and Son, 1968.

Garvard, H. S. D. "Wild Flowers of Northern China and Southern Manchuria." *Peking Natural History Bulletin*. Peking, 1937.

Glahn, Else. "Some Chou and Han Architectural Terms." *Bulletin of The Museum of Far Eastern Antiquities* (Stockholm), no. 50 (1978). p. 105–25.

_____. "On the Transmission of the Ying-tsao fa-shih." *T'oung Pao* (Leyden), vol. 61, nos. 4–5 (1975): 232–65.

Goodall, John A. *Heaven and Earth: 120 Album Leaves from a Ming Encyclopedia*. London: Lund Humphries Publishers, 1979.

Goodrich, L. Carrington. *Fifteenth Century Illustrated Chinese Primer*. Hong Kong: Hong Kong University Press, 1967.

_____. *A Short History of the Chinese People*. New York: Harper, 1943. Paperbound ed. London: Allen and Unwin, 1972.

Goodrich, L. Carrington, and Fang Chaoying, eds. *Dictionary of Ming Biography*. 2 vols. New York and London: Columbia University Press, 1976.

Granet, Marcel. *La Civilisation Chinoise*. Paris: Albin Michel, 1929.

Hackin, Joseph. *Studies in Chinese Art and Some Indian Influences*. London: India Society, 1937.

Harada, Yoshito. *Chinese Dress and Personal Ornaments in the Han and Six Dynasties*. Tokyo: Toyo Bunko, 1937.

Hay, John. *Ancient China*. London: Bodley Head, 1973.

Hentze, Carl. *Chinese Tomb Figures*. London: Goldston, 1928.

Herrmann, A. *An Historical Atlas of China*. Chicago: Aldine Publishing Co.; Amsterdam: Djambatan, 1966.

Hopkins, Lionel Charles. "Dragon and Alligator: Being Notes on Some Ancient Inscribed Bone Carvings." *Journal of the Royal Asiatic Society* (London), July 1913, pp. 545–52.

_____. "The Dragon Terrestial and the Dragon Celestial." *Journal of The Royal Asiatic Society* (London), pt. 1 (1931), pp. 791–806, pt. 2 (1932), pp. 91–97.

Hucker, Charles O. *The Censorial System of Ming China*. Palo Alto, Calif.: Stanford University Press, 1966.

_____. "Governmental Organizations of the Ming Dynasty." *Harvard Journal of Asiatic Studies* 20 (1958): 1–66.

_____. *The Traditional Chinese State in Ming Times*. 7th ed. (Tucson: University of Arizona Press, 1972.

Hughes, Ernest Richard. *Chinese Philosophy in Classical Times*. New York and London: E. P. Dutton and Co., J. M. Dent and Sons, 1942.

Hummel, Arthur W., ed. *Eminent Chinese of the Ch'ing Period*. 2 vols. Washington, D.C.: U.S. Government Printing Office, 1943–44.

Imbault-Huart, Camille. "Tombeaux des Ming près de Pékin." *T'oung Pao* (Leyden), no. 4 (1893): 391–401.

Johnston, Reginald F. *Twilight in the Forbidden City*. London: Gollancz, 1934.

Karlgren, Bernhard. "New Studies in Chinese Bronzes." *Bulletin of Far Eastern Antiquities* (Stockholm), no. 9 (1937): 1–117.

Karmay, Heather. *Early Sino-Tibetan Art*. Warminster, Eng.: Aris and Phillips, 1975.

Lai, T'ien-Ch'ang. *Chinese Calligraphy*. Seattle: University of Washington Press, 1973.

Laufer, Berthold. "Chinese Clay Figures." *Field Museum of Natural History* 13, no. 2 (1914).

Little, Mrs. Archibald. *Round About My Peking Garden*. London: Fisher and Unwin, 1905.

Lockhart, M. W. "Notes on Peking and Its Neighbourhood." *Royal Geographical Society Journal* 36 (1866): 150–51.

Loewe, Michael. *Everyday Life in Early Imperial China during the Han Period*. London: Batsford, 1968.

_____. *Imperial China*. London: Allen and Unwin, 1966.

Mahler, Jane Gaston. *Westerners among the Figurines of the T'ang Dynasty of China*. Rome: Istituto Italiano per il Medio ed Estremo Oriente, 1959. Serie Oriental Roma, vol. 20.

Mao Yi-sheng. *Bridges in China, Old and New*. Peking: Foreign Languages Press, 1978.

Medley, Margaret. *Handbook of Chinese Art* (1964). 3d ed. London: Bell and Sons, 1977.

Mennie, Donald. *The Pageant of Peking*. Shanghai: Kelly and Walsh, 1922.

Mirams, Dennis George. *A Brief History of Chinese Architecture*. Shanghai: Kelly and Walsh, 1940.

Mizuno, Seiichi. *Chinese Stone Sculpture*. Tokyo: Mayuyama, 1950.

Mo Tsung-chiang. "Architectural Decoration." *China Reconstructs* (Peking) 4, no. 9, (1955): 15–17.

Nagel's *Guide to China.* English version by Anne L. Destenay. Geneva: Nagel Publishers, 1968.

Needham, Joseph, *Science and Civilisation in China.* 6 vols. Cambridge: Cambridge University Press, 1954–81.

Oksbjerg, Erik. *Kinas Haver* [Chinese gardens]. Copenhagen: Rhodos, 1974.

Olsen, Eleanor. "A Tibetan Emblem of Sovereignty." *Oriental Art,* o.s. 3 (1951): 91–92.

Oriental Ceramic Society. *See* Arts Council of Great Britain.

Pelliot, Paul. "Bulletin Critique: 'Les Sépultures impériales des Ming' per G. Bouillard et Commandant Vaudescal." *T'oung Pao* (Leyden), no. 21 (1922), pp. 57–66.

————. "Obituary of G. Bouillard." *T'oung Pao* (Leyden), no. 27 (1930), pp. 454–57.

Pirazzoli t'Serstevens, Michele. *Chine: Architecture Universelle.* Fribourg: Office du Livre, 1970.

Polo, Marco. *The Travels.* Translated by R. Latham. Harmondsworth, Middlesex: Penguin, 1958, 1972.

Pratt, Keith. *Peking in the Early Seventeenth Century.* Oxford: Oxford University Press, 1971.

Prip-Møller, Johans. *Chinese Buddhist Monasteries.* Copenhagen and London: G. E. C. Gads Forlag, Oxford University Press, 1937.

————. "The Hall of Lin Ku Ssu, Nanking." *Artes* (Copenhagen) 3 (1935): 171–211.

Rawson, Jessica. "The Development of Archaistic Styles in Chinese Ceramics." Paper given at a symposium on Chinese ceramics held at Seattle Art Museum, July 1977.

Reischauer, Edwin O., and Fairbank, Jonathan K. *A History of East Asian Civilisation.* 2 vols. Boston: Houghton Mifflin, 1958, 1960.

Rennie, David Field. *Peking and the Pekingese.* 2 vols. London: John Murray, 1865.

Roberts, F. M. *Western Travellers to China.* Shanghai: Kelly and Walsh, 1932.

Rudolph, Richard C. *Han Tomb Art of West China.* Berkeley and Los Angeles: University of California Press, 1951.

Schlegel, Gustaaf. "Bulletin Critique: 'The Religious System of China' by J. J. M. De Groot, Book 1, part III." *T'oung Pao* (Leyden), no. 9 (1898), pp. 65–78.

Segalen, Victor. *Briques et tuiles.* Montpelier: Fata Morgana, 1975.

————. *Chine: La grande statuaire.* Paris: Flammarion, 1972. *The Great Statuary of China.* Translated by Eleanor Levieux. Chicago and London: University of Chicago Press, 1978.

Segalen, Victor; Voisins, Gilbert de; and Lartigue, Jean. *Missions archaéologiques en Chine.* 2 vols. Paris: Paul Geunther, 1923–24.

Shangraw, Sylvia Chen. "The Arts of China." *Oriental Art,* n.s. 22 (1976): 379–84.

Sickman, Lawrence, and Soper, Alexander. *The Art and Architecture of China.* Harmondsworth, Middlesex: Penguin Books, 1956. 1st paperback ed. based on 3d hardback ed., 1971.

Simmons, Pauline. *Chinese Patterned Silk.* New York: Metropolitan Museum of Art, 1948.

Sirén, Osvald. *Chinese and Japanese Sculptures and Paintings in the National Museum, Stockholm.* London: Edward Goldston, 1930.

————. *The Chinese on the Art of Painting.* Peking: Henri Vetch, 1936.

————. *Chinese Sculpture from the Fifth to the Fourteenth Centureis.* 4 vols. London: Ernest Benn, 1925.

————. *History of Early Chinese Art.* 4 vols. London: Ernest Benn, 1929–30.

————. *The Imperial Palaces of Peking.* 3 vols. Paris: Van Oest, 1926.

————. *The Walls and Gates of Peking.* London: Bodley Head, 1924.

Sitwell, Oswald. *Escape with Me—An Oriental Sketchbook.* London: Macmillan, 1939.

Skinner, George William. *The City in Late Imperial China.* Stanford: Stanford University Press, 1977.

Smith, A. *Chinese Characteristics.* Edinburgh and London: Oliphant, Anderson and Ferrier, 1897.

Spence, Jonathan. *The China Helpers.* London: Bodley Head, 1969.

————. *Emperor of China: Self-portrait of K'ang-hsi.* London: Jonathan Cape, 1974. Penguin Books, Peregrine Books, 1977.

Sullivan, Michael. *A Short History of Chinese Art.* 1st paperback ed. London: Faber, 1967.

Swallow, Robert William. *Sidelights on Peking Life.* Peking: China Booksellers, 1927.

Swann, Peter. *Chinese Monumental Art.* New York: Viking Press, 1963.

Thilo, Thomas. *Klassische chinesische Baukunst: Strukturprinzipien und Funktion.* Vienna: Tusch, 1977.

Tun Li-chen. *Annual Customs and Festivals in Peking* (1936). Translated by D. Bodde. 2d ed. rev. Hong Kong: Hong Kong University Press, 1965.

Villa, Brian Loring. "The Problems of Archaism in Ming Bronzes." *Oriental Art,* n.s. 23 (1977): 216–23.

Vogel, J. Ph. "Le Makara dans la sculpture de l'Inde." *Revue des Arts Asiatiques,* 6 (1929–30): 133–46.

Wang, Tuan, ed. *Ancient Chinese Patterns.* Hong Kong: Hung-t'u ch'u-pan-she, 1974.

Waterbury, Florance. *Early Chinese Symbols and Literature: Vestiges and Speculations with Particular Reference to the Ritual Bronzes of the Shang Dynasty.* New York: E. Wehye, 1942.

Watson, William. *Ancient Chinese Bronzes* (1962). 2d ed. London: Faber and Faber, 1977.

_____. *China before the Han Dynasty* (1961). 2d ed. rev. London: Thames and Hudson, 1966.

_____. "On Some Categories of Archaism in Chinese Bronzes." *Ars Orientalis* 9 (1973): 1–13.

_____. *Style in the Arts of China.* Harmondsworth, Middlesex: Penguin Books, 1974.

Werner, Edward Theodore Chalmers. *A Dictionary of Chinese Mythology.* Shanghai: Kelly and Walsh, 1932.

_____. *Social Life in Ancient China.* Yoevil, Eng.: Edwin Snell and Sons, 1950.

Willetts, William. *Chinese Art.* 2 vols. London: Penguin Books, 1958. Revised as *Foundations of Chinese Art: From Neolithic Pottery to Modern Architecture.* London: Thames and Hudson, 1965.

Williams, Charles Alfred Speed. *Outlines of Chinese Symbolism and Art Motives* (1932). 3d ed. rev. New York: Dover Publications, 1976.

Wu, Nelson I. *Chinese and Indian Architecture.* New York: Braziller, 1963. London: Prentice-Hall, 1963.

Yetts, Walter Percival. "A Chinese Treatise on Architecture." *Bulletin of the School of Oriental and African Studies* (London) 4 (1926–28): 473–92.

_____. "Notes on Chinese Roof Tiles." *Transactions of the Oriental Ceramic Society* (1927–28): pp. 13–42.

_____. *Symbolism in Chinese Art.* Leyden: The China Society, 1912.

Chinese Pamphlets

"The Thirteen Ming Tombs." Peking Publishing House, 1978.

"Ting-ling." Peking Publishing House, 1973. 2d ed., 1978.

Index

Page numbers are set in roman type, with tomb numbers enclosed in parentheses. Numbers for illustrations are italicized and placed at the end of an entry or subentry; "pl." indicates colourplates.

Building: as activity, 6; continuity in tradition of, 37, 38, 40; methods of construction, 38–40, 51, 90, 99, 174, 176; of vaults, 52, 149; of ramparts, 126; of stele pavilion, 194; use of basic units, 38–45; materials, 40, 66

Buildings: wooden, 37, chap. 4 *n*4; siting of (feng-shui), 38, 39; surface, on graves, 46, 49, chap. 5 *n*4, *45–47, 92, 131, 187*

Buttresses, 126, 130, *132*

Calendar, importance of, 181; reform of, 182; calculation of feast days, chap. 21 *n*3

Candlesticks. *See* "Five precious objects"

Cameron, Nigel, 39, 182

Cammann, Schuyler, 220

"Cannon of Dwellings," 7

Canton, 119, 131, 132, 182

Capital, moving of, 7

Ceilings: Gate of Heavenly Favours, Ch'ang-ling, 57; Sacrificial Hall, Ch'ang-ling, 68, *pl. 9*; Ching-t'ai's "spirit" pavilion, 196, *207*

Ceramic screen, 76, 92(4), 100, 103(5), 107(6), 114 (7), 137(9), 176(12), *103, 189*

Ceramic tiles: development of, 62; as door decoration, 62, 69(1), 82(3), 90(4), 135(9), 162, 168(11), 172(12); *pls. 16, 23, 149, 150*; as roof frieze, 43, 84(3), 92(4), 100(5), 107(6), 135, 136(9); on sacrificial oven, 62, 66; eave tiles, 62*n*, 67; of roof animals, 43, 62, 82, 92, 107, *68, 186*

Ceremonial rites: described by Bouillard, 2; purpose of, 7; performance of, 68, 185, 193, 211, 215, chap. 20 *n*3; dates of, 215, chap. 21 *n*3; described by Fonssagrives, 216–18. *See also* Rites; Sacrificial Hall; Sacrificial ovens

Chang, Empress (d. *1442*), 71

Chang, Empress (d. *1541*), 105

Chang, Empress (d. *1644*), 171, 179

Chang Ch'ü-cheng, 141, 156

Ch'ang-p'ing, 214

Chao Yi-kuei, 184

Characters on steles: importance of number of, 52. *See also* Chuan script

Charts, basis for, 3

Ch'en, Empress (d. *1528*), 120, 183*n*

Chen, Empress (d. *1592*), 133, 141

Cheng Ho (admiral), 6, 78, 85

Ch'eng-hua, Emperor, 97, 103, 104, 110, 111, 130; influence of Buddhism on, 14*n*

Cheng-te, Emperor, 97, 111, 118, 119

Ch'eng-tsu (Yung-lo), 70

Cheng-t'ung, Emperor, 87, 94–96, 105, 183*n*, 193; stopped immolation of concubines, 48*n*, 96

Chi, Empress (d. *1475*), 97

Ch'i, State of, 62

Chia-ching, Emperor, 141, 156, 183*n*, 201*n*; interest in tombs, 15, 16, 81, 84, 120, 215; reign, 120, 130–32

Ch'ien, Empress (d. *1468*), 87, 96, 103

Ch'ien-lung, Emperor, 16

Ch'i-lin: on P'ai-lou, 14; nature of, 14, 222–26; on Columns Supporting the Sky, 21; "Roaring towards the Sky," 21*n*, 225, *5, 17, 27, 43, 128, 185, 197, 237, 238*; on Spirit Road, 28, 204; on Dragon and Phoenix Gate, 36; on protective screen door, 47, 69, 82, 125, 135, 172; among roof animals, 62. *See also* Unicorn

China. *See* Porcelain

Ch'in dynasty, 37, 49, 70*n*, 71, 201*n*

Chin dynasty, 89, 201*n*

Chinese Oak, 76, 125

Ch'ing dynasty, 117; Western Tombs of, 2, 51, 137, 174, 216; at Ming Tombs, 19, 61, 137, 181, 185–92 passim, 208, chap. 6 *n*2; and trees, 54, 56, 145, 146

Ching-t'ai, Emperor, 87, 95, 193, 196–98; tomb prepared for, 87*n*, 159

Ching-te-chen, 85

Ching-ti. *See* Ching-t'ai

Ching Tien Chu. *See* Columns

Ch'i-wen, 62, 162, 211; origin of, 43, 220

Chou, Empress (d. *1504*), 87, 96

Chou, Empress (d. *1644*), 181, 185

Chou dynasty, 5*n*, 28, 38, 43, 70*n*, 219; bronzes, 49

Christianity, 157, 158, 182

Chu, Marquis of, 68

Chuan script, 70, 70*n*, 126, 194

Chuang-lieh (Ch'ung-chen), 187

Ch'ung-chen, Emperor, 181–85, 191, chap. 18 *n*2

Chu Ti. *See* Yung-lo

Chu Yüan-chang. *See* Hung-wu

Chu Yün-wen, 6

Chü Yung Kuan, 12

Clavichord, 158

Clocks, 158

Clothing, ceremonial, 15, 217. *See also* Costume; Mandarin squares; Sumptuary laws of *1391*

Coal Hill, 182, 192

Coffins: wood for, 53, 54; in Ting-ling, 151, 153; Concubine T'ien's, 185

Colour, 12, 15, 57, 216, 217; on steles, 16, 70, 73, 174, 186, 191; role of, 40, 43; on ceilings, 57, 68, 196; in tiles, 62

Columns: Hua Piao (flowery columns), 21; Ching Tien Chu (Columns Supporting the Sky), 21, 224; watch-towers, 24, *8, 15–17, 77. See also* Beacons

Conch shell, 149*n*

Concubines: forced death of, 48, 48*n*, 71*n*, 86, 96, 201; cemeteries of, 79, 96, 97, 122, 183, 183*n*. *See also* chap. 18

Confucian/Confucianism, 12*n*, 46, 70*n*, 110, 118, 179, 219

Confucius, 28, 224

Cormorant fishing, 11

"Corner stone": on wall enclosing south end of tumulus, 107, *113;* on ramp down to back area, 137, *169*

Photo Credits

Endpapers: Engraving of "Chinese View of the Ming
   Tombs" from Lewis Charles Arlington and William
   Lewisohn, *In Search of Old Peking* (Peking, 1935;
   New York: Paragon Book Reprint Corp., 1967),
   opp. p. 317
Figures 8, 62, 69: Yale Slide and Photograph Collec-
   tion
Figure 18: Mrs. A. Little, *Round About My Peking
   Garden* (London, 1905), opp. p. 130
Figure 45: Nigel Cameron and Brian Brake, *Peking:
   A Tale of Three Cities* (London, 1971), p. 116
Figure 171: Sir John Addis